GREY GHOST:

The Story of the Aircraft Carrier Hornet

CV-12, CVA-12, CVS-12

Including a Self-Guided Tour of the
Aircraft Carrier Hornet Museum
Alameda Point, California

Lee William Merideth

Rocklin Press
P O Box 64142
Sunnyvale, CA 94088

Manufactured in the United States of America.

Grey Ghost: The Story of the Aircraft Carrier Hornet
CV-12, CVA-12, CVS-12

By Lee William Merideth

Copyright © 2001
Lee William Merideth

Printing Number
10 9 8 7 6 5 4 3 2
Second printing May 2004

ISBN: 0-9626237-5-X

Rocklin Press
P O Box 64142
Sunnyvale, CA 94088
Phone: 408-944-0352
Fax: 408-944-0836
Email: rocklinpress@earthlink.net
www.rocklinpress.com

Illustrations by Phil Hall II at Nostalgia Graphic Design
Cover by James Zach

This book is printed on 50-lb., acid-free stock. The paper meets or exceeds the guidelines for permanence and durability of the Committee on Production Guidelines for Book Longevity of the Council on Library Resources.

This book is gratefully dedicated to the tens of thousands of former crewmen and pilots who served on and all too frequently gave their lives while serving on an aircraft carrier.

To the staff and volunteers of the Aircraft Carrier Hornet Museum, who are working to preserve the ship for future generations.

To Uncle Frank Hubof, a veteran of Saipan, Tinian and Iwo Jima, who was like a second father to me. *Semper Fi.*

And to my mother Eleanore and my late father
Edward W. Merideth, CWO-4, USN (RET),
who have always encouraged me to follow my dreams

Other Books by Lee William Merideth

1912 Facts About Titanic
Titanic Names: The Complete List of the Passengers and Crew

Guide To Civil War Periodicals, Volume II
Guide To Civil War Periodicals, Volume I
Civil War Times and Civil War Times, Illustrated
    30 Year Comprehensive Index

CONTENTS

Part I
History of the Aircraft Carrier *Hornet*, CV-12, CVA-12, CVS-12

Part II
A Self-Guided Tour of the Aircraft Carrier *Hornet*

HOW IT WORKS

Drawings

All Drawings by Phil Hall II at Nostalgia Graphic Design

Preface

History has obsessed me since I was a child.

I do not recall what it was that triggered my fascination with things past. Perhaps it was a book that lit the match that still burns so brightly; possibly a movie activated the passion I feel for the subject. Whatever its source, my obsession remains. Over the pasts couple of decades my interests have been focused primarily in three areas: the American Civil War, World War II naval history, and the story of RMS *Titanic*.

As a child I vowed to someday write the great American Civil War novel, only to discover years later that *Killer Angels* had already been written. Another contribution I pledged as a youngster to pen was a book about the horrific *Titanic* tragedy. *1912 Facts About Titanic* (originally published by Savas Publishing, and now in print by Rocklin Press, Sunnyvale, California), hit the shelves in February 1999. The book has been more successful than I could have hoped, and just went into its seven printing and first revision.

Once the *Titanic* project was completed, I began searching for another meaningful subject to write about. Of course, it had to be related to history and my preference was the Civil War. While I was working on my *Titanic* study I learned in 1977 that the aircraft carrier USS *Hornet* was being towed to the Alameda Naval Air Station (NAS) as part of a nine-month closing ceremony before the Base Realignment and Closure Commission turned the NAS over to civilian control. With a free day available, I visited the rather distressed looking hulk that had once been a proud fighting ship, one of the most decorated ships in our history.

I learned a lot about that great ship that day. One of the volunteers carefully explained that this was NOT the *Hornet* that carried Jimmy Doolittle and his men on the morale-boosting air raid on Japan. I also learned that *Hornet* was in the process of being turned over to a non-profit organization to be turned into a floating museum. It wasn't the Civil War, but it was one of World War II's most famous combat ships. A soon as I could, I signed on to be a docent on the Aircraft Carrier Hornet Museum. Let me confess now that I never served in the United States Navy. I can't swim and I would probably spend all my time at sea hanging over the rail watching my meals race toward the water. My military background consists of twenty years on terra firma in the United States Army and Army Reserves. Thus, when I became a docent, I had to learn everything from the keel up, literally. As it turned out, my interest in *Hornet* and role as a docent proved fortunate indeed.

In early 1999 at the Celebrate History Conference in San Francisco, Ted Savas of Savas Publishing Company, my good friend and original publisher of *1912 Facts About Titanic,* suggested I write a similar book about *Hornet.* The idea was an intriguing one. I knew that there were several excellent books for sale in the Hornet Museum Gift Show, but most were of the coffee table variety and much too expensive for the average *Hornet* visitor.

Initially, *Grey Ghost: The Story of the Aircraft Carrier Hornet* was going to be a history of the great ship as told by former crewmembers. However, as the book progressed and I spent more time working with other volunteers and speaking to thousands of visitors, it became apparent that I was working on the wrong book. Visitors invariably asked the same questions over and over: "How do the elevators work?""How do the planes get off the deck?" "What does [fill in the blank] do?" What was really needed was both a history of the ship and an explanation of what an aircraft carrier is and how it performs its myriad of tasks. And thus the book you are now holding in your hands was born.

Visitors to the *Hornet* tour only a small portion of the ship with a docent; the rest of the excursion is self-guided. While there is a lot to look at, there often is little in the way of description or explanation. As a result, I altered somewhat the focus of the book so that visitors can utilize it as a guidebook while wandering the many decks of the great ship. I also included sections called "How it Works," which explain, in laymen's terminology, how specific sub-systems operate and what they are used for. As more spaces on *Hornet* are opened to public view, it is my intention to include additional sections in future editions of *Grey Ghost.*

Many people and organizations have helped me with this book, and I would like to thank them for their thoughtful input and assistance: Teeodore P. (Ted) Savas of El Dorado Hills, California gave me the original suggestion for this book, provided valuable help along the way, and saved me from myself. Many members of the Aircraft Carrier Hornet Museum staff and volunteers provided input for this book, starting with Mr. Bob Rogers, formerly the Director of Marketing for the Aircraft Carrier Hornet Foundation, who provided considerable support for tracking down hard-to-find information. Bob also arranged for me to meet with several individuals who were able to provide me with some interesting insights into the *Hornet.* Albert Smith from the Aircraft Carrier Hornet Museum is one of the volunteers who has helped transform the ship from a rusting hulk that it was, to the gleaming museum it is today. Al took me on a first class tour of portions of the ship that aren't open to the public and probably never will be; the expedition into the bowels of the ship provided me with a real appreciation for the thousands of crewmen who served on *Hornet* and other aircraft carriers. "Chief" Bronson Parry, Oscar Robinson, Ken Gulley and Art Johnson, all volunteers who served on other *Essex*-class carriers, provided a wealth of information about how an aircraft carrier works. The Naval History Center and Larry Johnston of the National Archives provided considerable information and assistance with photo selection.

Tagging along on one of my tours was Doug Brentlinger, who knows everything anyone would ever want to know about steam turbine engines. Doug has the gift of being able to explain these engineering marvels so well that even I now understand them. Bob Rogers, Ted Savas, my good friend Bill Haley from Huntington Beach, California Fred Davis from San Jose, California and Connie Silveria from Tracy, California helped with proofreading and fact checking. Once the book was completed, several volunteers from the Hornet pointed out some much needed corrections. I would like to thank Dennis Teeguarden, Tony Clifford, Mickey Gaul, Oscar Robinson and probably some others whom I have not listed. Any errors that remain, be they of fact or punctuation, are my responsibility.

The excellent original drawings found in *Grey Ghost* were drafted by Phil Hall II, who resides in the wild country of the Sierra Nevada foothills in Central California. I have not yet had the pleasure of meeting Phil face-to-face, having found him (or I guess he found me) when I posted a request for a freelance designer on an Internet site. Phil spent over a year working, and then reworking, the drawings. They add significantly to the book and I am thankful for his efforts.

My late father, Edward Merideth, served as a gyro electrician in the south Pacific during World War II and retired from the United States Navy with twenty-three years under his belt. I think he would have enjoyed this book. After all these years, my mother Eleanore still prods me, as only mothers can, to finish the numerous projects I invariably find myself involved with. For years I've called her "Cyclone Momma," a name born from her proclivity to straighten, clean, wash, iron and organize my house whenever she drops by for a visit. Thanks, mom, for the constant and not always so gentle nudging and encouragement.

Lee William Merideth
Sunnyvale, California
May, 2004

Introduction

The sun had barely cleared the horizon on December 7, 1941, when more than three hundred aircraft from the Imperial Navy of the Empire of Japan struck the United States Pacific Fleet at Pearl Harbor, Hawaii. It was a Sunday, and the arrival of the white planes emblazoned with the Rising Sun emblem heralded one of the most infamous surprise attacks in military history. Two hours later the skies were empty, the last of the enemy's aircraft on their way back to the six large fleet aircraft carriers of the Japanese Combined Fleet steaming some 200 miles northwest of Hawaii. The surprise attack on Pearl Harbor left more than 2,000 dead Americans in its wake and propelled the United States into a war that already engulfed most of Europe, much of Asia, and a sizeable portion of North Africa. It also signaled the beginning of the end of Imperial Japan and Nazi Germany.

On December 8, 1941 at 12:20 p.m., President Franklin D. Roosevelt entered the chamber of the House of Representatives. Standing at the rostrum to a rousing ovation and supported by his son James, Roosevelt began a speech with words that will forever ring throughout the pages of history: "Yesterday, December 7, 1941," he began, " a date which will live in infamy, the United States of America was suddenly and deliberately attacked by naval and air forces of the Empire of Japan...."

The Japanese attack on Pearl Harbor was the culmination of failed diplomacy and Japan's desire to expand its influence into the central and south Pacific in order to procure a permanent source of oil, rubber, tin and copper—raw materials unavailable in Japan. Just as Germany's fast-moving armored panzer divisions had provided the blueprint for how much of the war in Europe would be conducted, Japan's Pearl Harbor gambit presaged many aspects of how the Pacific war would unfold. Many of the campaigns in the large-scale and complex Pacific war were either conducted by or dependent upon war planes launched from aircraft carriers, which were essentially mobile airfields operating far beyond the reach of the fleets of massive battleships the principal navies of the world had built at such great expense during the previous decades. The Sunday morning strike was intended to cripple the American Pacific fleet, so the Japanese pilots were instructed to attack and sink the aircraft carriers normally anchored within Pearl Harbor's protective confines. Fortunately for

America, none of her carriers were in port that fateful morning. Unfortunately for thousands of sailors and other fighting men, women and civilians serving on the battleships and other vessels, air bases, hospitals and support areas, the brunt of the attack was shifted in their direction.

By the time the air attack on Pearl Harbor was over, all eight of the American battleships anchored there were either sunk or seriously damaged and the attack was an almost fatal blow to the Pacific Fleet. Because of the damage inflicted, the Japanese government and military planners embarked on a massive campaign to overrun tens of thousands of square miles of the south and central Pacific, including Hong Kong, Malaysia, the Philippine Islands, Java and Wake Island. Thousands of American and allied soldiers, sailors and airmen would die trying to prevent the Japanese expansion, but with the American battleship force now resting on the bottom of Pearl Harbor, there was seemingly little the United States Navy could do to prevent this Japanese onslaught.

The inability to sink the American carriers, however, left Japan's new enemy with a powerful and lethal offensive strike capability. During the next year, the three original Pearl Harbor carriers and three of their sister ships (in conjunction with ground forces, submarines, air forces, and other naval surface units) rendered gallant service. Their efforts halted Japanese expansion, led to the bombing of the Japanese home islands, and turned the tide of the war irrevocably against Japan.

USS *Hornet*, CV-12 was the fourth ship of a new class of aircraft carrier designed just before the beginning of the war. The aircraft carriers of the *Essex*-class and a hundred smaller carriers carried the war directly to Japan, bypassing many of the Japanese-held islands and hastening the defeat of imperial Japan. Although not commissioned until late 1943, *Hornet,* CV-12 spent 18 months at sea and participated in every major campaign against Japan in 1944 and 1945. In later years *Hornet* served in the Cold War, Vietnam, and in her final days, as the prime recovery ship for the first two manned Apollo missions to the moon. After twenty-six years of service to America and twenty-seven years of uncertain fate and planned disposal, *Hornet* was saved by a dedicated group of individuals who felt that the most decorated ship in the United States Navy should be preserved so that future generations could tread her decks and ponder her remarkable and unique history.

The story of *Hornet,* CV-12 and her predecessor CV-8 is in many respects the story of the entire fleet of World War II aircraft carriers. The *Essex*-class carriers were the best designed and built ships of their time. More than one dozen carriers of the *Essex*-class were completed in time to see combat during World War II. Many suffered some of the heaviest damage the Japanese meted out during the entire war—and remained afloat. None were ever sunk. Instead, the inevitable passage of time and the cutters torch took their toll. Of the twenty-four *Essex*-class carriers, only four of them are still in existence as museum ships: *Intrepid* in New York Harbor, *Yorktown* at Patriot's Point in Charleston, South Carolina, *Lexington* in Corpus Christi, Texas and, as of mid-1997, *Hornet* in Alameda, California. The other twenty ships live only in the memories of the thousands of men who served on them.

Hornet's proud lineage began in 1775 as one of the first ships of the new Continental Navy; it continues to this day into the 21st Century with the McDonnell-Douglas F/A 18 Hornet, the most modern United States navy aircraft, currently flying off the flight decks of the latest generation of super aircraft carriers. The name *Hornet* will not be forgotten any time soon.

History of the

Aircraft Carrier
Hornet

CV-12, CVA-12, CVS-12

Why *"Grey Ghost?"*

The origin of the name "Grey Ghost" is obscure. Crew members tend to assign nicknames to their ships based upon some event or perception. Other *Essex*-class carriers were called "Oldest and the Boldest" (*Essex*), "The Fighting Lady" (*Yorktown*), "Hard Luck I" (*Intrepid*), "Big Ben" (*Franklin*), "Bonnie Dick" (*Bon Homme Richard*) and "The Blue Ghost" (*Lexington*).

Apparently *Hornet* was never given the call sign "Grey Ghost", so there isn't any official reason for calling her by that name. The origin of the name probably is related to two different events: earlier aircraft carriers with the same names had been sunk during the war and the *Lexington* was named "The Blue Ghost".

Each of the large aircraft carriers that were lost during World War II *(Yorktown, Hornet, Lexington, Wasp)* had a new aircraft carrier names for it. Since both *Lexington* and *Hornet* served all over the Pacific, they were like "ghosts"—especially since the Japanese never dreamed that we would name a new ship after a lost ship. That, after all, would to them be viewed as bad karma.

Lexington, CV-16 went through the war painted in a camouflage pattern called by the navy "Measure 21". This camouflage pattern consisted mainly of vertical stripes of different sizes, all painted Navy Blue, and was the only carrier with this type of camouflage. It seems to reason then, that *Lexington* would be known as "The Blue Ghost".

Hornet, was painted in "Measure 33/3A," a very light gray with the darker areas painted a medium gray. Overall, *Hornet* was very difficult to see from a distance and particularly in the mist and haze because she tended to blend into the background. Consequently, she acquired the name "Grey Ghost".

Why, then, is the "Grey" in Grey Ghost" not spelled "Gray?" Although many documents spell it both ways, most utilize the former, of "Grey." Consequently, I have decided to use that spelling in the title of this book.

Chapter 1

From One Through Six — The First *Hornets*

For most of its existence there has been a ship named *Hornet* in the United States Navy. The careers of these eight ships began with the first *Hornet*, a small ten-gun converted merchant vessel in 1775 to the present day *Hornet,* CVS-12, now a museum ship operated by the Aircraft Carrier Hornet Foundation in Alameda, California. This tradition has continued with the FA-18 Hornet, the current primary carrier-launched aircraft of the U.S. Navy.

■ The histories of the first six ships named *Hornet* provide a proud lineage for the current *Hornet*. They are ships mostly forgotten over time, but the history of America could not have been written without them and the thousands of other ships that have flown the American flag in defense of our nation. The lineage of *Hornet,* CVS-12, dates back to the earliest days of the American Revolution when the first *Hornet* was commissioned.

Hornet Number One: 1775-1777

In 1775 the Continental Congress authorized the outfitting of two small merchant ships into ten-gun sloops to help defend the American coast from British warships. These two ships were named *Wasp* and *Hornet*, seemingly because of the sting the enemy would feel from them. That these small ships would dare challenge the mighty British Navy was more a sign of determination, spirit and courage than of common sense.

Hornet was out-fitted with ten 9-pound cannons at Baltimore, Maryland in late 1775, and placed under the command of Capt. William Stone. She was assigned to Commander Ezek Hopkin's fleet in the Delaware River. There she remained for most of the following year, patrolling the rivers and coastline, looking for anything suspicious and maintaining a token presence for the Continental Navy.

■ In January 1777, Capt. John Nicholson assumed command of *Hornet,* and the ship successfully evaded the British blockade and helped escort a fleet of merchant ships to South Carolina. After returning to the Delaware River to do more patrolling, *Hornet* was stranded when the British captured the forts guarding Philadelphia in late 1777. In order to prevent her from falling into British control, Capt. Nicholson was ordered to destroy his ship, thus ending the brief career of the first *Hornet*.

Hornet Number Two: 1805-1806

If the career of the first *Hornet* was brief, the second *Hornet* had one even shorter. *Hornet* number two was another converted merchant ship, purchased by the United States Navy in Malta in 1805 and out-fitted with 10 cannons, converting her into a 71-ton sloop.

Hornet was commanded by Lieutenant Samuel Evans, and was assigned to blockade duty at Tripoli in North Africa with other American forces. She participated in the bombardment of the Turkish batteries at Derne. After United States Marines captured Derne, *Hornet* served off Tunis in the Mediterranean Sea to help suppress the Barbary Pirates in their attacks against merchant shipping.

On June 3, 1806, a severe storm tore away some of her masts and she sprang several leaks. *Hornet* sailed to Philadelphia where she was decommissioned and sold in September 1806.

Hornet Number Three: 1805-1829

Launched in Baltimore in July 1805, the third *Hornet* had a long and distinguished career that ultimately ended in tragedy. She was the first to be built as a naval vessel, and was a 440-ton, 20-gun brig.

Commissioned in October 1805, and commanded by Isaac Chauncey, *Hornet* first patrolled the east coast and then tracked down pirate ships in the Mediterranean. In 1807, *Hornet* returned to Charleston where she was decommissioned and put into storage.

■ In late 1807, Congress passed the Embargo Act. This act prohibited all international trade from American ports to persuade France and Britain of the value of neutral commerce. Subsequently, in late 1808, *Hornet* was recommissioned and sent to the Caribbean to patrol the coastal waters and enforce the Embargo Act.

In 1810 *Hornet* was sent to the Washington Navy Yard and was rebuilt. On June 18, 1812, the United States declared war on Britain (War of 1812), and three days later *Hornet*, along with three other warships, headed out to sea. During the next two months *Hornet* captured several merchant ships and a British privateer. *Hornet* then was assigned to Commander William Bainbridge's fleet and sent to South America, where she again captured several British merchant ships.

In February 1813 *Hornet* engaged in a 15-minute gunfight with the British brig *Peacock,* after which the British warship, having lost several men and rapidly sinking, surrendered. With almost 100 prisoners from various ships on board, *Hornet* headed for New London, Connecticut. After arriving in New London, she was blockaded there for a year.

■ When the blockade was lifted the following year, *Hornet* was ordered into the South Atlantic where she encountered the British brig *Penguin*, another ship similar in size to *Hornet*. During the ensuing battle, *Penguin's* captain was killed, *Hornet* rammed the ship and *Penguin* was forced to surrender. *Hornet* picked up *Penguin's* crew and sailed to the East Indies where she rendezvoused with another small American ship. These two ships then encountered the huge British 74-gun ship *Cornwallis*. Being severely out-gunned, the American ships had to flee, but *Hornet* had trouble staying out of range. When she came under fire from *Cornwallis*, *Hornet's* crew tossed everything they could overboard to lighten the ship: guns, ammunition, spare spars, sails, anchors, and lifeboats. Finally light enough to escape from *Cornwallis*, *Hornet* sailed for New York and arrived in June 1815.

After several cruises and a refit, for the next 14 years *Hornet* was used to patrol the coasts and areas around the Caribbean. Disaster struck the third *Hornet* on September 29, 1829, when off the coast of Tampico, *Hornet* sank in a severe storm, taking all 140 crewmembers with her to their deaths.

Hornet Number Four: 1813-1820

Although the third *Hornet* was already in commission, the Navy commissioned another small ship in 1813 and called it *Hornet*. The fourth *Hornet* was a small, 5-gun schooner. The little ship was used as a dispatch vessel between east coast ports from 1813 through 1820. It was then sold and became a private merchant ship.

Hornet Number Five: 1865-1869

From 1829 until the end of the Civil War in 1865, there wasn't a ship named *Hornet* in the U.S. Navy. That changed in June 1865 when the navy purchased the former Confederate blockade-runner *Lady Sterling* that had been built in England and captured off Wilmington, North Carolina in late 1864.

By the time *Hornet* number five had been fitted out with eight guns and commissioned in June 1865, the Civil War was over. Used primarily as an escort ship and later as a transport for discharged union army troops, *Hornet* was decommissioned in December 1865 after only six months of service. After being in storage for four years, *Hornet* number five was sold in June 1869.

Hornet Number Six: 1898-1910

Once again, for almost thirty more years there wasn't a *Hornet* commissioned in the U.S. Navy, but that changed when in April 1898 the navy purchased the former steam yacht *Alicia*, built in 1890. At 160 feet and 425 tons, the sixth *Hornet* was only capable of carrying five small cannons and four machine guns, but she was assigned blockade duty off Spanish Cuba.

Hornet's big day arrived on June 30, 1898, when, accompanied by two other small navy ships, *Hornet* first seized an English blockade-runner and later that day helped sink a Spanish gunboat in the Manzanillo harbor. Shortly thereafter, the three ships entered the harbor and engaged the Spanish forts guarding it.

A hit by an enemy shell burst *Hornet's* steam pipe disabling the ship, which then started to drift into shallow water and toward the enemy batteries. At about this time a small Spanish ship attacked *Hornet*, but a couple of well-placed shots sank the enemy. *Hornet*, still drifting toward shallow water, was finally towed out by one of her sister ships. No American sailors were lost during the entire day's combat.

■ After several more assignments, in mid-July 1898 *Hornet* and several other ships engaged the Spanish flotilla in Manzanillo harbor. In less than two hours they sank 13 ships, including four gunboats. This was done while also engaging the harbor's forts.

Returning to South Carolina, *Hornet* was decommissioned in October 1898 and served as a training ship. In 1902 *Hornet* was reassigned as a tender and in March 1910 sold to a private concern.

Perspective

The histories of the first six ships named *Hornet* in the U.S. Navy paralleled that of most other navy ships of their era: generally small ships, all but one purchased and converted from existing vessels, all but one commissioned for a specific purpose and then decommissioned. Only the third *Hornet* had been built as a warship and had a long history: all of the others were relatively short-lived ships. All had served honorably and contributed to the proud lineage of the name *Hornet*.

■ It would be thirty years before there would be another *Hornet* in the U.S. Navy. By then the entire nature of naval warfare had changed. The next *Hornet* would be purpose built and be the most technically advanced ship in the navy when it was commissioned. The next *Hornet* would be an *aircraft carrier*—a vessel not even imagined when the previous *Hornet* was sold in 1910, seven years after the Wright brothers made their first flight at Kitty Hawk.

Chapter 2

A History of the Aircraft Carrier

In November 1910, the same year *Hornet* number six was sold, Captain Washington Chambers built a small platform on the forward deck of the cruiser USS *Birmingham*. He then convinced a civilian pilot named Eugene Ely to fly an airplane off of the ship while anchored in Hampton Roads, Virginia. The takeoff, in a 50-horsepower Curtiss biplane, was successful. The first airplane launch from a ship had been made, although Ely had to land his plane at a local airfield.

Two months later Ely *landed* another airplane on a similar deck on the stern of the cruiser USS *Pennsylvania* while it was anchored in San Francisco Bay. This was a one-shot effort on Ely's part. Cables, nets and sandbags were placed on the deck to prevent the plane from crashing into the superstructure of the *Pennsylvania*. Had they not stopped his plane, Ely's flying days would have been over. As it was, his biplane survived the landing, and after having lunch with *Pennsylvania's* captain, Ely flew off. Ely, the world's first aviator to fly off and land upon a ship, died in a plane crash one year later.

■ Flying airplanes off makeshift decks covering the forecastle of armored warships were fun projects for the world's various navies during the time of peace, but they were totally impractical for wartime. Warships had their primary weapons systems on the forward part of the ship, and covering them over with a deck to launch an airplane would render the guns useless. Besides, no one had given much thought about how to recover an aircraft once it was launched. These were seemingly one-way missions.

In 1911 Glen Curtis developed the floatplane, one that could take off and land in the water. This solved some of the immediate problems; at least now the pilot could fly back to his ship, land next to it and then be hoisted back aboard. It also solved the need for a flat deck to launch from as the plane took off under its own power on the water. However, a floatplane could only take off and land in smooth water, seldom on the open ocean. Another problem was that the host ship had to stop in order to drop the plane into the water and then later stop to retrieve it.

■ By now, one of the primary principles of flight was well known. The speed of the wind over a wing was the important factor in getting an airplane aloft, not the speed of the airplane itself.

Thus, if a given airplane needed 50 knots of wind over the wing in order to achieve enough lift to get airborne, then that speed could be attained in one of three ways:

- Under its own power, the airplane could accelerate to the required speed using a runway of sufficient length to achieve that speed or;
- The airplane was flying into a 20 knot wind, then it only needed enough runway to accelerate to 30 knots, or;
- If the airplane was on a ship traveling at 20 knots and steaming into a 20-knot wind, the airplane only needed enough runway to accelerate to 10 knots.

About the same time as the floatplane was developed, a fourth option was created. Captain Chambers invented the catapult, a mechanism that could launch an aircraft in a style similar to a slingshot. This could eliminate any requirement for a large deck to launch from. All that was required was a short track for the airplane to travel on as it was being shot into the sky. Now a catapult could be mounted on a ship and a floatplane launched while the ship was in motion.

■ In November 1915 the first successful catapult launch was made by Navy Lieutenant Commander Henry C. Mustin off the stern of USS *North Carolina* in Pensacola Bay, Florida. By late-1915 several ships were fitted with catapults, a process that continued through World War II. Most cruisers and battleships had one or more catapults, usually located near the fantail (stern) or on top of one of the aft gun turrets.

■ Regardless of how the airplane managed to get airborne, landing it was still a problem. Anything but calm seas made landing a floatplane in water a hazardous task at best, and short decks lined with sandbags to bring an airplane to an abrupt halt just weren't practical.

However, the main purpose for the floatplane would be to search out the enemy fleet. During combat the floatplane would aid the gunners in spotting the fall of the shells from the big guns. Aerial combat by navy aircraft in World War I was extremely rare. Once the mission was completed, the pilot landed in the water close to the nearest ship and was picked up. The airplane was usually lost.

■ While several navies were working on the fundamentals of landing an airplane on board a ship, progress was made in several other areas. In 1912 a navy pilot carried a small dummy bomb up in his airplane and dropped it over the side, by hand. In 1914 a small cannon was test fired from an airplane, and later that year a small torpedo was launched from another airplane. Thus, by the eve of World War I most of the basics for utilizing aircraft at sea were either in place or were being considered.

■ While most of the navies of the world were at war in 1915, the U.S. Navy was trying to get the funds needed to continue experimenting with ship-borne aircraft. Research and development funds were scarce. Also hindering development at this stage and continuing until the eve of World War II were the "big gun" admirals in the navy who felt there was absolutely no use for an airplane in naval warfare because the battleship was the ultimate weapon.

Several studies were made during this time about how to develop a ship that could both launch AND recover aircraft AND be fast enough to keep up with the battle fleet AND be protected enough to allow some amount of survivability. With the entry of the United States into World War I however, all the studies were shelved and not dusted off until 1919. By the end of the war, even the "big gun" admirals realized the need for better fleet reconnaissance and the airplane seemed the obvious choice. A vessel that could provide this support was needed.

■ After the war, the navy started working on designs for building such a vessel, but once again budget constraints prohibited the building of one. However, the issue could be resolved by the use of one of several existing cruiser hulls under construction, but currently in limbo since the end of the war. Although a good idea at the time, neither Congress nor the navy would allow the hulls to be used for this purpose. All Congress would appropriate funds for was the conversion of a collier, USS *Jupiter,* into an experimental carrier named *Langley.*

Design work on *Langley* was completed by mid-1919, and in March 1922 the former *Jupiter* emerged from the Norfolk Navy Yard as USS *Langley,* CV-1.

■ *(The Navy designation CV does not have anything to do with carrier, as in aircraft carrier. The "C" stands for cruiser, a type of naval warship. Because the original carriers were built on converted cruiser hulls, they retained the "C". The "V" is the letter the Navy assigned to heavier-than-air aircraft. Thus, CV would mean a ship built on a cruiser hull designed to carry aircraft. Although only two carriers were built from cruiser hulls, the designation CV, with a suffix of "A" for Attack, "S" for Anti-submarine or "N" for Nuclear, etc., continues to this day.*

■ *Langley* was the first true aircraft carrier in that it had a full-length flight deck from which to launch or recover aircraft, and it had a large open area under the deck where aircraft could be stored or repaired. The landing deck was built above the existing superstructure of the ship, leaving only the ship's funnels extending above the deck on the port side. First one, and later a second catapult was mounted on top of the deck. Aircraft were assembled on the original deck of the collier and hoisted up to the flight deck on the single elevator. It took twelve minutes for a plane to be placed on the elevator, hoisted to the flight deck and prepared for flight. For protection, *Langley* was also equipped with four 5-inch guns.

Solving the landing problem was an issue that several teams of engineers tackled while *Langley* was being converted. The solution was for a series of cables to be stretched across the flight deck both fore and aft. The cables would be attached to hydraulic brakes. Aircraft would have a hook located on the bottom of the fuselage near the tail, and this hook would, hopefully, catch one of the cables. After engaging the cable, the hydraulic brake would engage and haul the aircraft to a stop. This method, with many modifications, is still in use today.

On October 17, 1922, Lieutenant V.C. Griffin, flying a tiny Vought VE-7 bi-wing off the deck of *Langley* made the first successful launch from an aircraft carrier deck while *Langley* was anchored in the York River, Virginia. Nine days later Lieutenant Commander Godfrey Chevalier, flying an Aeromarine, made the first landing aboard *Langley*. A month later another navy pilot made the first catapult launch from *Langley*'s deck.

In 1923 *Langley* began to accompany the fleet during annual maneuvers. From that time on the aircraft carrier would be a prominent part of all U.S. Navy fleet training.

Although too slow to operate with the fast combat ships of the fleet, it was perfect as a training platform for pilots, aircraft and equipment. *Langley* continued service as an aircraft carrier until the late thirties when part of its flight deck was removed and it was converted to a seaplane tender. Japanese aircraft sank *Langley* in the South Pacific on February 27, 1942.

■ Because of growing dissatisfaction with the role America played in World War I, the United States Senate in 1920 rejected the League of Nations and the Treaty of Versailles, which meant the United States felt it was best not to get involved in events in Europe. Thus, the navy no longer would have use for or could afford the large battleships, battle cruisers, and fleets of cruisers and destroyers that were then in commission or still under construction because of contracts issued during the war.

■ In November 1921 the Washington Naval Arms Limitation Conference was held, and America offered to scrap thousands of tons of ships under construction or in service. The resulting Five-Power Treaty (or Washington Treaty) signed in February 1922 established the famous 5:5:3 tonnage ratio between the United States, Great Britain and

Japan. For every five tons of large warship (aircraft carrier, battleship and battle-cruiser) construction in the U.S. and Great Britain, Japan was allowed three tons, while France and Italy were allowed 1.5 tons. There was a moratorium for ten years on capital ship construction, and a 35,000-ton weight limitation on battleships. Aircraft carriers would be limited to a maximum of 27,000 tons. Because it was already in commission, *Langley* was exempt from the limits.

■ It didn't take long for the navy to start working on a true aircraft carrier to replace *Langley*. On July 1, 1922, Congress authorized the construction of two aircraft carriers to be named *Lexington* and *Saratoga*. Actually, these ships were to be converted from two of the existing battle cruiser hulls that were supposed to be scrapped under the Washington Treaty.

Early design considerations called for several large-caliber guns to be included on aircraft carriers, primarily for anti-ship defense. It was assumed that aircraft carriers would have to defend themselves against fast-moving enemy cruisers that could get close enough to shoot at them. Prior to the final designs for the first two aircraft carriers, plans included sixteen 6-inch guns and up to twelve 5-inch anti-aircraft guns—almost as much armament as a cruiser. There even were plans to put torpedo tubes aboard in case an enemy warship managed to steam within torpedo range.

Smoke disposal was a major design factor. *Langley* didn't have an "island," the superstructure so familiar on all future aircraft carriers. Thus, there wasn't a permanent above deck funnel that would expel smoke high enough above the deck to keep it from being sucked back inside the ship or from blowing across the flight deck and blinding the pilots. *Langley's* funnels could fold down along the side of the ship so aircraft wouldn't crash into them. When in the "down" position, smoke would fill the ship. Several ideas were tried, and ultimately an island was added as part of the ship, and the funnel was routed up through it.

■ Washington Treaty limitations stated that the maximum weight for an aircraft carrier was 27,000 tons displacement, which was considerably less than the designers felt was required, especially for a conversion. There were six battle cruisers under construction when the Treaty was signed, and all six were expected to be scrapped as part of the Treaty. Theodore Roosevelt, Jr., Assistant Secretary of the Navy, arbitrarily decided that a carrier converted from a cruiser hull could displace up to 33,000 tons. This was still 3,000 tons less than was needed, so a loophole found in the Treaty was exploited which allowed up to 3,000 tons of extra deck armor to protect against air attack and underwater blisters to protect against torpedo attack. This weight could be added above the maximum allowable tonnage on existing capital ships, which also included ships under construction, i.e. the cruisers-now-aircraft carriers. Now naval architects could design an aircraft carrier up to 36,000 tons displacement, which is exactly the allowance they wanted.

■ On November 16, 1927, USS *Saratoga*, CV-3 was commissioned at Camden, New Jersey under the command of Captain Harry E. Yarnell. Less than a month later on December 14, 1927, the USS *Lexington*, CV-2 was commissioned at Quincy, Massachusetts under the command of Captain Albert W. Marshall. *Saratoga*, displacing 35,544 tons, and *Lexington displacing 35,689 tons, came in just under the 36,000-ton limit created by the loophole in the Washington Treaty.*

In anticipation of potential combat with other surface ships, both "*Sara*" and "*Lex*" were equipped with eight 8-inch guns in four turrets located on the starboard side, two ahead of and two behind the island. Additionally, there were twelve 5-inch guns for antiaircraft defense located in sponsons around the ships under the edge of the flight deck and numerous 3-inch guns placed wherever space could be found. There were also four torpedo tubes installed near the stern of the ships, but after fleet testing, they were removed.

The weight of the island, funnels and four gun turrets on the starboard side of the flight deck caused a considerable starboard list. To compensate, only one of three planned catapults (on the portside) was installed, and the ships had to carry ballast in the port side fuel oil tanks.

The hangar deck on both ships was completely enclosed and the flight deck was part of the hull structure, two items that would change on subsequent aircraft carriers. They had turboelectric drive propulsion systems (engines) that created 180,000 shaft horsepower (SHP) and could attain a sustained speed of 33 knots. Over 90 aircraft could be carried in the hangar and on the flight deck.

■ On January 11, 1928, Commander Marc A. Mitscher completed the first take off and landing on *Saratoga*. Mitscher would have a long history with both of the future *Hornets*.

During fleet exercises off Panama in January 1929, 69 aircraft from *Saratoga* made an undetected dawn attack on the locks in the Panama Canal. Although just a war game, its effects were not lost on naval officers who were developing new aircraft and carrier tactics.

In an even more profound demonstration, in 1932 both carriers participated in a dawn surprise attack on the fleet at Pearl Harbor. The aircraft attacked Pearl Harbor from the northwest and got away without the carriers having been found. Some of the foreign officers who were allowed to view the published results of the attack were senior officers of the Imperial Japanese Navy. They definitely did not forget what they had observed.

Until the beginning of World War II, both carriers were continuously refined and changed. As many as 50 additional .50 caliber machine guns were added, while the original 3-inch guns were replaced by 1.1-inch guns. Two additional catapults were added and the arresting cables were removed and later added again. The flight decks were lengthened and the forward ends were widened. Although both ships required a major modernization, neither could be spared from fleet duties. Consequently, by the time the war began in 1941, neither had been modernized, although *Saratoga* was completely modernized in 1942 after being torpedoed by a Japanese submarine. *Lexington* was lost at the Battle of the Coral Sea before she could be modernized.

■ At the urging of President Coolidge, in 1928 Congress authorized the construction of another aircraft carrier, this one to be built from the keel up. With two large carriers already in commission, there were only 69,000 tons available for new construction under the Washington Treaty limits. The new carrier would be considerably smaller to save on tonnage, which could be reserved for future carrier construction. The tonnage saved would allow the navy to build two more mid-sized aircraft carriers instead of one large one. Consequently, in September 1931 the keel for USS *Ranger*, CV-4 was laid at Newport News Shipbuilding and Dry Dock Company in Newport News, Virginia. Less than four years later, *Ranger* was commissioned, Captain Arthur L. Bristol in command.

Ranger proved too small to be considered a fleet carrier. Although it could carry 86 aircraft, its length at 769 feet, displacement of 14,500 tons and slow speed made it more in common with the later escort carriers of World War II, and in fact *Ranger* spent most of the war in the Atlantic serving as a training carrier.

Some of the design enhancements on *Ranger* were the gallery deck suspended below the flight deck. Provision was also made for two hangar deck catapults, however they were never installed.

Up until the time of the final design of *Ranger*, there was considerable controversy about the addition of an island; however, *Ranger* was equipped with a small one.

Three funnels to evacuate the smoke from the boilers were added on each side of the flight deck toward the stern. The funnels were hinged so they could be lowered during flight operations. Depending on the prevailing wind, one side or the other would be used to prevent smoke from blowing across the flight deck. The dual funnel design was ultimately rejected in future construction, as it was found to be impractical.

■ In 1934 the navy developed the flush-deck hydraulic catapult to replace the earlier cruiser-type launch rail and flywheel that were in use on *Saratoga* and *Lexington*. They and all of the World War II era aircraft carriers, were equipped with catapults in various numbers and locations. Although aircraft of the time were light enough that they could fly off a carrier deck without the use of a catapult, with a deck full of aircraft, there wasn't room enough for a 300 to 400 foot run-up before taking off. This meant that at least half the flight deck would have to be clear before an airplane would have enough room to take off. The inclusion of a catapult meant that several aircraft could be catapult-launched to clear the flight deck so the remaining aircraft could take off under their own power. Also, scouting floatplanes could be launched without having to clear the deck.

■ Here was a dilemma: if you store a large quantity of aircraft on the stern of the flight deck and you launch one of them, how do you land the airplane without having to move all of the stored aircraft parked on the flight deck? An airplane can be catapult launched, but it can't be landed. For this reason floatplanes were used whenever the sea was calm enough to land them next to the carrier and then be hoisted back on the deck with the deck crane. If the sea was too rough to land, the pilot could always bail out next to a rescue ship and the airplane would be lost.

During one war game, the captain of *Saratoga* wanted to launch two observation aircraft under their own power. To do so, he had to launch 38 aircraft already on the deck in order to launch the observation aircraft because they needed a longer flight deck to fly off. The 38 aircraft circled the ship until after the observation planes were off and the remaining 14 aircraft on the deck had been moved to the bow. Then the circling aircraft landed and the 14 other aircraft were spotted on the back end of the flight deck. When the two planes finished their mission and prepared to land, all 38 aircraft had to launch again because the deck was too full to land aircraft and the remaining 14 were pushed up to the bow and the landing process was repeated. Why didn't the aircraft just remain in the air? They didn't have fuel capacity to circle until the observation aircraft returned. In the meantime, *Saratoga* lost the war game because it took too long to get the observation planes airborne!

■ In 1929 Herbert Hoover was elected president. Hoover was a Quaker and a pacifist, and during his four-year term the navy laid down not one single ship. Testing, training and war games continued on all four of the navy's existing aircraft carriers, and navy architects continued to make plans for additional carriers when the authorization for them would be made sometime in the future. Franklin D. Roosevelt's election in 1933 made that happen.

■ In January 1930, the five naval powers that signed the Five-Power Treaty in 1921 met again at the London Naval Disarmament Conference. The primary ruling that came from this conference was the imposition of a 23,000-ton limit to all new aircraft carriers.

■ In 1931 the Japanese army attacked Manchuria. The League of Nations condemned Japan for the attack, so Japan just withdrew from the League (the United States had never joined). Then, in 1934 Japan announced they would no longer abide by the Washington Treaty after the end of 1936.

Throughout the latter part of the 1930's Japan expanded its invasion of China, and in 1937 it sank the *Panay*, an American gunboat, in China. This type of continued aggression convinced naval planners that Japan would eventually become a major opponent in the Pacific, and some planners thought that war with Japan was inevitable.

■ Franklin D. Roosevelt had been the Assistant Secretary of the Navy during World War I. No other politician of his time was more an advocate of both sea and air power, and it wouldn't be long before changes began to take place in the navy's ship building program. In mid 1933 Congress passed the National Industrial Recovery Act, and $238 million worth of funds were made available to construct 32 new warships, including two aircraft carriers. The Vinson-Trammel Naval Expansion Act of 1934 would bring the navy back up to the Treaty limit, which meant authorization for 102 more warships to be built by 1942.

Due to the Washington Treaty, the navy only had 54,500 tons available for aircraft carrier construction after *Saratoga*, *Lexington* and *Ranger* had been completed. The navy wanted three more carriers, so two hulls were laid down in 1934 that would displace 19,900 tons each, leaving 14,500 tons for one more future carrier similar to *Ranger*.

The two new aircraft carriers were laid down at Newport News, and on September 30, 1937, the USS *Yorktown*, CV-5 was commissioned, followed on May 12, 1938, by USS *Enterprise*, CV-6. These were the minimum size the navy felt was sufficient for fleet operations. They were 769 feet long and initially could carry up to 100 aircraft, although by the second year of the war they were carrying as many as 121 aircraft, many of them as spares stored overhead on the hangar deck. Meanwhile, the navy continued to modify the design of the ships and worked on designs for even larger carriers should the United States opt out of the Washington Treaty.

These carriers were really the first of the modern aircraft carriers. Several years worth of operational experience with the existing four carriers allowed navy designers to make numerous design modifications and enhancements. In reality, these carriers were the basis of the *Essex*-class carriers that would dominate aircraft carrier operations in World War II.

■ The navy had all sorts of expectations about how these ships should be designed. It wanted full anti-torpedo bulkheads for defense, a full armored flight deck, no island, four elevators, and two flight decks: the upper one for landing and the lower one, an extension of the hangar deck, to take off. The two flight deck idea wasn't that outrageous, because by this time the Royal Navy had two aircraft carriers that had a hangar deck that aircraft could fly off. The great advantage to the two decks is that you could launch an airplane from the bottom (hangar) deck and land another airplane at the same time on the flight deck.

Also of major concern was the speed of the carriers. Navy doctrine had carriers as being self-sufficient against an enemy cruiser, thus the 8-inch guns on *Saratoga* and *Lexington*. By the time the drawings for the two new carriers were completed, operational experience convinced the navy that the carriers would have to: (1) have their own escorts and (2) have ample speed to keep up with the escorting ships, usually cruisers, or about 32.5 knots. If carriers had their own escorts and could maintain that speed, they wouldn't have to steam with the battle fleet and could outrun most other types of warships. Carriers could perform scouting and screening, strike enemy forces away from the battle fleet, and could operate independently as their own task force.

When these carriers were being designed in the early 30's, the navy did not consider fighter aircraft to be a suitable defensive mechanism against enemy aircraft because radar hadn't yet been developed. By the time approaching enemy aircraft were detected, it would be too late to launch fighter aircraft. Consequently, the ships would carry a substantial number of antiaircraft weapons. Later, combat would show that even with radar and fighter cover, the antiaircraft defenses on the carriers were still inadequate.

■ Once reality set in, the navy found there wasn't any way to incorporate all of the changes because of the weight limitations, so they had to compromise. Gone were the 8-inch guns that *Saratoga* and *Lexington* carried on the flight deck, replaced by eight 5-inch guns located around the edge of the flight deck that were primarily used as a high-altitude antiaircraft weapon. The weapons of choice for close in defense were sixteen 1.1-inch machine cannons and twenty-four .50-calibre machine guns. Also, since these two ships were built from the keel up as an aircraft carrier, the flight deck was not part of the hull structure. A good portion of the sides of the hangar deck would be open to the elements (air and water), as both a weight saving device and because aircraft could warm up on the hangar deck prior to launch. The open sides were needed for ventilation. The hangar deck would become the armored deck, providing overhead protection above the fuel and ammunition storage and machine spaces.

Gone, too, was the plan for the second flight deck, or extension of the hangar deck. Added was a side launch catapult on the hangar deck so scout and observation airplanes could be launched without having to move all of the aircraft on the flight deck. There were also two flight deck catapults to launch aircraft off the bow.

Another design concept that was added was the addition of a double-ended flight deck, with arresting gear at both ends. The ships engines were designed so they could steam as fast *backwards* as forwards. This would allow the launch of aircraft over the stern if, by having to turn into the wind to launch aircraft, the ship would have to steam too close to the enemy. Pre-war war games found this to be the situation so many times that the navy was willing to expend the funds to include the double-ended flight deck.

The hangar deck kept growing in height, first to allow eight feet under the flight deck for a partial gallery deck. Later several more feet were added to accommodate the stowage of disassembled aircraft to be hung from overhead and not interfere with movement on the deck.

One of the biggest shortcomings was the location of the two engine rooms and the two fire rooms. The two fire rooms were located together forward of the two adjoining engine rooms. This was a poor design because if a bomb or torpedo penetrated either engine or fire room, chances are both rooms would be put out of commission. This design later contributed to the loss of the *Yorktown* and the first *Hornet*, CV-8.

■ On April 1, 1936, the keel of the next carrier, the 14,700-ton USS *Wasp*, CV-7 was laid down in Quincy, Massachusetts. *Wasp* was the first aircraft carrier to be built by the Bethlehem Shipbuilding Company and not by Newport News. Although similar in size to *Ranger, Wasp* had the same speed problems and was considered too slow for fleet operations. The most significant design change was the addition of a deck edge elevator in addition to the two flight deck elevators.

■ In December 1936 both the Washington Naval Treaty (Five-Power Treaty) of 1922 and the London Naval Treaty of 1930 expired. They were not renewed.

■ In response to the continued Japanese aggression in China, in May 1938 Congress, authorizing one billion dollars to expand the current navy to a two-ocean navy over the next ten years, passed the Vinson-Trammel Naval Expansion Act (Supplemental). Part of this expansion was the authorization to build two new 20,000-ton aircraft carriers to join the five that were already in service (*Langley* by this time had been converted to a seaplane tender). Included in the Vinson-Trammel act was the authorization to construct 3,000 naval aircraft of various types, and the fortification of the islands of Midway, Wake and Guam to help defend the eastern Pacific against any future Japanese expansion in that area.

By 1938 the navy realized that the design of all of the existing aircraft carriers was obsolete. For the previous seven years countless designs and modifications had been made toward building the carrier the navy really wanted, yet too many questions and continuous changes in the specifications meant the navy was about two years away from being ready to start construction of anything involving new design.

■ With the passage of the Vinson-Trammel Expansion Act, the expansion of the war in China and the political unrest being generated in Europe by Adolf Hitler, the navy decided that it would take the next best route toward getting at least one new carrier. The navy had a fairly successful design in *Yorktown* and *Enterprise*. With modifications developed over the past few years and the design changes incorporated into these two ships, the navy decided to build its next carrier based upon *Yorktown's* design. Consequently, the next carrier, number 8, would be a modified *Yorktown-class,* and the following one, number 9, would be a new class of its own.

On September 25, 1939, the keel of the USS *Hornet*, CV-8, seventh ship in the United States Navy to bear that name, was laid down at Newport News.

Chapter 3

USS *HORNET*, CV-8

When the navy was finally authorized to build two new aircraft carriers under the Vinson-Trammel Expansion Act (Supplemental) of 1938, the design of the next generation, or class, of ships was still long from being finalized. Instead of waiting for the design studies to be completed, the navy decided that the first carrier would be built for an emergency, utilizing the existing plans and modifications of the *Yorktown*-class carriers *Yorktown* and *Enterprise*.

The second carrier would be named *Essex,* and would incorporate all of the current and proposed changes. She would be the first carrier of a new class, to be called the *Essex*-class.

■ At 4:17 a.m. local time on September 1, 1939, Adolf Hitler launched the German Army on an invasion of Poland, inaugurating the European portion of what soon became World War II. Less than four weeks later, on September 25, 1939, the keel of the next *Yorktown*-class aircraft carrier, to be named USS *Hornet*, CV-8, was laid down at the Newport News Shipbuilding and Dry Dock Company at Newport News, Virginia.

■ Temporarily known as Hull No. 385 and launched on December 14, 1940, USS *Hornet*, CV-8 was christened by Mrs. Frank Knox, wife of the Secretary of the Navy. On October 20, 1941, only seven weeks before the Japanese attack on Pearl Harbor, USS *Hornet* CV-8 was commissioned at the U.S. Navy base at Norfolk, Virginia under the command of Captain Marc Mitscher. *Hornet*, CV-8 cost $32,000,000 to build, twice the cost of her two sister ships.

No two ships of the same class are ever built exactly the same, and *Hornet* was considerably different from *Yorktown* or *Enterprise*. *Hornet*, CV-8 was 827 feet long and 114 feet wide at the flight deck. The beam was 83 feet and the draft was 25 feet under full load. Hornet displaced 19,800 tons or 25,500 tons under full load. Four geared turbine engines generated 120,000 shaft horsepower to turn the four propellers and move *Hornet,* CV-8 through the water at 33 knots.

■ Senior Japanese Navy officers observed the results of the 1932 mock attack on the U.S. Navy ships at Pearl Harbor by aircraft from *Saratoga* and *Lexington*, something the U.S. Navy seems to have forgotten about. If Japan needed any validation of the potential to do severe damage to an anchored fleet, it came in late November 1940 when fewer than 20 aircraft from the British carrier *Illustrious* made a night attack on the Italian battleships in Taranto harbor in Italy. In a matter of a few minutes, the torpedo planes and bombers managed to severely damage three battleships and one heavy cruiser, at no loss to the attacking aircraft.

■ When Japan made the surprise attack on the United States Pacific Fleet at Pearl Harbor on December 7, 1941, and propelled the United States into war, *Hornet* CV-8 was off Norfolk on her shakedown cruise. *Hornet's* Air Group Eight along with the crew of the ship immediately began intensive training and war preparations.

On February 2, 1942[1] two Army B-25 "Mitchell" bombers were hoisted onto the flight deck at Norfolk. *Hornet* then put to sea, and shortly thereafter the two planes were flown off the deck under their own power to determine if such large aircraft could be successfully launched.

Hornet, CV-8 departed Norfolk on March 4 and passed through the Panama Canal. She arrived in San Francisco on March 20, docking at Pier 3 at Alameda Naval Air Station.

■ On April 1, 1942, sixteen of the B-25's were hoisted on the flight deck while all of *Hornet's* regular aircraft were stored on the hangar deck. Reporting on board *Hornet* was Army Lieutenant Colonel James H. "Jimmy" Doolittle and the volunteer officers and enlisted men attached to the bombers.

The next day *Hornet*, as flagship of Task Group 16.1, left Alameda with several escorts, enroute, so the crew thought, to Hawaii to unload the bombers, which were stored in double rows on the aft end of the flight deck. *Hornet* was steaming under sealed orders at the time. Late on the afternoon of April 2, Captain Mitscher announced over the public address system that *Hornet* was going to steam across the Pacific to within launching distance of Tokyo. The army bombers were going to fly off *Hornet's* deck and bomb Tokyo, the first chance the armed forces of the United States would have to inflict some type of damage to the Japanese homeland.

Task Group 16.2, comprised of *Enterprise* and her escorts, rendezvoused with *Hornet* on April 13. *Enterprise's* aircraft were to provide protective air support since *Hornet's* couldn't be used. Now under com-

---

1   *Several times I received draft copies of this manuscript back from my editor with the date February 2, 1942 circled in red. It turns out that it is the birthday of my good friend and editor, "Wild Bill" Haley. So, Bill, Happy Birthday!

mand of Admiral William F. "Bull" Halsey, the plan was to steam within 400 miles of Tokyo and launch the bombers on April 19.

■ Doolittle's airplane was going to launch at dusk, about three hours ahead of the remaining bombers, and he was going to drop incendiary bombs to guide the rest of planes to the targets. The targets were one or more large cities: Tokyo, Osaka, Nagoya or Kobe. Because they couldn't land back on *Hornet*, the bombers would fly another 600 miles and land at a friendly airfield in China. If the *Hornet* and *Enterprise* were only able to get to within 500 miles of Japan, the bombers would have only about 20 minutes of fuel remaining when they landed at the Chuchow (Zhuzhou) airfield in China.

On the morning of April 17 the fleet refueled from the accompanying tankers. *Hornet*, *Enterprise* and four escorting cruisers started a high speed run toward Japan, leaving the destroyers and slower tankers behind.

■ At about 3:00 a.m. on April 18, a radar contact from *Enterprise* detected two ships only ten miles away, so Halsey had the ships turn north, then west again to avoid the ships. Around 10:00 a.m. a scout plane from *Enterprise* dropped a message on *Enterprise's* flight deck (radio silence being in force) that a picket boat had been spotted 40 miles ahead, and that the plane itself had probably been spotted.

The weather at this time was horrible. The fleet was steaming in 45-knot winds and 35-foot swells, however, Halsey had the fleet continue ahead, trying to close the Japanese coast because they were still over 250 miles from the launch point. Unfortunately, just 30 minutes later another picket boat, previously hidden in the swells, was visually sighted by the fleet. This time Halsey knew the boat would be broadcasting the fleet's location. Halsey had one of the cruisers sink the picket and a second one that appeared in the swells while he and Doolittle discussed the options. They were still 650 miles from the Japanese coast, and the plan to launch at dusk wouldn't work. Now that they had been detected, the carriers would have to turn around and head back to Pearl Harbor. Doolittle either had to launch 250 miles short of the planned launch point and chance running out of fuel or abort the mission and return to Pearl. Doolittle chose to launch his aircraft.

There were only 500 feet of open deck to fly off, but Doolittle, now aided by a 50 knot headwind, managed to fly his bomber off the deck of *Hornet*, and during the following hour the other fifteen bombers followed him. The last bomber was launched 170 miles short of the planned launch point. As it left the deck, *Hornet* started to launch some of it's own aircraft to support those of *Enterprise*, who were now tracking down several Japanese picket boats. Ultimately, sixteen picket boats were attacked and all were either sunk or damaged.

Meanwhile, within a minute after the last bomber flew off *Hornet's* deck, Halsey ordered the little fleet to turn around and steam east. Doolittle's sixteen bombers and 80 crewmembers were now on their own.

■ Just before noon on April 18, radio operators on all of the ships were tuned into Radio Tokyo, listening to a propaganda program being broadcast in English. Shortly, the radio operators heard air raid sirens in the background and the broadcast abruptly switched to Japanese. Then, the station went off the air.

Flying in at just 2,000 feet, the bombers hit military and industrial targets around Tokyo and even damaged a new aircraft carrier, putting it out of commission for six months. Continuing to fly low and without the weight of the bombs, Doolittle's bombers continued flying west, evading Japanese fighters and antiaircraft fire. Because of the early launch, all of the planes were short on fuel, so once they had left Japan, the pilots were free to set their own course to China. One of them flew north and landed in Russia, the remaining fifteen either ditched in the ocean or crash landed in China. Of the 80 crewmembers, four died and seven were captured by the Japanese, three of whom were later beheaded by their captors.

The sixteen bombers did not do a lot of physical damage, but the raid accomplished its goal of providing a major American morale boost after four months of bad news and defeat since the Pearl Harbor raid. More important was the effect the raid had on the Japanese military leadership.

■ No foreign power had successfully attacked the Japanese home islands in over 400 years, and the Japanese military had promised the civilian government that no enemy aircraft would ever bomb a Japanese city. The Doolittle raid was a major slap in the face to the military.

The Japanese did not know where the bombers came from, the Japanese picket boats didn't get the word out about the carrier. Months later President Roosevelt told the American public that the bombers flew from "Shangri-La," the mythical city in James Hilton's novel *Lost Horizon*. Thinking they might have come from Midway Island, the Japanese high command decided to capture Midway to prevent future raids. The result of this decision would lead to the decisive Japanese defeat at the Battle of Midway less than two months later, which was the turning point of the war against Japan.

■ *Hornet*, CV-8 arrived back in Pearl Harbor on April 25, one week after launching Doolittle's raid, and spent five days in port prior to departing on April 30 for the south Pacific to participate in the Battle of the Coral Sea. Arriving after the battle, *Hornet* was able to escort the severely damaged *Yorktown* back to Pearl Harbor for repairs. It was during the Coral Sea battle that the U.S. Navy lost its first aircraft carrier. *Lexington* had taken a bomb hit which eventually led to a massive explosion from accumulated gasoline fumes. After several hours of trying to fight the resulting fires, the crew was ordered to abandon ship and was picked up by *Lexington's* escorts. As the ship burned, a destroyer launched two torpedo's into the hull and *Lexington* sank beneath the waves.

■ On May 26 *Hornet*, CV-8 arrived back at Pearl Harbor, departing two days later with the hastily patched up *Yorktown*. After rendezvousing with *Enterprise* northeast of Midway, *Hornet* became part of Task Force 16 under command of Admiral Raymond A. Spruance, whose Chief of Staff was Captain Miles A. Browning.

The U.S. Navy and other intelligence sources had cracked the Japanese naval code and knew in advance that Japan was planning an all-out attack on the island of Midway and the Aleutian Islands. With this information Admiral Chester W. Nimitz, commander of the Pacific Fleet in Pearl Harbor, planned to have his forces in place to intercept and surprise the Japanese fleet before it could attack Midway.

The three carriers (*Hornet*, *Enterprise* and *Yorktown*), eight cruisers and 17 destroyers of the combined Task Force 16 under Spruance, and Task Force 17 under Admiral Frank J. Fletcher, were going to face off against a large portion of the Japanese Imperial Fleet of six carriers, seven battleships, 14 cruisers and 42 destroyers. Things didn't look too promising for the American forces.

■ On June 3, Japanese forces attacked Dutch Harbor in the Aleutian Islands. Later that day B-17's flying out of Midway spotted and attacked the Japanese transport group that was carrying the troops that were going to land on Midway.

During the night of June 3-4, four Japanese carriers and their escorts under command of Admiral Nagumo approached Midway from the northwest, totally unaware that Fletcher and the three American carriers were only a couple hundred miles away to the east.

While the Japanese carriers were sending their planes to bomb Midway, American aircraft were searching out the Japanese fleet. While this is not a history of the Battle of Midway, one of the more dramatic events of the battle occurred when the sixteen TBD Devastator torpedo bombers of *Hornet's* Torpedo Eight managed to locate the Japanese fleet.

Flying in low and slow to launch their torpedo's against the Japanese carriers, the Devastator's were like sitting ducks. All sixteen were shot down, and only one of the 48 crewmembers, Ensign George H. Gay, survived. Meanwhile, *Enterprise's* Torpedo Six made a similar attack, losing ten of fourteen aircraft, followed by *Yorktown's* Torpedo Five, which lost eleven of thirteen aircraft. For over an hour the torpedo bombers of the three carriers sacrificed themselves, losing 37 of 43 air-craft and all but one of their crewmen.

However, they did not die in vain. All of the Japanese fighter planes were either down low to the water attacking the torpedo planes or were landing to refuel and rearm when the dive bomber squadrons from *Yorktown* and *Enterprise* came hurtling out of the sky. The dive bomb-ers struck three of the four Japanese carriers, sinking them all. Later that day the fourth carrier would also be sunk.

The Battle of Midway was a resounding defeat for the Japanese Navy, having lost four of its largest carriers, all veterans of the attack on Pearl Harbor. Not only were the carriers and several thousand crewmen lost, but so were all of their aircraft, and 300 of Japan's most skilled pilots who went down with the carriers.

■ It wasn't a one-sided victory for the U.S. forces, however, because some of the Japanese airplanes found *Yorktown* and managed three bomb hits on the carrier. Burning furiously, *Yorktown* was abandoned. When it didn't sink the next morning, a salvage crew went back on board and got a tow line to another ship in order to tow it back to Pearl Harbor. On the early afternoon of June 6, while under tow and with the destroyer *Hammann* alongside providing support, a Japanese subma-rine fired two torpedo's into *Yorktown* and one more into *Hammann*. The destroyer blew up and quickly sank, but *Yorktown* held on until the next morning when it, too, sank. *Hornet's* second sister ship had been lost.

After the British attack at Taranto, the Pearl Harbor raid, the loss of two British battleships off Singapore, the battles of the Coral Sea and Midway, no one could deny the power of the aircraft carrier striking force. With Midway, the initiative in the Pacific passed to the American forces. It would never stop.

When *Hornet*, CV-8 returned to Pearl Harbor after the Battle of Midway, Captain Mitscher was promoted to Admiral and turned com-mand over to Captain Charles P. Mason. While in Pearl Harbor, *Hornet* had it's hangar deck catapult removed since it had proven to be of little value.

■ On August 7, 1942, American Marine units successfully landed on Guadalcanal, one of the Solomon Islands, which was also scheduled to be a major Japanese stronghold. If the Japanese retained Guadalcanal, it would sever the line of communications between the United States and Australia. The subsequent campaign to retain con-trol of Guadalcanal would continue to draw in more and more of the combat forces of both sides. Japan didn't want to lose Guadalcanal and spent a large portion of its navy during the next six months trying to supply its troops and to defeat the U.S. Navy and Marine forces on the island.

The four remaining United States carriers in the Pacific, *Hornet*, *Enterprise*, *Wasp* and *Saratoga* were all sucked into the Guadalcanal meat-grinder along with several battleships and dozens of cruisers and destroyers.

■ During the Battle of the Eastern Solomons on August 24, *Enterprise* was struck by three bombs and had to retire to Pearl Harbor for repairs. Then, on August 31, *Saratoga* was struck by a torpedo fired by a Japanese submarine. It, too, had to return to Pearl Harbor for repairs.

Two weeks later on September 15th it was *Wasp's* turn. Three torpedoes fired by a Japanese submarine struck the carrier, and other torpedoes struck the new battleship *North Carolina*. *Wasp* was so severely damaged that it had to be sunk by an escorting destroyer. Now there was only one American aircraft carrier available for service in the Pacific – USS *Hornet*, CV-8.

■ *Enterprise* was quickly repaired and rejoined *Hornet* off Guadalcanal, taking up position off the Santa Cruz Islands to repel any attempted Japanese naval sortie. This was fortunate because the Japanese Combined Fleet was preparing to do just that.

In another major fleet movement four Japanese carriers, four battleships, ten cruisers and 30 destroyers were steaming toward Guadalcanal to re-supply the garrison there and, hopefully, to draw the U.S. fleet out and destroy it. *Hornet* and *Enterprise* plus one battleship, six cruisers and fourteen destroyers moved to intercept them. The First Battle of Santa Cruz Islands was fought on October 26, 1942.

■ Aircraft from the Japanese carriers found the American ships first, and *Hornet* became their primary target because *Enterprise* was hidden in a rain squall. *Hornet* was out in the clear and enemy bombers and torpedo planes focused all their attention on her.

In a seven-minute span, *Hornet,* CV-8 was struck by two damaged suicide planes, seven bombs and two torpedoes. Among other things, the electrical power was knocked out and the ship was plunged into darkness while fires raged everywhere.

In the meantime, *Hornet's* aircraft had found the Japanese fleet and dropped several bombs on the large carrier *Shokako*, one of the two remaining Pearl Harbor attack carriers, putting that ship out of commission for over a year. Meanwhile, enemy aircraft found the *Enterprise*, hitting her with two bombs and causing severe damage to the ship. *Enterprise* couldn't be sent back to Pearl Harbor for repairs because she was now the only operational aircraft carrier in the Pacific.

With the attacks over for the time being, the cruiser *Northampton* took *Hornet*, now dead in the water, in tow. By early afternoon over 850 wounded and non-essential crewmen had been transferred to escorting destroyers, and *Hornet* was being towed at four knots while the engineering crew struggled to fire up the undamaged boilers.

Late in the afternoon six enemy torpedo aircraft flew in out of the clouds and once again attacked *Hornet. Northampton* had to cut the tow line in order to evade the planes, but once again this left *Hornet* dead in the water. Five of the attacking planes were shot down, but one managed to launch a torpedo into the starboard side of *Hornet*. As *Hornet* began to list past 18 degrees, it looked like it might capsize, so Captain Mason gave the order to abandon ship at 4:25 p.m. He was the last person to leave the sinking ship.

To prevent *Hornet*, CV-8 from falling into enemy hands, two U.S. destroyers fired nine torpedoes and 300 5-inch shells into the hulk, but it refused to sink. Late that night Japanese surface forces were detected closing in on the ships trying to sink *Hornet*, so they left the scene, leaving *Hornet* burning from end to end.

Two Japanese destroyers eventually launched four more torpedoes into the hull, and finally, at 1:35 a.m. on October 27, 1942, USS *Hornet*, CV-8 sank into the 16,000-foot deep waters of the Pacific Ocean.

■ *Hornet* CV-8 was only one year and six days old. She would not be forgotten. She would be avenged.

...NAVY'S $31,000,000 AIRCRAFT CARRIER LAUNCHED.
NEWPORT NEWS, VA. THE AIRCRAFT CARRIER HORNET, CONSTRUCTED AT A COST OF $31,000,000, EXCLUSIVE OF ARMAMENT, WAS LAUNCHED TODAY. MRS. FRANK KNOX, WIFE OF THE SECRETARY OF NAVY, ACTED AS SPONSOR. THE NEW SHIP, THE NAVY'S SEVENTH, WILL GIVE THIS COUNTRY ONE MORE CARRIER THAN GREAT BRITAIN'S SIX....
(NATIONAL ARCHIVES, REFERRED HEREAFTER AS "N.A.")

NOTE THAT ONLY THE BASE OF THE ISLAND HAS BEEN CONSTRUCTED. ALSO, NOTE THE GAGGLE OF DIGNITARIES PRESENT ON THE PLATFORM AT BOTTOM, LEFT.

HORNET, CV8. PORT SIDE VIEW, LATE 1941
(AUTHOR'S COLLECTION, OR "A.C.")

Chapter 4

Hornet is Dead,
Long Live the *Hornet!*

In 1940 there wasn't any requirement to follow the restrictions imposed by the Washington Treaty or the London Treaty, both of which expired at the end of 1936. All of Europe and most of Asia was at war. Congress passed the "Two-Ocean Navy" Act in 1940, and the rapid construction of new carriers was put into motion. The navy could now build the optimal aircraft carrier that designers had been working on for years but couldn't build because of Treaty restrictions.

An improved *Yorktown* design was developed, and the first ship of this new class was named USS *Essex* after the Revolutionary War frigate. This new class would also be called the *Essex*-class. In February 1940, construction of the *Essex*, CV-9, was ordered and the keel was laid down at Newport News on April 21, 1941, just a few months before the attack on Pearl Harbor.

With the world at war and America apparently going to be sucked into it, President Roosevelt and Congress began appropriating funds to make major purchases for all branches of the services. In May 1940 Germany invaded Belgium, France and the other Low Countries, and the evacuation of the British and Allied forces from Dunkirk took place. This same month the Navy ordered construction of three more aircraft carriers, the first of which was to be *Bon Homme Richard*, CV-10, named after the Revolutionary War hero John Paul Jones' flagship. Its keel was laid at Newport News on December 1, 1941, just one week before the Japanese attack on Pearl Harbor.

Next in line would be *Intrepid*, CV-11, whose keel was also laid down at Newport News on December 1, 1941. The third carrier, ordered in May 1940, was going to be named *Kearsarge*, CV-12, named for the famous Civil War frigate that defeated the Confederate commerce raider *Alabama* off the coast of France in 1864.

■ *Essex* was launched on July 31, 1942, commissioned on December 31, 1942, and immediately headed for the Pacific to support the two remaining large aircraft carriers, *Enterprise* and *Saratoga*. Also commissioned on July 31, 1942 was the Japanese aircraft carrier *Hiyo*. Its destiny, in two years, would be to meet up with a group of pilots flying from a new US carrier named *Hornet*.

With the loss of *Yorktown*, CV-5 at the Battle of Midway in June, 1942, the navy decided to rename the hull being built as *Bon Homme*

Richard as *Yorktown*, CV-10. The new *Yorktown* was launched on January 21, 1943, commissioned on April 15, and it headed immediately to the Pacific. *Intrepid*, CV-11 was launched on April 26, 1943, commissioned August 16, 1943, and it too headed directly to the Pacific theatre.

■ On Slipway Number 8 at the Newport News Shipbuilding and Dry Dock Company, the same slipway that USS *Hornet*, CV-8 had been built less than two years before and from which *Essex*, CV-9 had just been launched, the keel and frame of hull number 395, USS *Kearsarge*, was quickly being constructed. The keel was laid down on August 3, 1942. Less than three months later USS *Hornet*, CV-8 was sunk at the Battle of Santa Cruz Island.

Crews worked around the clock to push construction of the ship because aircraft carriers were desperately needed in the Pacific. By September 1942, *Lexington*, *Yorktown* and *Wasp* were gone, and *Enterprise*, *Saratoga* and *Hornet*, CV-8 were holding the line against Japanese aggression. New aircraft carriers were needed, and nothing was allowed to slow their construction.

■ In August 1940, seven more aircraft carriers of the *Essex*-class were ordered by the navy, (CV-13 through CV-19) and in December 1941 two more were funded (CV-20 and CV-21). In August 1942 another ten carriers were authorized (CV-31 through CV-40), and finally in June 1943 two more were authorized, (CV-45 and CV-47). In all, 25 *Essex*-class carriers were ordered, and of those, 24 were actually built.

■ Construction of the *Kearsarge* continued at a rapid pace. Sub-assembled sections, machinery, tons of steel, propellers, parts in the tens of thousands, more steel and more parts all arrived at Newport News to be added to the new hull quickly taking shape.

The navy considers a ship as active until it is officially "stricken" from the list of ships. Some, such as the USS *Constitution* in Boston Harbor have never been "stricken" and are still considered to be on active duty. But eventually, if a ship is no longer available or needed to perform its mission, it is stricken from the list. Thus, on January 13, 1943, two and one-half months after being sunk at Santa Cruz, the USS *Hornet*, CV-8 was stricken from the Navy List of Active Ships. However, the navy wouldn't be without a *Hornet* very long. One week later, on January 21, 1943, hull number 395, USS *Kearsarge*, CV-12 was renamed USS *Hornet*, CV-12.

A new *Hornet* era had begun.

A New Class of Carrier

There was a group of very senior active duty and retired Navy officers called the General Board who met and studied and approved all long-range war plans or design specifications for new navy ships. Formed in 1900, the General Board had more power then the Chief of Naval Operations. The Board was responsible for aircraft carrier design based upon staff requirements and known or perceived needs.

In 1939, with a pending war against Japan, improved funding and the termination of the Washington and London Naval Treaties, the General Board finally had the opportunity to approve a totally new aircraft carrier, using all of the knowledge gained from previous carriers. This class of carrier had a target weight of 20,000 tons, but would not be limited to that weight in order to add all of the armor, machinery and aircraft that provided the optimum mix for the maximum punch. They were designed to operate against Japan in a war in the Pacific, so there would be room for a larger group of aircraft. While the carriers of the other principle navies were designed to hold a maximum of 50 or so aircraft, the *Essex*-class would hold double that, because one of the lessons learned prior to the war was that an additional (fifth) squadron of aircraft was needed. This would be a second fighter squadron, needed to help protect the fleet from enemy aircraft.

It was navy doctrine to utilize a "deck load strike," where all of the aircraft for a given mission were to be stored on the flight deck and launched at one time. Consequently, the deck had to hold all of the required aircraft and still have room to launch, which meant the deck had to be as large as possible.

■ Although no two ships are built alike, the twenty-four *Essex*-class carriers would all be built to the same general specifications. Certainly *Hornet*, CV-12, ex- *Kearsarge*, would be built to these initial design specifications for the *Essex*-class carriers.

■ *(From this point in the book, you, the reader, need to understand that* Hornet, *as launched in 1943, is considerably different than* Hornet *as it now resides as a museum. During its 27 years of active service,* Hornet *underwent many design changes and four major rebuilds. Since the narrative is in approximate chronological order, what you visit today may be considerably different than what was originally built.)*

■ On the morning of August 3, 1942, the keel of CV-12 was laid down at Newport News. The keel basically was an 870-foot long "I" beam made out of steel plates. Over time as more beams and plates were added, the shape or form of the ship became identifiable. Frames, beams and more plating were added. Hundreds of compartments were created and the ship grew higher and higher. When she was launched on August 30, 1943, just one year and three weeks after the keel was laid, *Hornet* was about 75% complete, the most noticeable item missing being the island. The rest of the decks were in, but much of the interior work had yet to be done. But *Hornet* was launched anyway, because

Slipway Number 8 had to be immediately put to use to construct another ship. The rest of the construction would be done while *Hornet* rested at the fitting out pier in the Portsmouth (Virginia) Navy Yard.

■ During that year while *Hornet* resided at Slipway Number 8, 2,000 construction workers, working from over 9,000 separate plans, worked three shifts, seven days per week hammering and cutting, riveting and welding. Although the keel was laid six months *behind* schedule, *Hornet* was launched six months *ahead* of schedule. A massive wooden scaffold containing over 56 miles of lumber had been built around the hull, it and tens of thousands of feet of hoses and electrical cable had to be removed before the ship could be launched.

■ Launch was scheduled for 11:36 a.m. on August 30, 1943. Secretary of the Navy and Mrs. Frank Knox, Captain Miles Browning, *Hornet's* first commander, and a platoon of high-ranking officers and officials from the Newport News shipyard were in attendance. Mrs. Knox was the ship's sponsor, and as such would christen the ship with the traditional breaking of the champagne bottle on the bow. Additionally, thousands of yard workers and their families, people who had worked on the ship for the past year, were in attendance along with a small army of photographers and reporters.

The launch did not take place as scheduled. There was an indefinite postponement announced when it was discovered that certain hydraulic equipment that was needed to give the hull a push so it would slide down the slipway under its own weight, was malfunctioning. About thirty minutes later, the equipment had been fixed, and at 12:17 p.m. Mrs. Knox broke the bottle of champagne on the starboard side of the hull, proclaiming, *"I christen thee Hornet."* (Mrs. Knox had also christened *Hornet*, CV-8, hull number 385, on the same slipway just three years earlier.)

It only took 35 seconds for *Hornet* to float free of the dock, and it was immediately pushed by several tugs across the bay to the fitting out dock. On a huge sign nearby, a hornet (the buzzing kind) was painted over the top of an outline of Japan. The sign read, "Hull 385 started it, Hull 395 will finish it." After *Hornet* was launched, Secretary Knox made a speech and remembered the previous *Hornet,* ending his speech with *"The Hornet is Dead, Long Live the Hornet!"*

■ The next part of getting *Hornet* ready for commissioning began immediately. The civilian yard workers now struggled to finish the ship, knowing they only had three months to do so. The island had to be completed, along with the masts, machinery, guns, electrical, plumbing and hydraulic systems. All of the living quarters and items required for crew use had to be finished, including the galleys, machine shops, engine and boiler rooms and the medical facilities.

On the date of her launch, some of *Hornet's* crewmembers reported aboard to begin the monumental task of testing, familiarization, testing, organizing and more testing. Even as additional crewmembers reported aboard on a daily basis, ever more work had to be done. Thousands of tons of material had to be ordered, received, inspected, loaded and stored in hundreds of compartments. In the age before the invention of the computer, everything had to be recorded on paper. Literally tons of paperwork was created to track all of this materiel. Everything from food to bunker oil, aviation fuel, lubricants, spare parts, spare clothing, medical supplies, laundry detergent, shop rags—everything, including tens of thousands of unique items—all had to be ordered, received, tallied, inventoried and stored.

■ On November 29, 1943, there was a brief interlude from all this commotion, for it was on this day that *Hornet* was officially commissioned as a United States Navy warship. It was a cold and windy day as 2,000 members of the crew formed up on the flight deck to take part in the commissioning ceremony. Once again, among the special guests were Secretary of the Navy Frank Knox and Mrs. Knox.

At 1:00 p.m. Mrs. Knox presented the battle flag from *Hornet*, CV-8 to Captain Miles Browning, and then Secretary Knox ordered *Hornet*, CV-12 placed into commission. Captain Browning accepted the ship and then issued his first order, which is customary at all commissioning ceremonies, to *"Set the watch."*

By 2:15 it was all over and everyone returned to work. There was still an enormous amount of work to be done before the ship could begin its first shakedown cruise.

■ The following day *Hornet* was placed in dry dock, and the water was pumped out so engineers could check everything that had been submersed for the past three months. On December 3 she was re-floated and moved to another dock where preparations continued. Now was when the boilers and engines, the catapults and other major subcomponents were tested. Tons of fresh food, along with over 200,000 gallons of aviation fuel and thousands of rounds of ammunition for the ship's guns was loaded. More crewmembers reported aboard, among them being the aviation crew who were assigned to Air Group 15, which would be the first of several groups assigned to *Hornet* during the next 26 years.

It was on December 20, 1943, that USS *Hornet*, CV-12, left Norfolk to begin her sea trials.

BOW VIEW, HORNET PREPARING FOR SEA TRIALS, DECEMBER 1943. NOTE THE THREE CAGED RADIO ANTENNA'S ON THE STARBOARD EDGE OF THE DECK (LEFT SIDE IN THE PHOTO), THE TWO TWIN 5 INCH MOUNTS IN FRONT OF THE ISLAND AND THE SINGLE QUAD-40 MILLIMETER GUN MOUNT HANGING OFF THE STEM (BOW) JUST BELOW THE FLIGHT DECK. PILED ON THE FORWARD ELEVATOR IS A STACK OF WHAT APPEARS TO BE DUFFLE BAGS CONTAINING THE CREW'S PERSONAL GEAR. (NATIONAL ARCHIVES)

Chapter 5

Return on Investment: Specifications

So what did the Navy get for its $69 million investment? *Hornet* specifications, typical of the early *Essex*-class carriers, were as follows: *(remember, these are the specifications when the ship was commissioned in 1943. Also, check the Glossary for an explanation of terms.)*

Overall Dimensions

Displacement:
Standard: 27,100 tons
Full Load: 36,200 tons
Length:
Overall: 876.8 feet
Waterline: 820.0 feet
Flight Deck: 846.0 feet
Width (beam):
Overall: 147.5 feet
Waterline: 93.0 feet
Flight Deck: 108.0 feet
Draft: (Under load:)   29.5 feet
Height: (height is measured from the waterline. Total height in the second column would be distance from the water line *plus* the designed draft of 29.5 feet).
Flight Deck: 52.3 feet / 81.8 feet
Hangar Deck: 25.5 feet / 55.0 feet
Navigation Bridge: 74.9 feet / 104.4 feet
Flag Bridge: 67.3 feet / 96.8 feet
Top of Mast: 193.5 feet / 223.0 feet
Hangar deck:
Length: 654.0 feet
Width: 70.0 feet
Height, to bottom of Gallery Deck: 17.5 feet

Engines and Mechanical

The propulsion system on *Hornet* consists of two engine rooms and four fire (boiler) rooms. The forward fire room is located amidships, below the island. Going aft, you begin with fire room #1, then fire room #2, forward engine room, fire room #3, fire room #4 and finally the after engine room. They were divided this way to prevent combat damage to one engine room from affecting the operation of the ship. *Hornet*, CV-8 had both engine rooms next to each other and a torpedo hit on one knocked them both out of commission.

Boilers: eight Babcock and Wilcox boilers, two in each of four fire rooms with 634 psi designed pressure.

Engines: four Westinghouse geared turbine engines in two engine rooms, with a total of 150,000 shaft horsepower. (The engines in the forward engine room turn the outside or "wing" propellers, and the aft engine room engines turn the inside propellers.)

Propellers: four, four-bladed propellers, 15.0 feet in diameter, made of solid manganese bronze, weigh 27,000 pounds or 13.5 tons each.

Propeller shafts: four, 20 inches in diameter. Outside shafts are 257.9 feet long and the inside shafts are 185.8 feet long.

Rudder: one rudder, 430 square feet in surface area.

Anchors: two, 30,000 pounds or 15 tons each.

Anchor chains: two, 1,100 feet long (or over 3 1/2 football fields). Each link weighs 120 lbs, approximately 900 links per chain, one chain weighs about 108,000 pounds or 54 tons. The anchors were located on either side of the hull. *(There was no anchor on the bow, or stem, as you see today. The port side anchor was moved to the stem in 1965 during the FRAM II conversion.)*

Armor Protection

Unlike aircraft carriers from other World War II navies and all modern aircraft carriers, *Hornet* and other *Essex*-class carriers did not have an armored flight deck. The Hangar Deck was the armored deck because it was considered a part of the ship's hull. The reason for this is covered elsewhere in this book.

Deck Armor:

Flight Deck:	.2" (or 3/16" thick) steel topped with 3.5" of teak wood
Hangar Deck:	2.5" thick STS (Special Treatment Steel, a heat tempered nickel chrome steel alloy)
Fourth Deck:	1.5" STS
Second Platform:	1.5" STS
Island:	1.5" STS

Side Armor:

Armor Belt:	2.5" to 4"
Bulkheads:	4"
Island:	1" on sides of the pilothouse

Anti-torpedo Defense:
Vital areas of the ship are protected by up to five bulkheads that enclose four "dead" areas that are designed to absorb the impact of a torpedo. The "dead" areas are compartments that can be used to store bunker oil, water or air (for buoyancy.)

Armament

5-inch / 38 caliber gun:
Four-2 gun turrets located on the Flight Deck, two in front of and two behind the island.

Four single mounts, located on sponsons on the port side Gallery Deck, two forward and two near the stern.

40 Millimeter antiaircraft:
32 total in eight-four gun mounts, later increased to 40 in ten mounts.

20 Millimeter antiaircraft:
46 total in single mounts, later increased to 55.

(Note: only four of the 5-inch/38 caliber guns survive today: two of the original port side guns and two on the starboard side, added in 1956.)

Miscellaneous

(Remember, these specifications are for Hornet *as she was built in 1943.)*

Catapults:
Flight Deck: One H-4B hydraulic on the port side of the flight deck.

Hangar Deck: One H-4B hydraulic to launch off the starboard side of the ship.

Elevators:
2-centerline on flight deck: 48.2 feet by 44.2 feet, capacity 28,000 pounds (14 tons)

1-side elevator: located off the port side. This elevator tilts up to allow passage through the Panama Canal and has a capacity of 18,000 pounds (9 tons)

(The elevators are numbered: the forward flight deck elevator is #1, the port side deck edge elevator is #2 and the aft flight deck elevator is #3.)

Arresting Gear:
Aft: 16 cross deck pendants (wires), Mark 4 system with five Davis barriers (nets stretched across the deck to catch the landing gear or propellers of any aircraft that missed the arresting cables. The Davis barriers generally caused serious damage to any aircraft that hit them

or would even turn it upside down. The barriers could be lowered after each landing so the aircraft could be taxied out of the landing area.)

Bow: 9 cross deck pendants, Mark 4 system with two Davis barriers. The forward arresting gear was added to allow aircraft to land on the bow of the ship if the aft part of the Flight Deck was damaged or the ship was steaming in reverse. They were impractical and were removed in 1944.

Fuel Oil: (bunker oil)
Capacity: 6937 tons
Usage:

Knots (speed)	Gallons per day	% fuel/day
15	46,150	3%
20	76,800	4.5%
25	131,334	8.4%
30	273,420	17.5%
33	414,800	25.5%

(Steaming at 25 knots, Hornet would have to be refueled about every ten days)

Aviation Fuel: 231,500 gallons
Crew:
Officers: 268
Enlisted: 2,363

Although designed for a crew of 2,500, by the end of World War II there were as many as 4,000 men assigned to *Hornet*. This was due to the addition of an extra fighter squadron, additional anti-aircraft guns, and the addition of an Admiral and his staff.

Chapter 6

Hornet Eagerly Heads West

All new ships participate in a "cruise" known as sea trials followed by another called the "shake down" cruise. Sea trials and shake down cruises are designed to allow the crewmembers to become acquainted with each other, all of the equipment, subsystems and the myriad of details required to run a ship. The navy standard for an aircraft carrier of the *Essex*-class was for two weeks of sea trials followed by four or five weeks of "shake down" so the ships crew and the aircrews could get some meaningful training time together. With all of Air Group 15 except the pilots on board, on December 20, 1943, *Hornet* departed Norfolk to begin her sea trials. The pilots would fly aboard later with their aircraft.

One of the first things Captain Miles Browning had to contend with during the sea trials was the orders he received to reduce them from the normal four weeks to two weeks because *Hornet* was desperately needed in the Pacific. During the two trials, every system and subsystem was checked out, and then checked again. Speed and turning tests, fuel consumption, catapults, radar, antiaircraft defenses, pilots, mechanics, ships crew, everyone and everything was tested. General Quarters sounded several times a day to see how responsive the crew was and to make them even better.

■ The most important group of individuals on *Hornet*, the reason for her very existence, were members of Air Group 15. While the ship was going through sea trials, the pilots and men of the air group were conducting carrier qualifications (or CARQUALS, as the navy calls them). Everything was being practiced and checked, including launches and landings, formation flying, navigation, communications and maintenance.

The first arrested landing (using the cross-deck pendant, or arrestor cables, to stop the aircraft) was made on January 1, 1944. Shortly thereafter the entire complement of Air Group 15 landed on *Hornet*: 16 TBF-1 Avenger torpedo bombers of VT-15, 36 F6F-3 Hellcat fighters from VF-15 and 32 SB2C Helldiver dive-bombers from VB-15.

■ After two weeks of sea trials in the Chesapeake Bay, *Hornet* returned to Norfolk for inspections and to take on more fuel. *Hornet* then left for her shake down cruise off Bermuda accompanied by several escorting destroyers. During this cruise, aircraft towed targets for the antiaircraft gunners to shoot at, and several of the ships towed floating target sleds for the pilots to practice divebombing. During this time, six aircraft were lost to landing accidents with the loss of three airmen. Unfortunately, they wouldn't be the last.

On February 1, *Hornet*, again, pulled into Norfolk for a two week stay, during which time additional training was conducted. New crewmembers were signed on. Complete inspections of all machinery and the ship's hull were made. Food, oil and other provisions were loaded. Finally, on February 14, 1944, *Hornet* departed Norfolk enroute to San Diego, California via the Panama Canal.

■ As usual, during the voyage to San Diego, continuous training, calls to General Quarters, flight operations and close maneuvering with the escorting ships was practiced 24 hours per day. By the time *Hornet* arrived in San Diego on February 27, the crewmembers had become pretty adept at their duties.

Before departing San Diego for Pearl Harbor, *Hornet* loaded well over 2,000 Marines and their gear and over 250 jeeps and other vehicles for the trip. Not being a troopship, there were no bunks available for the marines, so they were jammed into every space that could be found. With so many extra men on board, the ship's cooks had to resort to feeding everyone only two meals a day.

Also boarding in San Diego were a group of over 70 Spanish-speaking Mexican nationals who were drafted into the Navy (If you were living in this country, you were eligible for the draft!). They were assigned to the 20 mm antiaircraft mounts, where they became experts in the use of the guns.

There is a comment made in one of the orientation videos shown at Aircraft Carrier Hornet Museum that says, *"...the Hornet eagerly headed west...."* Every former member of the crew that the author has spoken to gets a big laugh out of that. As most have said, *"The Hornet may have been eager, but the crew surely wasn't!".*

■ Five days after leaving San Diego, *Hornet* docked at Pearl Harbor to offload the Marines. Then Captain Browning ordered the removal of Air Group 15, an incident that thoroughly upset all of the crewmembers, because, it seems, ever since *Hornet* had been launched, it had been a truly unhappy ship.

■ Captain Miles R. Browning, graduate of the United States Naval Academy class of 1917 and the first commanding officer of *Hornet*, by most accounts had a brilliant mind. He was an outstanding aviator and was assigned to be the Chief of Staff to Admiral Spruance during the Battle of Midway where he received the Distinguished Service Medal for his tactical leadership during that battle. He was a good friend of Admiral William F. Halsey who looked after his fellow officer and pilot, and after Midway Browning had been Halsey's Chief of Staff. Unfortunately, Browning was probably the most hated officer who ever commanded an aircraft carrier.

Spruance said he was *"unstable and evil-tempered, becoming angry, excited and irrational with little provocation, and that people hated his guts."* Another officer called Browning a *"...scowling martinet who prowled the bridge like a caged animal. Every order was a snarl and his subordinates reacted to him with fear and hatred. Pilots kept a discreet distance from him."*

Browning received much of the credit for the victory at Midway, but only because Spruance wasn't the type to seek credit for himself. However, during a later tour of Guadalcanal, Browning managed to antagonize Navy Secretary James Forrestal, who complained to Admiral Ernest J. King. King didn't like Browning anyway, calling him *"erratic and unreliable and no damn good at all."* King wanted him out of the navy.

Halsey liked Browning, and King liked Halsey, so in order to get Halsey to part with Browning as his Chief of Staff, King decided to assign Browning as the commanding officer of the first available *Essex*-class aircraft carrier, which happened to be *Hornet*. King later said, *"The idea was to get rid of him at once and if it took a new carrier, so be it."* King figured it was only a matter of time before Browning committed an act that would cause his removal from command and forced retirement.

■ When *Hornet* arrived in Pearl Harbor, Capt. Browning requested that Air Group 15, whose members had been with *Hornet* since the start of sea trials, be replaced because he felt they weren't combat ready. He requested Air Group 2, then in Hawaii, be assigned. The request was approved, and Air Group 15 and the crewmembers of *Hornet* sadly parted ways.

Air groups were normally assigned to a carrier for a certain length of time and then rotated with another air group when combat time, losses, or lack of aircraft required it. Such changes were expected. However, by having Air Group 15 transferred out at Pearl Harbor, the ship's crew and the members of Air Group 15 were totally dismayed. Captain Browning had created a major blunder as far as the crew was concerned–having trained together they wished to fight together. Air Group 2 had previously been on *Enterprise* and had rotated back to Pearl Harbor to bring on new pilots and do some training. Air Group 2 officially reported aboard *Hornet* on March 8, 1944.

■ People in high places were watching Capt. Browning and it is probably for that reason that on March 15, Admiral Joseph J. "Jocko" Clark came aboard and made *Hornet* his flagship. That afternoon *Hornet* left Pearl Harbor and headed west for the war zone.

A BRAND NEW HORNET. SPORTING A NEW STYLE OF "DAZZLE" PATTERN CAMOUFALGE. HORNET, CV-12 UNDERGOING TRIALS AT NEWPORT NEWS IN LATE 1943. (N.A.)

Chapter 7

Hornet Goes to War

On March 20, 1944, *Hornet* arrived at Majuro Atoll in the Marshall Islands, 2,000 miles west of Pearl Harbor, and was attached to Admiral Alfred E. Montgomery's Task Group 58.2, joining carriers *Bunker Hill*, CV-17, *Monterey*, CVL-26 and *Cabot*, CVL-28. *Hornet's* arrival in Majuro almost ended in disaster when Captain Browning, giving steering commands and not reading the charts correctly, almost ran *Hornet* aground. Admiral Clark saw what was about to happen and tried to convince Browning to change course, but Browning, as commander of *Hornet,* refused to do so. Only the intervention of several destroyers, all blowing their whistles to warn him, caused Browning to change course before he ran his ship aground.

(NOTE: Task Group 58.2 was one of four carrier task groups that made up Task Force 58 under command of Admiral Marc A. Mitscher, which was part of the Fifth Fleet under Admiral Spruance. Each task group generally consisted of four aircraft carriers and their supporting cruisers and destroyers. As carriers arrived or departed the war zone, the makeup of the task groups changed.)

■ Shortly after *Hornet* arrived, Task Group 58.2 left Majuro and *Hornet* crossed the equator for the first time on March 25. On March 29, a *Hornet* pilot scored the ship's first victory when he shot down a Japanese patrol plane, the first of many such encounters. The following day *Hornet's* pilots shot down nine more enemy aircraft. For the next week *Hornet* and Task Group 58.2 conducted raids on several Japanese-held islands, including Palau, Ulithi, Yap and other islands of the Caroline chain before returning to Majuro on April 6.

After a week at Majuro, *Hornet*, now part of Task Group 58.1, undertook operations against several enemy islands in support of General Douglas MacArthur's landings at Hollandia. Then *Hornet* and Task Group 58.1 joined up with the rest of Task Force 58 to attack Truk, the supposedly impregnable forward base of the Japanese Imperial Fleet. During the attack so many of Truk's defending aircraft were destroyed that eventually the decision was made to bypass the island and its 50,000 defenders and move 1,000 miles further north and invade the Mariana Islands.

■ Just before dawn one morning while Captain Browning was giving course changes, *Hornet* almost collided with a destroyer and then an aviation fuel tanker. Admiral Clark was so angry about the ship's handling that he berated Captain Browning in front of the whole bridge crew, something he had never done before.

On May 1 an aircraft returning from a mission landed on the flight deck with its bomb still attached. The bomb broke loose and penetrated the flight deck, exploding on the hangar deck near the present day passage to the escalator, killing two crewmen and wounding several more. The dead were buried at sea that afternoon.

■ On May 3, *Hornet* and the rest of Task Group 58.1 anchored at Kwajalein Atoll in the Marshall Islands, and a few days later moved over to Eniwetok. In the meantime, Admiral Clark was looking for some reason to relieve Captain Browning, but couldn't do so unless some overt act had been committed.

One evening over 2,000 of the off duty crewmen, including Admiral Clark and Captain Browning, were watching a movie on the forward end of the Hangar Deck when someone accidentally set off a fire extinguisher. Someone else yelled that it was a bomb, and a panic ensued. Before calm settled in and the movie resumed, one of the crewmen got knocked overboard and had to be fished out of the water. He reported that another crewman was also in the water, so the duty officer ordered the duty launch (boat) to search around the ship. Captain Browning cancelled the order, even after Admiral Clark recommended the search and a crew muster to count everyone.

Two days later the body of the second crewman was found in the bay. Admiral Mitscher called an immediate court of inquiry, which found Captain Browning guilty of negligence. On May 29, Admiral Mitscher relieved Captain Browning and assigned Captain William D. Sample to take command of *Hornet*. Morale immediately improved with the change. Captain Browning spent the remainder of his career as commander of the Naval Air Station in Leavenworth, Kansas. Meanwhile, Captain Sample quickly moved to prepare *Hornet* for its next mission in support of the marine and army assaults on the Marianas Islands of Saipan, Tinian and Guam.

■ June 6, 1944 was D-Day, the day Allied troops began the Normandy invasion in Europe. It was also the day *Hornet* and the rest of Task Force 58 once again steamed out of Majuro and headed west for the Marianas. With Admiral Mitscher in command of Task Force 58, things had changed considerably since the Battle of Midway just two years earlier. Task Force 58 now consisted of seven large and eight smaller carriers with a total of 934 aircraft, including Task Group 58.1 with *Hornet* and Air Group 2. Beginning on June 11, carrier aircraft began attacking the islands in preparation for the infantry assaults, and on that day *Hornet's* pilots were credited with shooting down 26 enemy aircraft.

■ For almost a year the navy had stationed submarines in those areas where aircraft were operating against enemy held islands. These "lifeguard" submarines were placed so they could retrieve crewmen from downed aircraft. If the crewmen were far enough from enemy guns, the submarine would surface and bring them aboard. If they were close enough to enemy guns to jeopardize the submarine, the pilots were told to try to swim out far enough for the submarine to pick them up. Hundreds of downed pilots and crewmen were saved in this manner during the war.

One of *Hornet's* aircraft was shot down during an attack on Guam on June 13, and the wounded pilot parachuted into the water too close to enemy guns for one of the assigned submarines to pick him up. In a dramatic rescue, the submarine *Stingray*, while submerged, approached the *Hornet* pilot who then tied his life raft to the raised periscope. The *Stingray* then slowly towed the pilot to sea out of enemy range before surfacing and taking the pilot aboard.

On June 12, several *Hornet* aircraft dumped thousands of leaflets over the island of Guam to warn the native population of the pending invasion. The Japanese defenders already knew the invasion was coming, but the navy wanted to warn the civilians. This actually had an interesting effect on the enemy. They couldn't believe we would announce our arrival unless we *weren't* planning an invasion. Thus, for a while the enemy even thought we were going to bypass Guam!

■ Military pilots are an aggressive group and it's always the goal of a fighter pilot to become an "ace." You become an ace when you can claim five confirmed kills, or shoot downs, of enemy aircraft. Kills are confirmed when at least two other pilots can claim they saw the event and describe the details *or* by the use of a gunsite camera mounted on the aircraft that records the event.

During the course of the war hundreds of fighter pilots became aces, and it was a testament of the quality of American pilots that by the middle of 1944 it was becoming commonplace for pilots to qualify as an ace. Many pilots were double or triple aces. As the war progressed, American pilots were becoming more skilled while the skilled Japanese pilots were mostly gone. The battles of the Coral Sea, Midway and actions around Guadalcanal had killed off most of the pre-war trained, highly skilled pilots. The average American carrier pilot had over 525 hours of flying time before he was assigned to a carrier, while the average Japanese pilot had less than 270 hours.

A new twist on the "ace" designation was the "ace in a day," where a pilot could confirm five enemy aircraft shot down in one day. On June 15, rookie pilot Lieutenant Lloyd Barnard, flying an F6F Hellcat on his first combat mission, became *Hornet's* first "ace in a day" while *Hornet's* Air Group 2 was attacking the enemy airfield on Iwo Jima.

■ After additional air strikes on Iwo Jima on June 16, Task Group 58.1 headed south to join up with the rest of Task Force 58 east of the Mariana's Islands. The navy had discovered that the main Japanese fleet was steaming toward Saipan to disrupt the invasion of that island.

■ Japan had lost a large part of its offensive punch at the Battle of Midway in June 1942. More of it had been whittled away during the Guadalcanal battles. By mid-1943 the major ships of the Imperial Japanese Navy were being kept at secure locations around Japan and in the South Pacific, waiting for the opportunity to steam out and take on the U.S. Navy in one grand and decisive battle. The pending invasion of the Marianas Islands, particularly Saipan which was considered by Japan as sacred territory, made it imperative that the Japanese Navy make an all out attempt to disrupt the invasion and defeat the U.S. Navy. *Hornet*, a unit of Task Group 58.1, as part of Task Force 58, was about to do battle with the Japanese fleet.

■ On June 15, the enemy fleet was discovered east of the Philippines by American submarines. Two large enemy forces consisting of nine aircraft carriers containing 450 aircraft, six battleships, 13 cruisers and 27 destroyers were steaming east toward the Marianas. In addition, there were almost 1,200 land-based enemy aircraft in the Philippines and Marianas. It was the largest concentration of Japanese naval forces during the entire war, however it was also the least trained and most inexperienced.

The Japanese commander's plan was to draw Task Force 58 out west of the Marianas and keep his fleet about 400 miles away from it. His aircraft could then attack the American ships and fly about 200 miles to the islands to refuel and rearm. They could then fly back to their carriers while striking Task Force 58 again on the return flight. By doing this, the enemy commander could keep his carriers far enough away from the American carriers so their aircraft couldn't attack him due to the lack of enough fuel to make the round trip.

■ Facing the Japanese fleet was also the largest American fleet assembled to that time: seven heavy carriers (i.e. *Essex*-class), eight light carriers and eleven smaller escort carriers, seven battleships, 21 cruisers, 62 destroyers and 25 submarines. All told, there were over 600 ships in the American fleet and invasion forces. There were also 950 aircraft on the carriers. The resulting Battle of the Philippine Sea became one of the largest sea battles in history. Amazingly, not one of the surface ships of either side ever saw an enemy ship. It was be a battle involving only aircraft and submarines.

The Battle of the Philippine Sea

The morning of June 19 found most of Task Force 58 about 100 miles northwest of Guam and about 600 miles due east of the Japanese fleet. Admiral Mitscher only had a vague idea of the location of the Japanese fleet because there hadn't been any sighting reports since the previous afternoon. The enemy knew exactly where Task Force 58 was because shortly after dawn several Japanese aircraft from Guam flew out of the clouds and bombed a destroyer. There wasn't any damage to the ship, but before the enemy aircraft were shot down, they were able to radio Task Force 58's position to the Japanese fleet.

Up until that morning, it was thought that Task Force 58 had destroyed most of the aircraft on Guam during several days of attacks, however, during the evening over a hundred enemy aircraft had been flown in from other Japanese-held islands. Consequently, it was decided to do another series of air strikes on Guam. For this, aircraft from Task Group 58.1, including *Hornet*, were ordered to conduct nonstop attacks on the island's airfields. Dozens of enemy aircraft were shot down over Guam and many more on the ground, many of them accounted for by *Hornet's* pilots.

Admiral Mitscher had anticipated the enemy plan to "shuttle" attack his forces, (fly from the carriers to Guam, refuel and fly back to the carriers) so he decided to keep fighter aircraft over the island all day, again including some from *Hornet*.

Although Task Force 58 didn't know where to find the Japanese fleet, the enemy certainly knew where Mitscher's ships were because of the earlier sighting by the Guam-based aircraft. Consequently, shortly after 9:00 a.m. and 400 miles from Task Force 58, the Japanese commander launched the first of several aircraft raids on Task Force 58.

■ The first enemy attack involved 70 aircraft followed shortly after by another strike force of 128 more. At 9:50 a.m. radar finally detected the first attack coming in from the west. Mitscher ordered every non-fighter aircraft still on his carriers to be launched and to circle east of Guam so they wouldn't get in the way of his fighter aircraft and would be safe from enemy attack. Then Mitscher ordered up most of the 450 fighter aircraft he had available to go out and intercept the enemy.

However, it was an American submarine that struck first. At 9:10 a.m. a torpedo from the submarine *Albacore* tore into the Japanese commander's flagship, the new carrier *Taiho*. Although the commander survived, the carrier rolled over and sank several hours later. *Albacore* actually fired two torpedoes, but in a supreme act of self-sacrifice, one of the Japanese pilots who had just taken off from the *Taiho* saw the second torpedo and dove his aircraft into it, thus exploding the torpedo and himself. This was a portent of things to come a few months later.

■ It was the worst slaughter of aircraft in the war. The 198 aircraft of the first two enemy strikes didn't have a chance against the 450 fighters that Mitscher sent after them. One pilot commented that it looked like "an old-time turkey shoot," and forever after the air combat on June 19 would be known as the Great Marianas Turkey Shoot. One junior pilot flying off the new *Lexington*, CV-16, shot down seven planes with only one load of ammunition to become an "ace in a day." From 10:30 a.m. until around 3:00 p.m., the crystal clear sky over Task Force 58 and for 60 miles to the west was full of aircraft. In a rare atmospheric occurrence, aircraft were leaving contrails which provided a great spectacle for the crews of the ships.

The third Japanese strike of 47 aircraft and the fourth strike of 82 aircraft met the same fate as the first two. If that wasn't enough for the Japanese, shortly after noon the submarine *Cavalla* pumped three torpedoes into the side of the huge carrier *Shokaku*, starting fires that ultimately caused it to explode and sink. Both *Taiho* and *Shokaku* sank within a half hour and in sight of each other. *Taiho* was Japan's newest aircraft carrier, *Shokaku* was one of the two remaining carriers of the original Pearl Harbor attack. In addition to most of the crews, twenty-two aircraft went down with the carriers.

■ Meanwhile, American pilots had shot down at least 328 enemy planes flying off the carriers and another 50 from ground bases, or 378 aircraft in just a few hours. Only one battleship was damaged by a bomb, and 23 aircraft were lost, most of the pilots being rescued.

Hornet's pilots were busy that day. Ensign Wilbur Webb and Lieutenant Russell Reiserer became an "ace in a day" and, because he shot down six aircraft, Webb was awarded the Congressional Medal of Honor. Webb made a famous radio transmission, announcing, *"I have forty Jap planes surrounded and need a little help!"* During the course of the battle, *Hornet* pilots would receive credit for shooting down 52 enemy planes.

■ By late afternoon, Fifth Fleet commander Admiral Raymond A. Spruance still didn't know where the Japanese fleet was located as none of the submarine reports had reached him, so with the exception of sending out scouting aircraft, no attempt was made to attack it. Besides, as far as Spruance knew, all of the Japanese carriers, battleships and over 200 aircraft were still lurking around somewhere west of the American fleet. Although several of the senior admirals tried to get Spruance to steam toward the enemy fleet, Spruance wouldn't do so because he still had to protect the vulnerable invasion forces off Saipan. It wasn't until after 8:00 p.m. that the Fifth Fleet steamed west to intercept the enemy fleet.

■ At dawn on June 20, search aircraft were sent out to find the enemy fleet, but it wasn't until late afternoon that it was discovered 275 miles northwest of the Fifth Fleet. Admiral Mitscher, making quick calculations, knew that if he launched his aircraft they would arrive over the enemy fleet with less than 30 minutes of daylight to make the attack and the pilots would have to fly back to the carriers and land in the dark, something most of them were not trained to do. However, this might be his last chance to attack the enemy fleet so Mitscher ordered the launch of 216 aircraft. *Hornet's* pilots did score a carrier though. Early in the day, aircraft from *Hornet* and *Bunker Hill* attacked and sank the 29,000 ton carrier *Hiyo* northwest of the island of Yap.

■ At 4:10 p.m. *Hornet* and the other carriers launched a deck load of aircraft. Another deck load launch was planned, but after the first aircraft were airborne, it was discovered that the enemy fleet was 60 miles further west then originally reported. The second launch wouldn't arrive before dark, so it was cancelled. Meanwhile, the pilots of the first strike, figuring fuel consumption, discovered that the additional 60 miles would mean many of them would run out of fuel before they could return to their carriers.

The thought of ditching in the ocean at night wasn't something the pilots were too keen on, but they continued their mission. Ditching alone would reduce the chances of getting rescued, so Lieutenant Commander J. D. Arnold, commander of *Hornet's* Air Group 2 decided that if it came to that, all of *Hornet's* aircraft would ditch together so they could join up and await rescue.

At 6:40 p.m. the sun was setting and after two hours of flying time and 300 miles, the aircraft found the Japanese fleet. There was only 30 minutes of daylight left. Time was so short that no attempt was made to coordinate the attack, so everyone attacked whatever ship they could find. With planes attacking from every direction, the Japanese carriers launched their remaining 75 fighter aircraft while every gun in the fleet, including the 18-inch main guns from the huge Japanese battleships, fired at the attacking aircraft. Although the Japanese fighter aircraft shot down 20 of the attacking aircraft, the American fighter aircraft shot down 65 of the enemy planes while the torpedo and dive-bombers attacked the enemy carriers.

Hornet's dive-bombers managed to hit and severely damage the *Zuikaku*, last of the Pearl Harbor strike force, and in fact they were credited with sinking the large carrier. However, *Zuikaku* survived to fight another day.

In the end, during the night attack, three enemy carriers were badly damaged and one light carrier and two oilers sunk along with the 65 aircraft sent up to defend the fleet, but it wasn't the decisive finish to the Japanese fleet that Mitscher had hoped for.

■ Now the pilots faced the long flight home, many with fuel tanks already over half empty. The sky was clear and dark. There was no moon, and the pilots, many injured or with damaged aircraft, few trained to fly at night and all of them fatigued, now faced a long flight home and probably a nighttime ditching into the water. For the next two hours, the pilots fought fatigue and tension trying to make it back. A few damaged aircraft ditched enroute, but most of the aircraft made it into the general vicinity of the carriers of Task Force 58. Then the mass ditching began as whole groups of aircraft ran out of fuel while trying to find the carriers in the dark.

Procedure called for the deck landing lights to be on, which they were, but the tired pilots found it difficult to distinguish between the deck lights and the stars. So it was the decision of Admiral "Jocko" Clark in *Hornet* to order every ship in his Task Group to turn on all of their lights to guide the returning aircraft. Ships even turned on their searchlights and the destroyers fired star shells to help.

The first of the recovered aircraft was a *Hornet* plane that landed on the *Lexington*, and for the next two hours aircraft landed on any deck they could find. Many crashed upon landing, some tried to land on cruiser decks, others ditched alongside, hoping to be picked up. Many of the aircraft that did land were immediately pushed over the side after the crew was removed to free up the flight deck for the next plane. Ninety-eight aircraft were lost during the return flight and the deck landings, but 100 aircraft managed to land. Of the aircrews that ditched, the ships of the fleet saved 160 men while 38 were lost.

Hornet's deck crew was kept busy trying to recover aircraft, and several crashed on the deck or missed the barriers and ended up falling overboard. After all the aircraft were landed, the flight officers on *Hornet* discovered that over half of the 56 aircraft that had been launched hadn't returned. By next morning all but 12 of the missing aircraft were found on other carriers. During the remainder of the day, 11 of the downed crews were fished out of the Pacific, leaving only one aircraft and its two crewmen that were never found or accounted for.

Hornet's record for the day was one carrier and three oilers sunk, one battleship, two carriers and three destroyers damaged.

■ Overall, Japanese losses during the Battle of the Philippine Sea were catastrophic. Three carriers were sunk, three seriously damaged, 480 aircraft and all of Japan's trained carrier pilots were lost. Without trained pilots, the remaining aircraft carriers were useless as offensive weapons. It was a result of the battle that the Japanese military would resort to the kamikaze, or one-way mission.

The remainder of the Japanese fleet escaped to fight and sacrifice themselves on another day. The great air battle of the Philippine Sea, the Marianas Turkey Shoot, was over. *Hornet*, however, was just getting started.

Chapter 8

Into the Storm: July–October 1944

After the Japanese fleet retired from the Philippine Sea, all of Task Force 58 except "Jocko" Clark's Task Group 58.1 returned to Eniwetok for refit and resupply. *Hornet* and the rest of Task Group 58.1 steamed north to attack Iwo Jima and the Bonin Islands once again. Three enemy air attacks were made on the Task Group but none of the aircraft got close enough to do any damage. Aircraft from *Hornet* were credited with shooting down 67 of them on June 24 alone.

Next, *Hornet* and Task Group 58.1 joined the fleet at Eniwetok for several days before setting out on another air strike on Iwo Jima. During this voyage to Iwo Jima *Hornet* passed the 50,000-mile mark. On July 3, *Hornet* was credited with another 35 kills. For the remainder of July 1944 *Hornet* was involved in several more air strikes on Guam, Ulithi and other islands.

■ After only four months in command of *Hornet*, Captain Sample was promoted to Rear Admiral. While at sea on August 2, Captain Austin K. Doyle reported aboard, and on August 8 assumed command of *Hornet* so Admiral Sample could move into another assignment. *Hornet* continued to steam with Task Group 58.1 and struck the Bonins again before returning to Eniwetok on August 9 for two weeks of rest and recovery (R&R) for the crew and ships. During the raid on Iwo Jima, *Hornet's* aircraft found a nine-ship convoy and with the assistance of the other carriers of the Task Group sank every one of them.

■ Admiral "Jocko" Clark's Task Group 58.1 had made so many raids on the Iwo Jima/Bonin Islands that *Hornet* and its Air Group 2 became known as the "Jocko Jima Retta–Clark Island Group." The "Jocko Jima Development Corporation" was formed by *Hornet* crewmen, who became "shareholders." They were issued certificates good for free land on the Bonin Islands after the war, signed by Admiral Clark.Whether anyone ever tried to redeem their certificate is unknown, presumably, none of the receipients had any intention of every going back to the Bonins!

■ While anchored at Eniwetok on August 26, Admiral Mitscher boarded *Hornet* to honor the ship and crew for their outstanding efforts during the past few months. During an impressive ceremony Admiral Mitscher awarded over 200 major awards to 124 crewmen, including the following:

Navy Cross	13
Legion of Merit	2
Silver Star	4
DFC or Gold Star	86
Bronze Star	1
Purple Heart	13
Air Medal or Gold Star	83

Admiral Mitscher also made the comment, *"When I was aboard the* Hornet *[as captain of CV-8] the last time, I thought she was the greatest ship in the Navy; but now that I am back I find that she is even better."*

■ While *Hornet* and Task Force 58 were at Eniwetok for what was the fleet's last major campaign break for several months, Air Group 2 was reorganized. The change meant the 18 torpedo (SBD), 36 bomber (SB2C) and 36 fighter (F6F) aircraft were changed to 18 torpedo bombers (TBM), 24 dive bombers (SB2C) and 54 fighters (F6F), a total of 96 aircraft.

Throughout the fleet, the SBD torpedo planes were now retired from service and replaced by TBM's. The SB2C pilots were checked out in the F6F so they could switch aircraft as needed. This meant that all fighter aircraft could serve as bombers, which allowed significant operational improvements.

After the debacle of the night operations during the Battle of the Philippine Sea, all carrier pilots now had to be night qualified, so the Eniwetok stay was a busy one for the pilots, all of whom spent the night hours practicing night launches and landings.

Also during this time napalm (a mixture of gasoline and a jelling agent) and rockets, both 5-inch and 11.75-inch, became available for general use.

It had been over five months since *Hornet* left Pearl Harbor. Under normal operating procedures, *Hornet* would have gone back to Pearl for refit and to pick up a new air group. Because of combat requirements, this procedure now changed. From now on, new pilots would train on whatever carriers were in Pearl Harbor or San Diego and then be ferried to the fleet on the next available transport. This meant that there weren't going to be any trips back to Pearl Harbor for *Hornet,* or any carrier, unless combat or other damage required it.

One final change occurred on August 26. While Admiral Mitscher was on *Hornet* awarding medals, Admiral William F. Halsey, Jr. relieved Admiral Spruance as commander of the Fifth Fleet. Spruance would return to Pearl Harbor to begin planning future operations against Okinawa while Halsey commanded the fleet. Part of the change was the fleet designation itself. While Halsey commanded it, Fifth Fleet became Third Fleet, and Task Force 58 became Task Force 38.

■ On August 29 it was once again time for *Hornet* to head out to sea. *Hornet*, Task Group 38.1, now commanded by Adm. John S. McCain and the rest of Task Force 38, under Adm. Mitcher, along with 15 other aircraft carriers and over 1,000 aircraft, attacked islands in the Western Carolines and Southern Palau groups. Air attacks were also conducted against Cebu, Davao, Mindanao and other islands of the Philippines. Throughout the month of September *Hornet's* aircraft were in daily combat. By now *Hornet's* fighter squadron VF-2 was the top fighter squadron in the fleet with more victories than any other fighter squadron had ever had up to the time. Twenty-eight of the 50 fighter pilots were confirmed "aces." Every single day from September 1 through September 16, *Hornet's* aircraft were in combat. Then, on September 26, *Hornet's* pilots were credited with sinking one destroyer and seven auxiliary ships.

In late September a single enemy bomber managed to sneak in below *Hornet's* fighter cover (or CAP: Combat Air Patrol). The enemy pilot flew down the length of the flight deck and just 50 feet above it. The bombs the pilot tried to drop on the deck didn't release in time and fell into the water, its shrapnel injuring several more crewmen, two of whom died the following day. With every gun on *Hornet* and the surrounding ships firing at him, the pilot then made three more strafing runs down the deck, shooting up several aircraft and wounding several crewmen on *Hornet*. By now the CAP had arrived and the enemy pilot disappeared into the clouds. The pilot was never caught, he was both very brave and very lucky.

■ The huge American fleet now numbered over 300 combat ships and 800 service, supply and transport ships. It was no longer efficient to send the fleet back to Pearl Harbor, and by now even Eniwetok was too far away. A new anchorage large enough to accommodate the fleet was needed. The navy picked Ulithi Atoll in the Caroline Islands, located south of Guam and equally about 1,200 miles from Iwo Jima and the Philippine Islands. Occupied on September 23, within a short time Ulithi became the largest fleet anchorage in the world.

While at Ulithi on September 29, Air Group 2 was detached and returned to Pearl Harbor for a well-deserved rest. Air Group 11 reported on board to replace them.

The 10,000th arrested landing on *Hornet* occurred on October 4, 1944. This was almost ten months to the day of the first landing on January 1, 1944. That same day *Hornet* and the rest of the fleet rode out the first day of a three-day typhoon that prevented any operations from taking place.

■ While Ulithi was going to be the forward fleet anchorage, it was still too far from the combat zone to send ships during the planned extended operations against the Philippines, Formosa and Bonin Islands.

Consequently the At Sea Logistics Service Group was formed with 34 fleet oilers, 11 escort carriers and 45 destroyers divided into four replenishment or "service groups." Each service group would refuel at Ulithi, then steam to a rendezvous with one of the carrier task groups somewhere outside the extreme range of enemy aircraft. The service group would refuel the ships of the task group and supply replacement aircraft and pilots before returning to Ulithi for more fuel. The use of the service groups meant the carrier force could remain on station in the combat areas for a much longer time.

■ On October 7, Task Force 38 steamed out of Ulithi for extended operations. On October 10, *Hornet's* aircraft conducted air strikes on Okinawa and Nansei Shoto, islands considered part of Japan's inner defense line. Task Force 38 destroyed over 100 enemy aircraft and 19 warships during the day. Twenty-one aircraft were lost, but lifeguard submarines picked-up all except two of the crews.

■ Next, *Hornet* was involved in a three-day air attack on Formosa. On October 12 over 1,300 air sorties were flown from the 15 carriers of Task Force 38, followed by over 900 more the next day. The Japanese were expecting the attacks, and although over 500 enemy aircraft were destroyed, enemy fighters and intense ground based anti-aircraft fire shot down 82 American planes. Several American ships were damaged, including two cruisers, but all survived and were sent back to Ulithi for repair. Japanese pilots reported serious damage to all of Task Force 38, which prompted the commander of the Japanese fleet to send out several ships to "finish off" the fleet, but he soon learned the truth and recalled the ships.

October 13 saw another "first" for *Hornet*: her antiaircraft gunners shot down their first two enemy airplanes. Also, that morning one of *Hornet's* returning aircraft landed on the deck with its machine guns charged. The guns fired, shooting up the deck, destroying seven aircraft and injuring 12 crewmen.

October 14 was a bad day. Although *Hornet's* pilots were credited with 15 kills, seven aircraft and their crewmen were lost.

On October 15, while *Hornet* aircraft were attacking enemy installations on Luzon, *Franklin*, CV-13, became the first U.S. aircraft carrier in almost two years to be damaged by enemy aircraft. Three aircraft attacked *Franklin* and one dropped a bomb on the flight deck, killing 3 sailors and wounding 22 more.

From October 16 through October 18 *Hornet's* aircraft continued the attacks on Luzon in preparation for the invasion of the Philippines by General Douglas MacArthur's forces, which was to take place on October 20. On October 17 *Hornet's* aircraft were credited with 24 kills and on the 18th with 40 more. From October 12 through October 18, 30 of *Hornet's* aircraft and 12 pilots were lost.

■ On October 19 a new Japanese air unit was activated in the central Philippines. Called the Special Attack Corps, it will be forever known by it's more popular name, the kamikaze, suicide planes flown by volunteer pilots on a one-way mission.

The Battle of Leyte Gulf

MacArthur's landings on the island of Leyte in the Philippines could not go unanswered by the Japanese Combined Fleet and an all out effort was planned to disrupt the landings. Three separate enemy fleets were going to converge on the Leyte beaches from the north, south and west. While the western and southern forces contained only battleship, cruiser and destroyer units, the northern force comprised the remainder of the Combined Fleet's carrier strike force.

■ It is significant that the carrier units of the Japanese Combined Fleet had run rampant over most of the Pacific and Indian Oceans only two years earlier. Now Japan resolved to send its few remaining aircraft carriers on a one-way decoy mission to draw the American carriers away from the Leyte beaches so their battleships could shell the landing beaches and sink the transport ships supporting the landings. This force, known as the "northern attack force," contained four of Japan's seven remaining carriers, which between them contained only 116 aircraft. The resulting battle is much too complex to cover here, and only the "central attack force" concerned *Hornet* and its crew.

■ From October 20 through the 23, aircraft from Task Force 38 pounded enemy units on Leyte and the surrounding islands. On October 23 an enemy land-based plane bombed and sank the light carrier *Princeton* CVL-23, the first American carrier lost since the earlier *Hornet*, CV-8, in 1942.

Hornet and the rest of Task Group 38.1 was refueling at sea on October 24 when word was received that the enemy fleet had appeared undetected amid the sixteen escort carriers and their escorts just north of the landing beaches on Leyte. The "central attack force" consisting of four battleships, (including *Yamato*, the world's largest), eight cruisers and eleven destroyers came up on a small escort carrier group consisting of six escort carriers and six destroyers or destroyer escorts. The American carrier group was primed for annihilation.

The aircraft from the escort carriers and the small destroyers protecting them made a valiant effort to distract the huge Japanese battleships so the carriers could get away, but it was hopeless. The battleships had twice the speed of the carriers, and huge guns that could strike a target 15 miles away.

■ In the meantime, all of Halsey's battleships and carriers of Task Force 38 (except McCain's Task Group 38.1 with *Hornet*) were pounding north looking for the four Japanese carriers. Halsey was totally unaware that this was a decoy force intent on drawing his carriers away from the Japanese battleships now shelling the escort carriers. The Japanese carriers, basically without protection, were being sacrificed to allow their battleships the opportunity to sink the transports, which ultimately they failed to do. Thus, Halsey and Task Force 38 were too far away chasing the enemy carriers to help the hapless escort carriers facing the Japanese battleships and cruisers north of Leyte.

Task Group 38.1 terminated its refueling and immediately steamed west toward the Japanese battleships while launching every aircraft that could fly. Meanwhile, the Japanese were having problems of their own. The little American destroyers attacked the battleships, doing minor damage but causing the breakup of the enemy formation. Aircraft from the escort carriers, armed only with anti-personnel bombs to drop on the enemy ground forces, dropped them on the enemy ships. When they ran out of bombs and ammunition they still made dry strafing runs on the ships to draw fire away from aircraft that did have ammunition.

The escort carrier *Gambier Bay* CVE-73 was sunk, and two other carriers were seriously damaged while all six of the destroyers and destroyer escorts were either sunk or severely damaged. However, the Japanese commander thought he had sunk several large aircraft carriers and cruisers. With the arrival of all of the aircraft from McCain's Task Group 38.1, the enemy commander decided he had done all the damage he could, so he turned around to head for home. For the next two days he suffered almost continuous air attacks, but for the most part, the battle was over.

■ Up north, Halsey's carriers eventually found the decoy carriers. During the ensuing battle, Halsey's aircraft sank all four of the carriers, including the *Zuikaku*, last of the carriers involved in the Pearl Harbor attack.

The Battle of Leyte Gulf (or Second Battle of the Philippine Sea) was actually four separate battles, but in the end the Japanese Navy almost ceased to exist. Japan lost one heavy and three light carriers, three battleships, six heavy and one light cruiser, eight destroyers, plus all 116 of their carrier-based aircraft and pilots. American losses were one light and one escort carrier and two destroyers, plus 40 aircraft.

■ The Japanese fleet would never again pose a serious threat to U.S. forces. However, on October 25, the last day of the battle, another American escort carrier was lost. The *St. Lo*, CVE-63, was struck by the Divine Wind, a kamikaze, in the first attack of its type. *St. Lo* sank in 30 minutes. It was only the first of over 300 ships that would become the victim of the Divine Wind.

JUNE 30, 1944. ADM. MITCHER PRESENT-
ING AWARDS TO HORNET'S CREW. (N.A.)

HORNET, SOMEWHERE IN THE PACIFIC. EARLY 1945. (A.C.)

BOW VIEW OF HORNET. NOTE THE TALL RADIO MAST TO THE LEFT. THIS MAST IS ON A HINGE AND ROTATES 90 DEGREES SO IT WON'T SNAG THE WINGS OF AIRCRAFT. NOTE ALSO THE JACOB'S LADDER BOOM EXTENDING OFF THE PORT SIDE OF THE SHIP. (N.A.)

HANGAR DECK CATAPULT. AN F6F HELLCAT IS PUSHED TAIL-FIRST OUT THE PORT SIDE CATAPULT EXTENSION IN PREPARATION FOR A LAUNCH. (N.A.)

THE AIRCRAFT IS LAUNCHED THROUGH THE HANGAR DECK AND OUT THE STARBOARD SIDE. NOTE THE CATAPULT EXTENSION. THE PILOT ALSO HAD TO CONTEND WITH A SUDDEN 25-30 KNOT CROSSWIND AS THE PLANE LEFT THE HANGAR DECK. (N.A.)

Launching Aircraft...

F6F HELLCAT PREPARING TO BE CATAPULTED OFF THE DECK. NOTE THE "V" SHAPED LAUNCH BRIDLE THAT WILL DROP AWAY AS THE PLANE IS LAUNCHED. (N.A.)

AN F6F CATAPULTED OFF HORNET'S DECK. NOTE TWO BARRELS FROM THE FORWARD TWIN 5-INCH MOUNT AND THE RADIO MAST LAYING AT 90 DEGREES OFF THE SIDE OF THE FLIGHT DECK. (N.A.)

ANOTHER F6F BEING LAUNCHED, THIS TIME WITHOUT A CATAPULT, US-ING WIND, HORNET'S SPEED AND FLIGHT DECK LENGTH TO GAIN SPEED. (N.A.)

HORNET'S PILOTS RUN-NING FOR THEIR AIRCRAFT PRIOR TO A STRIKE (N.A.)

SOMETIMES YOU WANT ALL OF THE DECK YOU CAN GET. HERE A FULLY-LOADED F6F PILOT TAKES OFF AT AN ANGLE TO GAIN A FEW MORE FEET OF DECK. IN THE FOREGROUND ARE THE BARRELS OF A QUAD-40MM GUN MOUNT. EXTENDING OFF THE SIDE OF THE DECK ARE THE RADIO MASTS. (N.A.)

...and then Landing

SOMETIMES YOU MAKE A GOOD LAND-ING...

A TBF AVENGER MAKES A SAFE LAND-ING (N.A.)

...AND SOMETIMES YOU DON'T.

AN F6F LOSES ITS TAIL PRIOR TO DROP-PING INTO THE SEA. THE PILOT WAS RES-CUED. (NATIONAL AR-CHIVES)

(ABOVE)
CREWMEN SCRAMBLE FOR COVER AS A TBF'S LANDING GEAR COLLAPSES
AND ITS PROPELLER CHURNS WOODEN SPLINTERS FROM THE DECK. NOTE
ARRESTOR CABLES STRETCHED ACROSS THE DECK.
(BELOW)
AN SB2C NOSES OVER AND CATCHES FIRE WHILE CREWMEN DRAG OVER
A DOZEN HOSES ACROSS THE DECK TO FIGHT IT. THE PILOT SURVIVED, THE
PLANE WENT OVERBOARD. (BOTH NATIONAL ARCHIVES)

Chapter 9

"The Same Yesterday, Today and Forever"

The continuous activity during the past several weeks had taxed the fleet and the aviators' nerves to the limit. Most of the ships were low on food and ammunition, items not easily re-supplied at sea. Finally, on October 26 McCain's Task Group 38.1 departed for Ulithi for replenishment, arriving on October 29.

On October 30 three carriers from other task groups, *Franklin*, *Belleau Wood* and *Intrepid* were struck by kamikaze aircraft, causing serious damage and much loss of life.

Also on October 30 Admiral Mitscher, whose assistance was required by Admiral Spruance at Pearl Harbor, turned over command of Task Force 38 to McCain. Admiral Alfred E. Montgomery assumed command of Task Group 38.1, raising his flag on *Hornet*.

Hornet and Task Group 38.1 left Ulithi on November 2 and steamed to the Philippines where they bombed airfields on Luzon destroying over 400 enemy aircraft, most of them on the ground. *Hornet* pilots were credited with shooting down 29 of the aircraft that did manage to get airborne.

■ On November 11, over 300 aircraft from Task Group 38.1 attacked and sank an entire nine-ship Japanese convoy. They sank four escorting destroyers and five transports that were carrying over 10,000 soldiers. There were so many aircraft in the air at one time that it was almost impossible to coordinate them, and several midair collisions were narrowly avoided. *Hornet's* pilots were credited with sinking one destroyer and damaging another.

On November 13 *Hornet's* aircraft flew into Manila Bay and bombed several enemy transport ships, destroyed an ammunition train, and downed ten enemy aircraft. The following day four more transports were hit and two aircraft downed. When Task Group 38.1 left the area that evening, 15 transports and one cruiser had been sunk, and 43 other transports damaged or sinking.

On November 19 *Hornet* aircraft struck Clark Field outside of Manila and sank a large freighter in Subic Bay. *Hornet* was now ordered back to Ulithi. While enroute to Ulithi, *Hornet's* pilots bombed enemy forces on the island of Yap, primarily for target practice. *(At this stage of the war, the navy had bypassed over 100 islands containing enemy troops. None of these islands had any aircraft and no way to be re-sup-*

plied. They were left to wither, and as such used for target practice for new pilots and refresher training for experienced pilots returning to fleet anchorages.)

■ *Hornet* arrived at Ulithi on November 23 and spent almost three weeks there re-supplying and giving the crew a rest. To help relieve the stress everyone was granted shore leave on one of the small islands that was set aside for recreation and beer parties.

Whenever *Hornet* was anchored, crewmen were allowed to go swimming off the ship at designated times. Swimming call was always an exciting event in an area teeming with sharks. Before anyone was allowed to go into the water, some of *Hornet's* launches (small boats) were dropped into the water and a detachment of armed Marines loaded into them. Their goal was to shoot any sharks seen in the area of the swimmers. Crewmen would then climb down into the water on nets, or the more hearty ones jumped in from the deck edge elevator. During this stay in Ulithi, one anxious marine saw a shark and shot at him four times. Unfortunately, his rifle was aimed at the bottom of the launch he was standing in. The holes allowed enough water into the launch to sink it, giving the launch crew and one embarrassed marine a dunking of their own. It is presumed the shark got away.

■ While *Hornet* was at Ulithi, four more carriers including *Intrepid* (again), *Essex*, *Hancock* and *Cabot* were struck by kamikaze aircraft off Leyte. *Intrepid* was so badly damaged it had to return to California for repair.

With all of Task Force 38 now back at Ulithi, it was time to try to figure out some way to combat the kamikaze threat, which was doing serious damage to the carriers and destroyers of the fleet. The immediate answer was to have more fighter aircraft and better radar coordination. The carriers would give up some of their bombers in exchange for more fighters. But now there was both a pilot and an airplane shortage. The solution was to train marine pilots to land their F4U Corsairs on the carriers' deck, an event that was implemented immediately.

Not only were *Hornet's* crewmen working under a lot of pressure, but so were the admirals commanding the four Task Groups. Fortunately, the navy had foreseen this and had planned for rotating the admirals as necessary. Consequently Admirals McCain and Montgomery were sent back to Pearl Harbor to help plan the next offensives and train new carriers coming on line.

■ The day after arriving in Ulithi, Admiral "Jocko" Clark, one of the replacement admirals having just come back from leave, once again boarded *Hornet*, this time as a visitor. There was much cheering among the crewmen.

Before leaving Ulithi for Pearl Harbor, McCain and his staff worked up some new steaming formations to try to combat the kamikazes. A screen of radar picket destroyers would now steam 60 miles ahead of the task groups to provide earlier warning.

New CAP (combat air patrol) procedures were also introduced. There were special groups of fighter aircraft at three different altitudes (low, medium and high) on each quadrant around the task group. These CAP fighters were flying dawn-to-dusk and were relieved as necessary. Another group was flying protection for the destroyers. While yet another group would intercept all returning flights to make sure an enemy plane hadn't snuck in. Any aircraft that failed to make an identifying turn on approach was shot down.

Over enemy airfields, the plan was to have three groups of aircraft available, one over the field, one enroute to replace them and the last group returning to the carrier to be refueled. This would allow constant coverage over the airfield and prevent any enemy aircraft from taking off. At night, special night fighter units would perform the same mission.

The planning and training for all this was done at Ulithi during the time *Hornet* was there. In preparation for its next mission and because of the loss of so many carriers, Task Force 38 was now divided into three task groups instead of four. *Hornet* became one of five carriers in Task Group 38.2, now commanded by Admiral Gerald F. Bogan, who flew his flag on the new *Lexington*, CV-16.

■ *Hornet* left Ulithi on December 12, and on December 13 passed the 100,000-mile mark. Starting on December 14 and for the next four days, *Hornet's* aircraft attacked targets in the central Philippines, managing to sink a large transport ship and downing six enemy aircraft.

While searching for a refueling site on December 17 and 18, the fleet steamed into a horrendous typhoon. On *Hornet*, aircraft broke their lashings and careened around the hangar deck or fell off the flight deck into the water. Some were tossed into other aircraft and considerable damage was caused aboard ship. Overall *Hornet* weathered the storm and was ready to resume operations on December 19. The same can't be said for three destroyers that were lost with all hands. Over 800 men, several ships and 140 aircraft from Task Force 38 were lost. *Hornet* and the rest of Task Group 38.2 limped back to Ulithi to clean up the mess and replenish. Christmas was spent at Ulithi, and Santa Claus even made an appearance.

■ After Christmas, *Hornet* and Task Group 38.2 left Ulithi. For the next three weeks they bombed enemy targets on Luzon, Formosa and French Indo-China. In Cam Ranh Bay, *Hornet's* pilots sank a cruiser, a destroyer, three oilers and three transports while damaging 16 other ships. Further attacks on Formosa damaged two more destroyers. During this cruise, *Hornet* completed its 15,000th arrested landing and lost an average of two aircraft every day. On January 21, two kamikaze's struck *Ticonderoga. Langley* and *Essex* were also hit, and *Hancock* suffered severe damage when one of its own planes dropped a bomb on the flight deck when landing.

■ *Hornet* arrived back in Ulithi on January 26 for two weeks of replenishment. On February 1, Air Group 11 departed *Hornet*, bound for Pearl Harbor to train new pilots. Admiral Clark came on board and presented 73 members of the air group with hard earned awards, including:

Navy Cross	10
Legion of Merit	1
Silver Star	1
DFC	13
Air Medals	41
Purple Heart	7

The following day, Air Group 17 reported on board, having spent the previous month in Guam becoming qualified. *Hornet* departed Ulithi for several days of CARQUAL for the new pilots. The air group was determined to be ready for the combat that everyone knew would soon follow.

■ On February 3 American forces liberated Manila. Although enemy resistance in the Philippines would continue for months, for all purposes the navy's portion of the Philippines Campaign was over. During the campaign from September 1944 to February 1945, Task Force 58/38 had destroyed thousands of enemy aircraft, sunk or damaged the major portion of the remainder of the enemy fleet and a million tons of enemy merchant shipping. With long range aircraft based in the Philippines, roving carrier task forces and dozens of submarines covering all of the shipping routes, any enemy ship trying to steam from the oil fields in Indo-China to the Japanese homeland faced almost certain destruction. The long-range blockade of Japan was now in full force.

■ On January 26, Third Fleet, Task Force 38 once again became Fifth Fleet, Task Force 58 as Admiral Spruance replaced Halsey, and Mitscher replaced McCain, who rotated back to Pearl Harbor to begin planning future operations. For the upcoming operations on Okinawa and Iwo Jima, four new *Essex*-class carriers arrived for duty: *Bennington, Randolph, Shangri-La* and *Bon Homme Richard.*

Hornet and the rest of Task Force 58 left Ulithi on February 10, 1945. *Hornet* was part of Task Group 58.1, now commanded by Admiral "Jocko" Clark, flying his flag once again on *Hornet*. A week later *Hornet* pilots bombed targets in Tokyo, the first time carrier-based aircraft had attacked that city since the Doolittle raiders had been launched from *Hornet,* CV-8, 34 months earlier. On February 20 *Saratoga* was hit by three bombs and two kamikaze aircraft and had to return to Pearl Harbor. The light carrier *Bismarck Sea* was sunk by a single kamikaze.

For the next two weeks *Hornet* pilots made air strikes on several targets in Japan and supported the marine assault on Iwo Jima before returning to Ulithi on March 4 for two weeks of resupply. On the night of March 11 while the crew watched a movie on the hangar deck, a stray Japanese kamikaze crashed into the flight deck of the *Randolph* which was anchored just a few feet off *Hornet's* bow. The resulting explosions killed or wounded 125 of the *Randolph's* crew. The previously damaged *Franklin, Intrepid* and *Bataan* rejoined the fleet. Within a week *Intrepid* would be damaged by another kamikaze, as would *Yorktown, Enterprise and Belleau Wood*. Two more struck the new *Wasp,* killing and wounding 370 crewmen.

■ *Hornet* departed Ulithi on March 14, on a 40 day operational campaign off Okinawa and Japan. *Hornet's* pilots flew missions on 32 of those days, flying over 4,000 combat sorties. Kamikaze pilots attacked the ship over 100 times, and her antiaircraft gunners fired more ammunition than they had during the previous year. During the Okinawa campaign, over 3,000 kamikaze pilots sank 34 American ships, and damaged over 360 more.

■ Two pilots became "ace in a day" on March 18. On March 19 an enemy airplane dropped two bombs on the loaded flight deck of *Franklin*, setting the ship on fire and killing 724 crewmen and wounding 260 more. Valiant efforts saved *Franklin*, but she had to return to the United States, never to see combat again.

On March 24 *Hornet* pilots spotted an enemy convoy of seven ships and sank every one of them. Air strikes supporting marine landings on Okinawa continued until April 7. On April 6 alone, almost 900 enemy aircraft attacked the American fleet around Okinawa, most of which were kamikaze. Few of the 900 aircraft survived. By the end of the day, three U.S. destroyers and three supply ships had been sunk, and 11 destroyers and several supply ships had heavy damage.

■ On April 7 *Hancock* was hit by a kamikaze, which killed or wounded 150 crewmen. During the day, search aircraft spotted an enemy surface force speeding toward Okinawa. The Japanese Navy still had a few ships left, but not enough fuel to do much with them. Watching thousands of young Japanese pilots kill themselves in kamikaze attacks, the Japanese Navy decided to sacrifice the rest of their fleet in a similar mission. The super-battleship *Yamato* (at 72,000 tons the largest ship in the world), two cruisers and ten destroyers were making a one-way trip to Okinawa, hoping to beach *Yamato* near the American landing forces and then use her huge 18.1-inch guns to shell the beaches. Since *Yamato* only had enough fuel for a one-way trip, it was a super kamikaze mission.

Pilots from *Hornet* were the first to attack *Yamato*, placing four torpedoes and three bombs into the huge ship. Over 280 aircraft were involved in the attacks on *Yamato* and the other Japanese ships. Ten torpedoes and numerous armor-piercing bombs hit the huge battleship, and it finally rolled over and sank, taking most of its 2,700 crew with her. Of the entire fleet, only three destroyers survived. Once again, the world's largest battleship had been taken out by carrier-launched aircraft.

Kamikazes hit *Enterprise* on April 11 and hit *Intrepid,* for the fourth time on April 16. On April 12 *Hornet* counted arrested landing number 20,000, and her pilots shot down 33 more enemy aircraft.

■ By the middle of the month, *Hornet* and Task Force 58 had been at sea for over two months, and under almost daily attack. Everyone was dogged tired, and there seemed to be no end in sight. Day after day enemy aircraft pounced on the fleet, and every day at least one ship was hit.

The commander of the anti-aircraft screen in Task Group 58.1 sent Admiral "Jocko" Clark a message, "See Hebrews 13, verse 8." Clark read the passage in his bible and circulated it to the fleet. It read: *"Jesus Christ, the same yesterday, and today and forever."*

■ On April 14 *Hornet* pilots shot down 19 aircraft, and on April 15 contributed to a total of 45 more aircraft downings. Similar activities continued until April 28 when Task Group 58.1 finally left the area and headed back to Ulithi. During the eight week cruise *Hornet* pilots flew over 4,200 sorties, shooting down 245 enemy planes and destroying 110 more on the ground. Over 20 ships were sunk, and as many as 130 more probably sunk or damaged.

Hornet arrived at Ulithi on April 30 for nine days of R&R for the crew, and re-supply for the ship. On May 8 word was received of the surrender of Germany and the end of the war in Europe. *Hornet's* crew could only hope Japan would quit soon, too.

■ On May 9 Task Group 58.1 headed out to sea once again, and two days later *Hornet's* pilots were providing air support for the American troops on Okinawa.

Bunker Hill, CV-17, another *Essex*-class carrier and Admiral Mitscher's flagship, was hit by two kamikazes on May 11, killing 400 crewmen and wounding another 264. Among the dead were most of Mitscher's staff and a large number of fighter pilots killed in their ready room. *Bunker Hill* was out of the war. Mitscher transferred his flag to *Enterprise*. On May 14 another kamikaze struck *Enterprise*, causing serious damage and sending her back to the states for repairs. So Mitscher transferred to *Randolph*.

Before the war in Europe ended, the British Navy had sent four aircraft carriers to the Pacific to help out. During the Okinawa campaign, all four were struck by kamikazes. No one was safe.

■ From May 11 to May 17, *Hornet's* pilots continued to bomb targets on the Japanese home islands, claiming another 11 aircraft shot down and 22 destroyed on the ground. The largest aircraft manufacturing plant in Japan was destroyed before it could manufacture a single plane.

On May 17 *Hornet* passed the 150,000-mile mark, and spent the next several days bombing targets on Okinawa and Japan.

Admiral Halsey replaced Admiral Spruance on May 27 so Spruance could start planning the invasion of the Japanese homeland. Fifth Fleet once again became Third Fleet, and Task Group 58.1 became 38.1. Admiral McCain replaced Admiral Mitscher who went back to the states for a much needed rest.

■ On June 3 another severe storm was detected bearing down on Task Force 38, and Halsey ordered the fleet to steam west to try to get out of its path. Unfortunately, Halsey forgot that Task Group 38.1 and *Hornet* were refueling and were right in the path of the storm.

On June 5 Halsey ordered Task Group 38.1 to steam in a direction that put it right in the middle of what was quickly becoming another typhoon. At 5:30 a.m. Admiral Clark ordered all his ships to maneuver independently to try to avoid damage.

Hornet began to encounter 100-foot waves which crashed down on the flight deck. The ship was bobbing like a cork in the mountainous seas. The wind picked up to 110 knots (126.5 miles per hour) and gusts hit 125 knots (144 miles per hour).

Hornet would climb to the top of a wave, the bow being completely out of the water, then plunge 50-60 feet down to the bottom of a trough. As *Hornet* struggled to recover, it would ride to the top of another huge wave and repeat the action. Every time *Hornet* hit the bottom of a trough, another wave would crash over the flight deck. *Hornet* would also roll side to side as much as 45 degrees, which equaled a 90-degree swing. Crewmen couldn't walk down a corridor except with one foot on the wall and the other on the floor. Finally the stress was too much, and one towering wave crushed 40 feet of the forward end of the flight deck. Twisted steel beams and splintered wood was all that remained of the deck. During the 24 hours of the typhoon, *Hornet* and the rest of the fleet struggled to survive.

The next day the storm abated, and on June 8 *Hornet* launched most of its aircraft to transfer them to other carriers. The aircraft were trying to be launched over the forward end of the deck even though a 40 foot section was now missing. One airplane spun out after trying to take off because the deck was creating turbulence that the pilots were having trouble navigating. Admiral Clark then ordered the ship to steam in reverse while launching the remaining aircraft off the stern. This was the first and only time any aircraft carrier launched aircraft over the stern during the war, but the *Essex*-class carriers were designed to do this very thing.

Soon enough repairs to the flight deck were made to allow aircraft to launch over the bow. For the next several days *Hornet* supported attacks on targets on the Japanese homeland before retiring to Leyte Gulf on June 10 for some R&R.

■ Much celebrating took place on June 15 when Captain Doyle announced that *Hornet* was going to return to San Francisco for repairs. Admiral Clark left that day to return to Guam for other duty. Finally departing Leyte Gulf on June 19, *Hornet* arrived at Pearl Harbor on June 29, and then at Alameda, California on July 8, 1945, after having not tied up to a dock for over 18 months.

After unloading aircraft and ammunition, *Hornet* was placed into dry dock at Hunters Point Navy Yard to begin repairs and an overhaul.

Captain Doyle was replaced by Captain C.R. Brown on August 1. By August 12 all of the repairs had been made, and *Hornet* sported a new coat of paint in time to host over 100,000 visitors who came aboard in one day to view the veteran ship. Shortly, *Hornet* began sea-trials to check out the repairs, and after a month, on September 13, 1945, *Hornet* returned to Alameda. By then the war was over, Japan having surrendered on September 2.

POUNDING THROUGH STORM-TOSSED WAVES, ALL FLIGHT OPERATIONS ARE SUSPENDED. THE FORWARD EDGE OF THE FLIGHT DECK AND FORWARD RADIO MAST HAVE BEEN CRUSHED BY WAVES. CREWMEN WATCH FROM BEHIND THE PALISADE PLACED TO PROTECT AIRPLANES. (N.A.)

What the enemy couldn't accomplish, nature did. Over 24 feet of Hornet's Flight Deck has been crushed by a huge wave during the June 1945 typhoon. After 18 months at sea, Hornet and its crew has its ticket home. (National Archives)

Chapter 10

Magic Carpet Ride

Now that the war was finally over, there was an urgent need to bring home over a million men and women and millions of tons of material that were located at hundreds of bases and camps strung out all over the Pacific. In an operation the navy called "Operation Magic Carpet," every available, suitable ship was used to transport the troops and material back to the states.

Depending on their immediate needs, ships involved in Magic Carpet either transported service members from forward areas to Pearl Harbor where they were picked up by a ship going to the states, or ships would make the trip from the forward areas to the states and return. *Hornet* was involved in both types of cruises.

■ After *Hornet* completed its sea trials on September 13, 1945, and returned to Hunters Point, 3,500 bunks, 5 high, were built for enlisted men, covering the entire Hangar Deck. Additional head (restroom) and shower facilities were also built, and extra bunk space for officers was created wherever room could be found. In all, *Hornet* would carry about 3,500 men and 500 officers on each of her five Magic Carpet cruises.

■ *Hornet* departed San Francisco on September 18 for her first Magic Carpet cruise, and arrived in Pearl Harbor on September 23. Two days later, *Hornet* left Pearl Harbor with a full load of troops and arrived back in San Francisco on September 30, and the troops were unloaded at Alameda.

Two days later, *Hornet* once again departed for Pearl Harbor for its second Magic Carpet Cruise. While at Pearl Harbor, *Hornet* was assigned to perform carrier qualifications for two air groups before picking up 800 navy yard workers and their families. *Hornet* then returned to San Francisco where it arrived on October 20.

■ Air Group 19 embarked at San Francisco for transport to Pearl Harbor. After leaving San Francisco, *Hornet* docked at Monterey, California for two days for Navy Day celebrations while 30,000 people toured the ship. *Hornet* departed Monterey and arrived at Pearl Harbor on November 3. Air Group 19 unloaded its gear, and another 4,500 servicemen and civilians boarded for the trip back to San Francisco. Departing Pearl Harbor on November 8, *Hornet* steamed into another severe storm, which did extensive damage to exposed platforms and catwalks. It also didn't help the nerves of the thousands of non-sailors suffering severe seasickness down on the Hangar Deck who probably thought *Hornet* was going to sink and take them with it. *Hornet* arrived in San Francisco on November 12 and unloaded its grateful passengers.

Magic Carpet cruises were becoming shuttle cruises now, and once again, on November 16, *Hornet* left San Francisco on its fourth Magic Carpet cruise, this time steaming directly to Guam for its next load of passengers. *Hornet* was ordered to travel from Guam to Seattle, where she arrived on December 14, just in time for its homesick passengers to celebrate Christmas. *Hornet's* crew would spend the holidays at sea, having departed Seattle on December 20 for its fifth Magic Carpet cruise.

Once again picking up its passengers in Guam, *Hornet* arrived back in San Francisco on January 28, 1946, having made its last Magic Carpet cruise.

■ The navy now had an abundance of aircraft carriers, and many more were still being constructed. At the end of the war there were 98 aircraft carriers of various sizes on active duty, and 21 more being built. Eighteen more were cancelled. Several of the *Essex*-class carriers never saw action during World War II, some of them being commissioned well into 1946. By this time, the navy had a new type of carrier about to be launched, the much larger *Midway-class.*

■ It was now time to start decommissioning procedures for some of the *Essex*-carriers, 19 of which were scheduled to be placed in reserve, and *Hornet* was no exception. On February 4, 1946, Captain Brown was replaced by Captain Charles F. Coe as commander of *Hornet.*

On March 12, *Hornet* was placed into dry dock at Hunters Point to begin inactivation preparation. The water was pumped out of the dry dock and work progressed to inspect all the hull plates and replace any rivets or parts that needed replacement. On March 18, *Hornet* was refloated and tugs moved her to another dock where preparations continued. Everything above the waterline was tested, painted and sealed against the weather. Dehumidifiers were added, and the ship was sealed.

Hornet and *Intrepid* were placed on Inactive Status, "In Commission, In Reserve" together on August 14 and assigned to the San Francisco Reserve Group. A skeleton crew remained until the final move to Inactive Status, "Out of Commission, In Reserve" on January 15, 1947. The remainder of the crew was ordered elsewhere, and *Hornet* was now just another one of the dozens of aircraft carriers permanently parked, awaiting further orders to be re-commissioned or disposed of. *Hornet* would remain that way for the next four years.

■ While *Hornet* was taking its four-year leave, the Navy was busy developing new aircraft and the carriers to operate them. Early jet fighters were being developed, as were improved propeller driven aircraft. Many of the older World War II aircraft were still in the arsenal. However, as new jet aircraft were developed and placed into service, it was becoming clear that the existing *Essex*-class carriers would need substantial modifications in order to carry them.

Operating jet aircraft from carriers posed many new problems. They used a lot of fuel, the aircraft were heavy, and they were underpowered. Their higher speed made it more difficult to land, and they did not accelerate as fast as propeller driven airplanes. Rolling takeoffs weren't possible, so they had to be launched by catapult. Existing catapults weren't heavy enough, and the elevators were too small to transport aircraft between the decks.

By the outbreak of the Korean Conflict in June 1950, there were only two of the new *Midway*-class and four of the last-built *Essex*-class carriers on active duty. The navy was forced to begin recommissioning some of the *Essex*-class carriers, and 17 of them were pulled out of "mothballs" between 1950 and 1955 and modernized.

■ *Hornet* was reactivated and recommissioned on March 20, 1951, under the command of Captain Francis L. Busey. After sea trials and various tests were completed, *Hornet* departed San Francisco on April 10, passed through the Panama Canal and arrived at the Brooklyn Navy Yard on May 1. Command of *Hornet* now passed to Commander G.C. Merrick and *Hornet* was decommissioned again on May 12 to begin her first major modification.

SCB-27A Modernization Program

In 1948 the Navy realized that the *Essex*-class carriers would need extensive modifications to handle newer aircraft, so two different modernization plans were developed. The Navy called them the SCB-27A and SCB-27B plans. Since the older *Essex*-class carriers would get the SCB-27A modifications, this is what *Hornet* underwent while at the Brooklyn Navy Yard. The modifications cost $50 million, a major expense considering that the ship only cost $69 million to build.

The SCB-27A designs were the minimum alterations necessary to permit *Essex*-class carriers to operate current or proposed aircraft without major structural changes. The changes for *Hornet* included:

- The Flight Deck was cleared of some of the obstructions by removing the four dual 5-inch gun turrets in front and behind the island. The size of the island itself was reduced by removing all antiaircraft guns, realigning the engine room uptakes and angling them aft to the starboard side. The redesigned island allowed for a huge mast to carry all of the support antennas and radars.

- The Flight Deck was reinforced and strengthened to accommodate a 52,000-pound airplane. The two centerline elevators (numbers 1 and 3) were enlarged to 44 feet by 58 feet and strengthened to hold a 40,000-pound airplane while the deck edge elevator on the port side was strengthened to hold a 30,000-pound aircraft. Now heavier aircraft could be armed and fueled on the Hangar Deck, raised to the Flight Deck on the centerline elevators and later moved back down to the Hangar Deck on the deck edge elevator after its fuel and bombs had been used or removed.
- New heavy-duty Type H-8 hydraulic catapults were added, one to replace the portside catapult and a new one on the starboard side of the Flight Deck. The new catapults could launch a 40,000-pound airplane. The Hangar Deck catapult had already been removed. New Mark 5 arrester gear replaced the older Mark 4 gear.
- The forward bomb elevator on the starboard side was enlarged to handle a 15-foot, 16,000-pound package (a nuclear weapon).
- Many pilots had been lost during the war when bombs detonated near the pilot ready rooms on the Gallary Deck. New pilot ready rooms were built under the armored Hangar Deck. Because of the weight and bulk of the equipment pilots had to carry up to the Flight Deck, a high speed escalator was added to the starboard side.
- Because the four Flight Deck mounted 5-inch gun turrets had been removed, two new sponsons were built on the starboard side and four single mount 5-inch guns were added. All 20-millimeter guns were removed and replaced with 14 twin 3-inch/50 caliber antiaircraft guns.
- Hull blisters were added to compensate for the extra weight on the Flight Deck. All side armor was removed and 1.5-inch blister plating was substituted.
- When *Hornet* was built, the Hangar Deck was not divided into three sections, or "bays." Experience showed that fires starting on the Hangar Deck were almost impossible to fight and severe damage was always the result. During the reconstruction, two sets of huge rolling blast and flameproof doors were added that could be rolled shut to divide the Hangar Deck into three Hangar Bays. Improved water and foam firefighting equipment was added.
- The entire radar system was upgraded and improved.

■ While undergoing the modernization program, *Hornet* "donated" a 40 foot by 60-foot section of her bow to her sister ship *Wasp* who had lost hers during a collision with an escorting destroyer. The bow section was sliced off, towed to the dry dock holding *Wasp*, and welded back on that ship. A new one was then built for *Hornet*.

On October 10, 1952, *Hornet* was officially re-designated CVA-12, the "A" for "Attack." Finally, on September 11, 1953, *Hornet* was recommissioned, Captain Milton A. Nation commanding. Three weeks later, *Hornet* steamed out of Brooklyn and started her sea trials, returning to Bayonne, New Jersey on December 17. Air Task Group 181 was on board for the sea trials, and on December 8, *Hornet* landed its first jet, an F2H-3 Banshee. *Hornet* next called on Norfolk, Virginia, then Mayport, Florida and Guantanamo Bay in Cuba before returning to Mayport and unloading ATG 181. *Hornet* next went to Bayonne and into dry dock for her post-shakedown inspection.

■ Since *Hornet* was based on the west coast, the navy decided to send it to California the long way, via the Atlantic, Mediterranean and Indian Oceans, on an around-the-world cruise. The eight-month cruise started on May 11, 1954 with Air Group 9 embarked, and ended in Manila Bay in late June when *Hornet* joined the Pacific Fleet. On July 19 Captain Nation was relieved by Captain F.A. Brantley.

Six days later, *Hornet* was sent out to find the survivors of a British commercial airliner that had crashed off the Chinese island of Hainan. *Hornet* aircraft searched for survivors, and several were found. An air force plane picked up the survivors, who told the rescuers that the plane had been shot down by Chinese aircraft.

The following two days *Hornet* pilots continued the search, this time with a full CAP flying cover. On July 25, two Chinese aircraft attacked three unarmed planes flying search missions from the carrier *Philippine Sea*. The search aircraft got away, and aircraft from *Hornet* immediately attacked the Chinese planes, shooting both of them down in an event dubbed the "Hainan Incident." After serving several more months in the Pacific, *Hornet* returned to Alameda in mid December 1954.

■ From January to May 1955 *Hornet* steamed between San Francisco and San Diego, training pilots for newly assigned Air Group 7. On May 4, *Hornet* departed San Francisco for Pearl Harbor and then on to Japan where she conducted operations and training until returning to San Diego on December 10.

In January 1956, *Hornet* was ordered to Bremerton, Washington to start her next major modernization, called SCB-125 by the navy. On January 28, 1956, *Hornet* was placed into dry dock at the Puget Sound Naval Ship Yard. Another chapter in the career of *Hornet* had closed, and a new one was about to begin.

OVER 3,600 BUNKS ARE INSTALLED IN HORNET'S HANGAR BAY IN PREPA-
RATION FOR ITS ROLE AS PART OF "OPERATION MAGIC CARPET", SERVING
AS A TRANSPORT TO BRING HOME THE TROOPS AFTER THE END OF THE
WAR. (N.A.)

NOVEMBER 1945, HORNET DOCKED AT PIER 3, ALAMEDA NAVAL AIR
STATION, THE SAME DOCK THE HORNET MUSEUM IS CURRENTLY TIED TO.
NOTE THE FISHING PIER IN THE BACKGROUND AND THE LARGE PARKING
LOT TO THE LEFT. AT TOP IS THE SAN JACINTO (CVL-30), A LIGHT CAR-
RIER. NEXT IS HORNET, THEN ENTERPRISE, CV-6, AND AT THE BOTTOM,
SARATOGA, CV-3, SOON TO BE SUNK AT THE BIKINI ATOMIC BOMB TEST.
(N.A.)

UNDERWAY REPLEN-
ISHMENT (UNREP).
NAVY OILER REFUELS
HORNET AND A DE-
STROYER AT THE SAME
TIME IN 1954. WHIP
ANTENNAS HAVE RE-
PLACED THE RADIO
MASTS. TWO QUAD-40
MILLIMETER ANTIAIR-
CRAFT GUNS IN TWO
GUN TUBS EXTEND BE-
YOND THE BOW. (N.A.)

RECOMMISSIONED AS AN ATTACK CARRIER, HORNET LEAVES NEW YORK
CITY IN OCTOBER 1953. THE CREW IS LINED UP AROUND THE FLIGHT
DECK. (N.A.)

HORNET IN THE SUEZ CANAL, JUNE 5, 1954. (NATIONAL ARCHIVES)

Chapter 11

Another Face-Lift
and Then Vietnam

The idea of providing an angle off the flight deck that would become the landing deck on an aircraft carrier was a simple idea that originated with the British Navy. The straight flight deck of an aircraft carrier had always posed an unresolved problem for carrier operations. You couldn't launch and recover aircraft at the same time, and any remaining aircraft couldn't be stored on the aft end of the flight deck because it had to be left empty for landings. Remaining aircraft had to be moved to the bow of the flight deck for storage.

With an angled deck, aircraft could land on the angled portion, freeing up the bow to continue catapult launchings. If an aircraft missed the arrestor cables when landing, the plane could go around and make another attempt. Furthermore the area between the angle and the catapults could be used to store aircraft.

The Navy began studying the idea in 1951, and the *Midway* and *Wasp* were fitted with angled decks for experimental purposes in 1952. The Navy soon started the modernization process to upgrade some existing carriers with the angled deck.

The use of jet aircraft posed another problem for pilots and the landing officers trying to direct them down onto the deck. The paddles used by the landing officers could only be seen about a half-mile, too short a time for pilots to react to the signals. The British again came up with the solution, a Mirror Landing System, and a later modification called the Fresnel lens system.

The SCB-125 Program

The Navy's SCB-125 modernization program was designed to add the angled flight deck and other improvements to the carriers that had been given the SCB-27A upgrade, including *Hornet*. There were several major noticeable improvements made to *Hornet*.

- The angled flight deck was added on the port side.
- The gun tub on the bow was removed and the bow was enclosed. The navy called this a "hurricane" bow, and it was designed to prevent the type of damage *Hornet* suffered during the typhoon in 1945. (Does anyone wonder why it isn't called a typhoon bow?)

- The number 3 centerline elevator was removed and the hole sealed. A new, larger folding elevator was added to the starboard side, aft of the island.
- Primary Flight Control, or "PRI-FLY" was moved to the aft end and top of the island. Fully enclosed, it was weatherproof and afforded an unobstructed view of the entire flight deck.
- Since aircraft attempting to land could now "go around," only four arrestor wires were needed, and these were upgraded to the Mark 7 type. The remaining wires and all but one of the Davis barriers were removed.
- The Mirror Landing System was installed on the port side gallery deck.
- Additional soundproofing and air conditioning was added to some compartments.

In late January 1956 *Hornet* entered dry dock at Bremerton, Washington to begin the SCB-125 modernization, which was completed in August 1956. Sea trials followed, and on August 17, 1956, *Hornet* departed for her shake down cruise under the command of Captain W.W. Hollister.

During the next few months *Hornet* ran tests, training and carrier qualifications for various air groups. In January 1957 Air Group 14 reported aboard, and on January 21 *Hornet* departed for a six-month deployment with the Seventh Fleet in the western Pacific.

In May *Hornet* threw her number 2 propeller and bent the shaft, so a trip to Japan and two weeks of repair was the result. In June, off the Chinese coast, Chinese antiaircraft gunners shot at two of *Hornet's* aircraft, but other than some minor damage, both aircraft returned to *Hornet* safely. *Hornet* returned to San Diego in late July.

■ Captain Hollister was relieved by Captain Thomas F. Connolly on August 12, 1957, and *Hornet* spent the rest of the year conducting training around the California coast before heading to the western Pacific in January 1958 for another cruise. Air Group 4 was embarked at this time. After a routine cruise, *Hornet* returned to Alameda in early July. On June 27 *Hornet* was re-designated CVS-12, the "S" standing for antisubmarine, and headed to Bremerton, Washington for refit and conversion to her new role.

Captain Marshall D. White relieved Captain Connolly on August 25 and within four months *Hornet* was back at sea. She completed her sea trials on December 18, 1958, and then steamed to San Diego for four months of training. In April 1959 *Hornet* again departed for the western Pacific in her new roll as an antisubmarine warfare (ASW) carrier. As an ASW carrier one of the more noticeable changes was the addition of helicopters, which became a significant portion of the assigned aircraft.

■ By May 1959, 1,000 helicopter and a total of 53,000 arrested landings had been completed. In November, Captain White was relieved by Captain Ernest E. Christensen, and *Hornet* returned home to Long Beach in time for Christmas.

Hornet's next cruise to the western Pacific started in March 1960. Captain Christensen was relieved by Captain David C. Richardson in November, and *Hornet* returned to San Diego, again in time for Christmas.

In February, 1961 *Hornet* was dry docked at Bremerton for a four month overhaul, returning to Long Beach in October, where Captain Hoyt D. Mann relieved Captain Richardson. In November, *Hornet* crewmen were used to help fight the famous Hollywood Hills fire that devastated the Los Angeles suburb. Other crewmen helped with the cleanup after the fire, and *Hornet's* two 1,000KW diesel generators were used to feed electricity into the Southern California power grid.

Hornet started her seventh WestPac Cruise in June 1962. In September Captain Ellis J. Fisher relieved Captain Mann. Once again, *Hornet* arrived back in Long Beach in time for Christmas.

■ While in Long Beach, four of the remaining 5-inch guns were removed during a short overhaul, and later *Hornet* completed another shake down and training cruise before returning to Alameda. Captain Fisher was relieved on September 25, 1963, by Captain J.I. Hardy. In early October 1963 *Hornet* departed for her eighth WestPac cruise to the western Pacific.

In the Sea of Japan a *Hornet* aircraft crashed into the flight deck during an attempted landing, killing or wounding several crewmen. In April *Hornet* returned to Long Beach, then steamed for San Francisco where she underwent another modernization and conversion called FRAM II.

FRAM II Conversion

By the mid-sixties most of the *Essex*-class carriers were beginning to exceed the designed life of their hull, and the Navy had to decide to either modernize them again or place them in Inactive status. Twelve of the remaining carriers were picked for the FRAM (Fleet Rehabilitation and Modernization II) program. Part of the FRAM II program was to determine exactly what condition the hull was in and estimate the probable life of the ship. Other FRAM II improvements were:

- Installation of the SQS-23 sonar in the bow dome under the bow of the ship for ASW self-defense.
- Move the port side anchor to the bow so it wouldn't interfere with the new sonar dome.
- Redesign and upgrade the Combat Information Center (CIC).
- Installation of a closed-circuit television system.

• Addition of aluminum planking on the landing portion of the flight deck to help strengthen the deck.

The FRAM II conversion was completed in February 1965. *Hornet* then started a refresher-training cruise and ended up in Long Beach in March.

Vietnam Cruises

On July 1, 1965 Captain W.M. Pardee assumed command and on August 11 *Hornet* departed for the western Pacific for the ninth WestPac Cruise with Air Group 57 on board. *Hornet's* first Vietnam cruise was spent supporting navy and marine aircraft on an around-the-clock SAR (search and rescue) mission. Her helicopters, armed with M-60 machine guns, flew inland flights in support of strike aircraft, while *Hornet's* assigned A-4E Skyhawk jet aircraft flew 110 combat missions off another carrier. In January 1966 a *Hornet* pilot and three crewmen from VS-35, flying an S-2F Tracker, were lost at sea off North Vietnam. During the cruise, *Hornet* made several trips to Japan, Hong Kong and one to Australia, in addition to visiting Iwo Jima and later traveling to the exact spot off Santa Cruz Island where *Hornet*, CV-8 had been sunk in 1942.

Arriving back in San Diego in early March 1966, *Hornet* entered dry dock for overhaul. Captain Van V. Eason assumed command from Captain Pardee on April 1, 1966.

■ In June and July *Hornet* served as a school ship for over 300 midshipmen from the United States Naval Academy, steaming off Hawaii before returning to Alameda in time for the Fourth of July. Following this, *Hornet* served as the Prime Recovery Ship for the unmanned Apollo AS-202 space shot, recovering the capsule on August 25, 300 miles north of Wake Island, before returning to Long Beach for the balance of the year.

Air Group 57 reported aboard *Hornet* in February 1967 in preparation for deployment to Vietnam. Captain Gordon H. Robertson relieved Captain Eason on February 27, and *Hornet* left for her tenth WestPac Cruise on March 27, 1967.

■ *Hornet* supported Seventh Fleet units in and around Vietnam and the Gulf of Tonkin. During that time she tracked Soviet submarines, and was over flown by several Soviet aircraft. On May 23 an SH-3 helicopter with four crewmen was lost off the coast of Vietnam. On June 23, Captain Robertson made the 100,000th arrested landing on *Hornet*. After several trips to Japan and Hong Kong, *Hornet* returned to Long Beach, arriving on October 28, 1967. *Hornet* entered dry dock in Long Beach in late November and remained there or tied up to a pier, undergoing overhaul, until May 1968.

After completion of the overhaul, which included replacing portions of the wooden flight deck and removing and balancing the propellers, Captain Jackson A. Stockton replaced Captain Robertson. After several months of sea trials and shake down cruises, *Hornet* departed for her eleventh WestPac and third Vietnam Cruise, arriving in Japan on October 26, 1968.

Arriving in the Gulf of Tonkin shortly after the bombing halt, *Hornet's* pilots conducted surveillance and ASW operations before stopping at Hong Kong and Japan. *Hornet* remained off Vietnam for most of the remainder of the cruise, finally returning to San Diego on April 13, 1969.

Hornet's service off Vietnam and her last WestPac Cruise was over. However, the tired old ship still had a couple of significant missions to accomplish.

WHAT A PILOT SEES WHEN LANDING. HORNET NOW HAS AN ANGLED DECK. FIVE ARRESTOR WIRES CROSS THE DECK JUST ABOVE THE "12". TO THE RIGHT OF THE DARK PORTION OF THE DECK IS THE FOUL LINE. ON THE LEFT EDGE OF THE DECK IS THE MIRROR LANDING SYSTEM, AND IN THE FOREGROUND IS THE LANDING SIGNAL OFFICER ON HIS PLATFORM. THE HORIZONTAL WHITE LINE ON THE END OF THE DECK IS THE RUNDOWN. BELOW IT ARE TWO GUN TUBS WITH A QUAD-40 IN EACH. (N.A.)

ABOVE: AN F-2 TRACKER WARMING UP PRIOR TO A MISSION. THE PLANE IS STILL CHAINED TO THE DECK TO PREVENT IT FROM ROLLING OVERBOARD DURING A STORM. NOTE THE EXTREME LIST OF THE FLIGHT DECK. (N.A.) BELOW : ANOTHER F-2 PREPARES TO LAND. NOTE THE FOUR ARRESTOR CABLES AND HOW NARROW THE DECK APPEARS AGAINST THE LARGE WINGSPAN OF THE TRACKER (N.A.)

Chapter 12

Hornet Joins the Space Age

APOLLO 11

On May 23, 1969, Captain Carl J. Seiberlich reported aboard and relieved Captain Stockton. On June 1, Captain Seiberlich notified the crew that *Hornet* would be the Prime Recovery Ship for the upcoming Apollo 11 Lunar Landing Mission.

On June 16 *Hornet* set out on a weeklong training cruise. Loaded on the ship at Long Beach were over 125 military and civilian personnel with all of their equipment: recovery teams, NASA, ABC Television, General Electric. Several trailers and communication huts were loaded on the Hangar Deck. Then *Hornet* departed for Pearl Harbor.

At Pearl Harbor, two modified Airstream trailers were loaded, one of which would become the Mobile Quarantine Facility (MQF), and the other a backup unit. Also loaded was a full-scale mockup of the Apollo Command Module to be used for training while enroute to the recovery area. Finally, over 250 members of three specialized recovery teams were loaded with all their gear.

■ Three C1-A Traders, four E-1B Tracers and eight SH-3D Sea King helicopters were being carried on *Hornet* to assist in the recovery efforts. Four of the SH-3Ds would be launched for the recovery of the capsule. Two would carry the swimmers from Underwater Demolition Team 11 and their equipment. The helicopters, known as Swim 1 and Swim 2, would drop the swimmers next to the Command Module *Columbia*. The swimmers would assist the astronauts in getting out of the capsule and into another helicopter, which would take them back to *Hornet*. The fourth helicopter would film the whole event. Flying above all of this were two of the E-1Bs that would provide communications between the recovery units, *Hornet,* and Hawaii.

■ One of the primary concerns that had to be dealt with was the possibility of the astronauts bringing some sort of unknown biological contamination back from the moon's surface. Much of the training was geared toward biological decontamination of the lunar module and the astronauts, both in the water and on the ship. The Mobile Quarantine Facility was going to be home for the astronauts for several days.

■ For a week *Hornet* and the rest of Task Force 130 trained for the recovery of the heavy lunar capsule, completed 16 simulated exercises and trained backup crews to cover every contingency. *Hornet* departed Hawaii for the recovery area on July 12.

By July 14 *Hornet* was stationed at the Primary Abort Area 1,600 miles southwest of Hawaii in case Apollo 11 had to abort the mission during its first orbit around the earth. Since the launch was successful and Apollo 11 was on its way to the moon, *Hornet* then moved to the Prime Recovery Area.

■ Astronaut Neil Armstrong was a former Navy pilot, having flown an F9F Panther off *Essex* for 78 combat missions over Korea. Michael Collins was a former Air Force test pilot, and Edwin Aldrin was a former pilot who flew 66 missions over Korea in an F-86 Sabre Jet.

Astronauts Armstrong, Aldrin and Collins made their rendezvous with the moon on July 20, 1969. Meanwhile, *Hornet* and her crew continued to practice for the recovery 1,200 miles southwest of Pearl Harbor.

The weather at the landing site was getting progressively worse, in fact so bad that it was unacceptable. On Wednesday afternoon July 23, Captain Seiberlich was informed that the new splashdown site was 250 miles closer to Hawaii, so *Hornet* and the rest of the task force steamed at flank speed to the new area in order to be in place by Thursday morning.

■ At 5:12 a.m. on July 24, Marine One landed on *Hornet* with President Richard M. Nixon, Secretary of State Henry Kissinger and Apollo 8 astronaut Frank Borman to observe the splashdown of the astronauts in their capsule *Columbia*. They had flown in Air Force One to Johnston Island, about 250 miles from *Hornet*, then by Marine One to the *Hornet* via a stopover on the communications ship USS *Arlington*, ex-USS *Saipan*, CVL-48.

The Apollo 11 Command Module entered the earth's atmosphere somewhere over the Mariana Islands at 22,300 mph. It was soon in visual contact by *Hornet's* aircraft and picked up on *Hornet's* radar. During reentry, communications were lost between *Hornet* and the Command Module for about 4 minutes because of friction created by the re-entry. Shortly after four minutes the astronauts heard a message being broadcast from *Hornet*, *"Apollo 11, Apollo 11. This is Hornet. Hornet, over."* Armstrong replied, *"Hello Hornet, this is Apollo 11 reading you loud and clear."*

At 5:50 a.m. Swim 1 announced, *"Splashdown. Apollo 11 has splashdown."* Splashdown had occurred eleven miles from *Hornet* and one mile from the aiming point. The Command Module hit the water so hard that it tipped upside down, but provision had been made for that and several small balloons were inflated to turn it back upright.

■ While two UDT members attached a floatation device around the Command Module, another opened up the hatch and tossed in three biological suits for the astronauts to put on, then promptly closed the hatch. When the astronauts were ready, the hatch was opened, they climbed out into a raft and the hatch was closed, sealed and wiped down with an antibacterial solution. After decontaminating each other, the astronauts and swimmers were hoisted into Helicopter 66, a SH-3 Sea King, for the flight back to the deck of *Hornet*. Meanwhile, Swim 2 remained with the capsule.

After landing on *Hornet's* Flight Deck, the helicopter was towed to elevator number two, (port side deck edge), lowered to the Hangar Deck, then towed to within a few feet of the Mobile Quarantine Facility. The astronauts, still in their biological suits, walked out of the helicopter and into the trailer. Then the door was shut and sealed behind them. Along with the three astronauts sealed in the trailer were two other men—Dr. Bill Carpentier and engineer John Hirasaki. Carpentier would tend to the physical well-being of the astronauts while Hirasaki had many roles. He cooked, did maintenance and was the person who would reenter the Command Module and retrieve the moon rocks and some of the personal gear left on board.

After they showered and changed into clean uniforms, the astronauts chatted through a window and intercom with President Nixon. A sign hanging above the trailer proclaimed *"Hornet + 3."* After a few minutes, the President was led back to the flight deck, where he talked to Captain Seiberlich and some of the crewmen. One of the crewmen proclaimed, after being congratulated by the President for a job well-done, *"Sir, we're Hornet!"*

■ Once Marine One departed, *Hornet* steamed over to the Command Module and gingerly slipped up next to it. With the module bobbing in the water on the starboard side of the ship next to elevator number 3, the ship's crane was used to hoist the module up to the elevator and then place it in a cradle, where it would remain until it reached Houston. The module and cradle were moved next to the MQF, and a sealed plastic transfer tunnel was attached to it so John Hirasaki could open the hatch and enter the module to retrieve the moon rocks.

The following day the astronauts, from inside their trailer, participated in some official ceremonies, including the re-enlistment of several of *Hornet's* crewmen. Also during the day two separate sets of sealed containers containing the moon rocks and other items were flown off *Hornet* and sent to Houston by two different routes, one via Johnston Island and one via Hawaii. They were then transferred to larger aircraft and flown to Houston.

Meanwhile, stamp collectors had sent over 250,000 pieces of mail to be cancelled by *Hornet's* Post Office to commemorate the day Apollo 11 landed. Since there was only one cancellation seal, it was an around-the-clock operation for the next several days to cancel the stamps, although they were all dated July 24. On July 26 *Hornet* steamed into Pearl Harbor with the Command Module proudly displayed on the flight deck. A broomstick hung from the mast indicating the mission had been a clean sweep.

■ After docking, the Mobile Quarantine Facility, with its five passengers, was lifted off the deck of *Hornet* and towed to Hickam Field where it was put on a transport plane and flown to Houston. Once there, its five passengers were moved out of the MQF into a roomier complex where they spent the next two weeks in quarantine.

The Command Module was also unloaded, trucked to Hickam Field and flown to Houston. *Hornet* returned to Long Beach.

APOLLO 12

Back in Long Beach, *Hornet* made several training cruises around the area awaiting her next assignment. Those orders came in September when it was announced that *Hornet* would now become the Prime Recovery Ship for Apollo 12, which had an all-Navy crew.

Hornet departed for Pearl Harbor on October 27 to begin preparation for the recovery that would take place in November. Upon reaching Pearl Harbor, *Hornet* picked up two more Mobile Quarantine Facilities (the Airstream trailers again) and another crew of technicians. *Hornet* departed Pearl Harbor, her destination this time was the Primary Abort Area in case the mission had to abort during its first orbit.

On this trip it was former Naval pilots Charles Conrad, Alan Bean and Richard Gordon who were the astronauts. After making a successful landing on the moon and completing their mission there, the Command Module *Yankee Clipper* returned to earth. At 10:01 a.m. on November 24, 1969, Apollo 12 splashed down less than two miles from *Hornet*. Once again the rescue UDT members arrived on the scene in a few minutes and the astronauts were recovered, flown back to *Hornet* and placed in the Mobile Quarantine Facility. It was almost an exact repeat of the Apollo 11 mission, only it went much more smoothly. Hanging above the MQF this time was a sign that read *"Three More Like Before."*

After picking up the command module, *Hornet* returned to Pearl Harbor with another broom attached to her mast. After off-loading the module and the MQF, *Hornet* departed the next day for Long Beach, where she arrived on December 4.

Hornet was now selected to be the Prime Recovery Ship for the January 1970 recovery of Apollo 13. However, that date was pushed back to April to allow more training time for the astronauts and recovery crews. This meant that another ship would have to take *Hornet's* place, for it had been announced that *Hornet* was going to be decommissioned in June, and that it had a destiny with a dry dock in Bremerton, Washington to begin deactivation.

The 27-year active career of the aircraft carrier USS *Hornet, CV-12, CVA-12, CVS-12* was about to come to an end.

TWO VIEWS OF HORNET TAKEN IN THE LATE 1960'S. (ABOVE) AN S-2F TRACKER IS UNFOLDING ITS WINGS ON A CATAPALT IN PREPARATION FOR LAUNCHING. (BELOW) HORNET NOW HAS A HURRICANE DECK, THE EN-CLOSED PORTION OF THE FO'C'SLE ON THE BOW. ALSO PRESENT IS THE RADOME, THE LARGE ROUND OBJECT ON THE AFT END OF THE ISLAND. BE-LOW IT IS A LARGER ROUND NASA TRACKING ANTENNA USED ON THE APOLLO MISSIONS. (N.A.)

THE CREW OF APOLLO 11: NEIL ARMSTRONG, MICHAEL COLLINS AND EDWIN "BUZZ" ALDRIN. (N.A.S.A.)

A SATURN ROCKET BLASTS OFF ON JULY 16, 1969, CARRYING THE APOLLO 11 CAPSULE AND CREW FOR A RENDEZVOUS WITH THE MOON. (N.A.S.A.)

(ABOVE) THE APOLLO 11 COMMAND MODULE SHORTLY AFTER SPLASH-DOWN. THE THREE ASTRONAUTS ARE IN THE LIFE RAFT. (BELOW) PRESIDENT NIXON AND OTHER VIP'S STANDING ON VULTURE'S ROW WATCH AS THE ASTRONAUTS ARRIVE ON HORNET ON JULY 24, 1969. (BOTH N.A.)

ABOVE: THE HORNET MUSEUM MQF SITS WHERE THE APOLLO 11 AND APOLLO 12 MQF SAT. THE MQF IS OPEN FOR INSPECTION. THE CHAIR IS NOT ORIGINAL, BUT PROVIDES NICE PERSPECTIVE RELATIVE TO THE SIZE OF THE MQF.
BELOW: THE HORNET MUSEUM'S APOLLO CAPSULE IS IN SERIOUS NEED OF RESTORATION.

Chapter 13

An End...

In October, 1969, Admiral J.D. Bulkeley and a staff of officers and senior enlisted men boarded *Hornet* for a four day "*Hornet* INSURV," or Inspection and Survey. Shortly after the inspection was completed, a Navy Ships' Disposition Review Board reviewed the results of the survey, and on January 15, 1970, it was announced that *Hornet* would be decommissioned as of June 30, 1970.

The navy has two basic choices about what to do with a ship that has been decommissioned: it can be "stricken" and disposed of (or scrapped, being the common term, cutting the ship up and making razor blades from it), or it can be retained in inactive status as a "mobilization asset" (or "mothballed" as it is usually called). In *Hornet's* case, the ship would be mothballed and she would receive regular maintenance to keep the ship in the best possible condition while it was mothballed.

■ During her final days prior to steaming to Washington, *Hornet* conducted CARQUALS for several squadrons. On February 20, 1970, Commander Gerald Canaan flying an S-2E Tracker and co-piloted by Admiral Norman C. Gillette made the final arrested landing on the deck of *Hornet*. It was number 115,445. A few days later *Hornet* received her sixth and final "E" award for overall battle excellence.

On March 2, 1970, *Hornet* tied up to a dock at the Long Beach Naval Shipyard to begin the long deactivation process, as non-essential parts were removed for storage or other use. On March 30, with only a skeleton crew to maintain the ship for the run up to the Puget Sound Naval Shipyard at Bremerton, *Hornet* began her final voyage under her own power. The Hangar Deck was full of personal items and automobiles as the remaining crew was being transferred to Washington.

Hornet arrived at the Puget Sound Naval Shipyard at 9:30 a.m. on April 2, 1970. Tugs pushed her into a dry dock, and at 10:30 a.m. the engines were shut down for the last time. At the same time, her status changed from "In Commission, In Service" to "In Commission, In Reserve."

While in dry dock, the hull was painted, repaired where necessary and corrosion-proofed. The propeller shafts were secured, the boilers and engines drained of water and fuel, key components were removed, and the ship prepared for storage.

At 8:00 a.m. on June 30, *Hornet's* crew was mustered for the decommissioning ceremony. Several senior officers and civilian dignitaries were present. At 10:40 a.m. *Hornet* was officially placed "Out of Commission, In Reserve." The final watch was secured and the crewmen marched down the gangplank and on to other duties. The last person to leave the ship stopped at the top of the gangplank, faced the stern and saluted the flag of the grand old ship. Captain Carl J. Sieberlich, 23rd and final commanding officer of *Hornet* had just given the final salute.

■ For weeks work continued on *Hornet* to prepare her for storage. All equipment was cleaned, lubricated and covered in preservative. All external openings were closed or covered over and sealed. Elevator number 3 was removed and placed on the deck. Steel "huts" were placed over the four remaining 5-inch guns, radars and directors, then sealed and dehumidified. Under the waterline around the hull a series of electrical wires were placed. When activated, the "cathodic protection system" would help protect the steel hull from the elements in the salt water. The interior was divided into nine sealed zones. Massive dehumidifiers maintained the humidity in each of the "zones" at a constant 40 percent humidity.

Once all work was completed, *Hornet* was towed over to the Naval Inactive Ships Maintenance Facility (NISMF) at Bremerton, Washington. During the next 14 years she would be joined by her sister ships *Bon Homme Richard*, CVS-31, *Bennington*, CVS-20, *Oriskany*, CVA-34, and the battleships *Missouri* and *New Jersey* plus a whole fleet of smaller ships. As far as anybody knew, *Hornet* would live out her days tightly sealed against the weather, waiting for the time when the Navy decided she was no longer needed.

While in this mothball status, internal systems were constantly checked, and every 90 days a crew of inspectors checked the interior to look for deterioration. In 1973 a 3-inch thick blanket of foam was sprayed on the Flight Deck to protect the wood from the Washington weather.

In 1984, after 14 years of residing at one pier at Bremerton, *Hornet* was pushed to another pier, recently vacated by the *Missouri*, which was being recommissioned. Her new home at *Missouri's* old pier gave *Hornet* great visibility from the nearby freeway. There, *Hornet* remained for the next ten years.

■ A detailed inspection of *Hornet* was made in 1987 to see if the navy had any further use for her. The inspections showed that every one of her systems was obsolete. Although the hull itself was in good condition, time and technology had passed *Hornet* by.

In late 1988 *Hornet*, *Bon Homme Richard*, *Oriskany* and *Bennington* were recommended for disposal. On August 19, 1989, *Hor-*

net was stricken from the navy's rolls and all maintenance funding was terminated.

■ In March 1989 the USS Hornet Historical Museum Association Inc. of Bremerton, Washington applied to have the navy consider placing *Hornet* in the Navy's Ship Donation Program. In September 1989 the navy did just that, allowing for donation as a naval museum. Although the Walt Disney Corporation showed some interest in preserving *Hornet* as an attraction next to the *Queen Mary* in Long Beach, the only formal bid was made by the USS Hornet Historical Museum Association. The navy now placed *Hornet* on "Donation Hold" to prevent any further removal of equipment.

In December 1991, during the time the Hornet Association was conducting financial studies and searching for a permanent home for her, *Hornet* was designated a National Historical Landmark.

Funding was slow in coming, and the navy extended the "Donation Hold" status twice, but in the end, the Hornet Association could not obtain the funds needed to save the ship. In late 1992 the Defense Reutilization and Marketing Service (DRMS) appraised *Hornet's* value at $200,000. In January 1993 a bidding notice was placed, and eleven bids were received, the high being $200,000 by Astoria Metals Corporation of Portland, Oregon.

■ Astoria Metals now owned *Hornet,* but had a problem finding a place to scrap it. It was well known that *Hornet* was a floating toxic-waste dump full of lead, asbestos, waste oil, PCB's and other items. Astoria Metals planned to scrap *Hornet* at the Port of Astoria, Oregon, but state officials and local residents were concerned about contamination of the Columbia River and even the Portland Ship Repair Yard was ruled out.

While trying to find a place to scrap *Hornet*, Astoria Metals now got into a scrape with the Environmental Protection Agency about removing *Hornet* from Puget Sound. Someone had to pay for the removal of over 1,300 items containing PCB's before the ship could be moved, and neither Astoria nor the navy was willing to pay for the work. The navy decided that since Astoria bought the ship as-is, then Astoria had to pay for the cleanup. The EPA eventually decided that the navy was responsible.

Because the navy needed the pier *Hornet* was tied too, it paid to have *Hornet* towed to Long Beach for temporary storage by a seagoing tug that was going to tow another *Essex*-class carrier, *Ranger* from Long Beach to Bremerton. On September 24, 1994, *Hornet* made her first voyage since 1970, being towed at 3.8 knots (4.4 mph) back down to Long Beach. The navy, which had just made $200,000 for selling *Hornet* as scrap, now paid $140,000 in towing charges and insurance to tow it to a temporary site. In the meantime, Astoria Metals had given up on its attempt to scrap *Hornet* in the Portland area, and applied for and received permission to scrap it at the old naval shipyard at Hunters Point, San Francisco, California.

■ Meanwhile, *Hornet's* sister ship *Bennington* was sold to a foreign company and, because of the EPA requirements, towed to India and scrapped on a beach. *Oriskany* was sold to another company and towed to San Francisco for scrapping in 1996.

■ After spending all of three weeks at Long Beach, *Hornet* was once again under tow, this time to Hunters Point where she arrived on October 23, 1994, to await her destiny with a cutting torch.

By this time Astoria Metals probably wished it hadn't bought the ship. Its contract with the DRMS required that *Hornet* be disposed of in a certain amount of time or Astoria would be in default and *Hornet* would return to the DRMS for resale. Unfortunately for Astoria Metals, *Hornet* now resided in California, which had some of the strictest EPA regulations. Astoria was having trouble trying to develop a plan to scrap *Hornet* that would be acceptable to the EPA and the state of California. Each of the different contaminants would have to be addressed separately and Astoria Metals was running out of time.

Chapter 14

...and a Beginning

Across from the former Hunters Point Naval Shipyard on the other side of San Francisco Bay is the now closed Alameda Naval Air Station. By the end of World War II over 25,000 aircraft had passed through the huge base, which was built in the early 1940's to support the construction, overhaul and shipment of naval aircraft.

Alameda has several deep-water docks for large ships, and it was from Alameda that Colonel James H. Doolittle's aircraft were loaded on *Hornet*, CV-8, for the air raid on Tokyo.

Throughout World War II, Korea, Vietnam and the Cold War, Alameda's three piers served as the homeport for over a dozen aircraft carriers, including *Hornet*, CV-12.

In time, the navy found little use for Alameda, a huge plot of land close up against Oakland, California and just across the bay from San Francisco at the foot of the San Francisco–Oakland Bay Bridge. Thus, in the early 1990's when the Cold War military reductions were taking place, Alameda Naval Air Station was picked by the Base Realignment and Closure Commission to be closed down and transferred to the city of Alameda for other use by the middle of 1997.

■ The last commander of Alameda NAS was Navy Captain Jim Dodge. When it was announced that Alameda would close, Captain Dodge decided that the base should go out in style. Captain Dodge and his staff decided on a five month celebration that would end with a huge open house during Fleet Week 1995.

Captain Dodge had heard about the rusting hulk at Hunters Point, and part of his plan was to try to "borrow" it and use it as a focal point for his five-month celebration. That deteriorating hull happened to be *Hornet*, and now fate intervened.

■ At a very opportune time in early 1995, Captain Dodge met with the managers at Astoria Metals. Astoria was still in the process of working up a salvage plan for all of the toxic material residing inside *Hornet's* hull. Former Navy Captain Jim Bruckner of Astoria liked Captain Dodge's idea to use *Hornet* for the base closing celebration, especially if it meant that the time it was on display at Alameda wouldn't count against his deadline to get his approvals needed to scrap the ship.

■ Several months of legal proceedings now took place. Neither the Defense Reutilization and Marketing Service nor the Naval Sea Systems Command (NavSea) was excited about the idea because of concerns about liability. Besides, they were trying to get *Hornet* scrapped, not loaned out to be the centerpiece of a base closing celebration. Eventually, however, approval was given as long as Captain Dodge assumed full liability for the plan. *Hornet* would be towed to Alameda for five months, and AMC would get its contract extension.

On May 11, 1995, *Hornet* was moved from Hunters Point during a three-mile, four-hour voyage, and was pushed into place at the north side of Pier 2 at Alameda, the same pier that *Hornet*, CV-8, loaded the aircraft for Doolittle's Tokyo raid 53 years before. This was also *Hornet's* first visit to Alameda in 30 years. Waiting for *Hornet* at Pier 3 was the huge nuclear carrier *Carl Vinson*, CV-70, sporting a new coat of paint. *Hornet*, after 25 years of neglect and decay looked absolutely pathetic next to the *Carl Vinson*.

During the next few weeks hundreds of volunteers cleaned up years of accumulated debris on the Flight Deck and painted the island and several compartments, including the bridge and pilothouse.

On May 20, the five-month celebration for Alameda Naval Air Station began, and over 9,000 people boarded *Hornet*, even though the only area open was the flight deck. On July 21, *Hornet* was opened for public viewing, and by now the Hangar Deck and portions of the Second Deck were ready for visitors.

■ In July a new organization entered the scene that would have a significant affect on *Hornet's* future. The non-profit Aircraft Carrier Hornet Foundation (ACHF) was formed to accomplish what the Seattle group could not—preserve *Hornet* as a museum for future generations.

■ Throughout the summer groups gathered on *Hornet* for celebrations, including 1,500 visitors celebrating the 50th anniversary of VJ Day, the day Japan surrendered and ended World War II. On October 6, 1995, Fleet Week began and Alameda Naval Air Station held a four-day open house with *Hornet* once again the center of attention. Numerous aircraft, including a B-25 Mitchell bomber, were hoisted upon the flight deck and were open for viewing. Over 30,000 visitors boarded *Hornet* during four days to tour the ship and view the dozens of displays that had been set up for the event. Hundreds of volunteers helped with crowd control, and the ACHF sold T-shirts and collected names of people who were willing to assist with the continued restoration.

A special ceremony was held honoring three of the surviving Doolittle raiders and over 100 survivors of the several ships that conducted the raid. Also honored was Ensign George Gay, the sole survivor of Torpedo 8 from the former *Hornet,* CV-8, that had been decimated at the Battle of Midway. Ensign Gay had recently died and his ashes had been scattered over the site of the battle.

■ Once Fleet Week was over, *Hornet* was scheduled to be towed back to Hunters Point and returned to Astoria Metals to begin the scrapping process. Astoria Metals suggested that, because of the overwhelming local support for *Hornet*, that Astoria and the ACHF contract with Naval Sea Systems Command to allow for the completion of fund raising to save *Hornet*.

By this time, Astoria had determined that there wasn't going to be any profit in scrapping *Hornet* because of all of the EPA concerns that still hadn't been resolved. However, NavSea rejected the plan and ordered the scrapping to proceed.

In October ACHF filed a lawsuit in San Francisco against NavSea, maintaining that NavSea hadn't completed a Section 106 review and to gain a temporary restraining order to prevent *Hornet* from going back to Hunters Point. Completion of the Section 106 Review was required because *Hornet* had been declared a National Historical Landmark in 1991, and could not be disposed of without a proper review.

In early October *Hornet* was towed to a temporary site in Oakland to free up pier 2 for other use. In mid-October NavSea finally agreed to put *Hornet* in the "Donation Program" for one year to allow ACHF to develop a plan to raise funds to make *Hornet* into a museum. *Hornet* would have to remain in Oakland and be closed to visitors, and any qualified organization that could come up with a workable plan could bid for the ship.

In November 1996 the Aircraft Carrier Hornet Foundation submitted its application and plan to NavSea. No other organization had applied. Although NavSea wasn't convinced that funding was available, it still placed *Hornet* in an official "Donation Hold" status in early 1997. After the Section 106 Review was completed, it was determined that NavSea should never have sold *Hornet,* and made the sale to Astoria Metals invalid. The way was now clear to save *Hornet* as a museum.

■ By the time Fleet Week 1998 was held, the Aircraft Carrier Hornet Foundation and hundreds of volunteers had cleaned and painted enough of the ship to have its official Open House. On October 16, 1998, a Gala Ball was held on the Hangar Deck and thousands of people participated in the grand dinner and the dancing to a live orchestra that followed throughout the evening.

The following day, October 17, 1998, a Recommissioning Ceremony was held on the dock next to *Hornet*, and that day the ship was officially opened to the public. Thousands more attended the ceremony and visited the ship for the first time while aircraft from the History of Naval Aviation Air show and the Blue Angels flew overhead. USS *Hornet*, veteran of two wars and two Apollo space missions, now has a permanent home and a dedicated group of people to look out for her.

Long Live Hornet!

A Self-Guided Tour of the

Aircraft Carrier
Hornet

CV-12, CVA-12, CVS-12

Chapter 15

Aircraft Carrier 101

Basic Flight Operations

There are millions of qualified and licensed private, commercial and military pilots in the world. All of them would agree that every time you take-off or land on an airport runway you are battling the forces of nature and gravity.

Under the correct set of circumstances, getting an airplane off the ground is a relatively simple matter, given enough wind over the plane's wings and a long enough runway to gain the speed to acquire that wind. And, with a long runway, if you have an engine problem, you have a reasonable chance to stop before you crash into something.

Landing an airplane is more difficult because downdrafts, updrafts and crosswinds can affect a landing. So can a myriad of other events and ultimately, if you run out of fuel or you get the correct set of circumstances, you will crash into the ground.

■ Relatively few pilots have the training, skill and ability to become qualified as a *carrier* pilot. It has just been in the past few years that any women were given the opportunity to become carrier qualified. With very few exceptions, all of the pilots are either Navy or Marine pilots. Flying an airplane off of or landing on a carrier deck is so difficult that only the best pilots are allowed to do it.

■ At its lowest common denominator, the sole purpose for spending millions of dollars during World War II, and billions of dollars currently on an aircraft carrier, can be summed up in one statement: an aircraft carrier is designed to transport aircraft and pilots to a given place, to launch those aircraft and pilots so they can perform a given mission, and then safely land those aircraft back on the deck. Regardless of the overall mission of the carrier and its escorting ships, if it can't successfully launch and land aircraft, there really isn't any need for the carrier.

In order to get an aircraft airborne, you have to have enough wind crossing over and under the wing to cause lift. It is not how fast an aircraft is traveling that gives it lift, it is the speed of the wind over the wings. Although this may not make sense, it is the nature of aerodynamics.

An earlier chapter listed how that wind speed could be attained, but it bears repeating here.

LAUNCHING AN AIRPLANE

To achieve a 50 knot takeoff speed, an airplane requires a
long runway to accelerate to that speed.

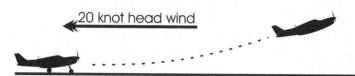

To achieve the same 50 knot takeoff speed with a 20 knot
head wind, an aircraft only has to accelerate to 30 knots
and requires less runway.

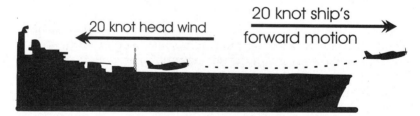

To achieve the 50 knot takeoff speed with a 20 knot head
wind and ship's forward motion of 20 knots, an airplane only
needs to accelerate to 10 knots and requires less runway.

The catapult can propel the airplane to the 50 knot takeoff
speed without any head wind or ship's forward motion.

Launching an Airplane

(Or, how do you get a big airplane off of that little deck?)

Let's assume that a given aircraft needs 50 knots (57.5 miles per hour) of wind across the wings in order to gain enough lift to become airborne. Most small private aircraft flying today need about 50 knots to get airborne.

If you have a long enough runway and flat calm (or no wind) then the aircraft, under its own power would accelerate to 50 knots, at which time the wind would be sufficient and the aircraft would become airborne, or let's say at 4,000 feet of runway. If there is any wind blowing down the runway, let's assume 5 knots (5.75 miles per hour), then the aircraft could take off at around 3,500 feet of runway. Airport runways are built so that aircraft can take off into the prevailing wind. That doesn't mean the wind will always blow down the length of the runway, which is why they are designed to be long enough so aircraft can accelerate to enough speed to take off without any wind.

One of the main advantages of an aircraft carrier is that it can turn into the prevailing wind. It doesn't make any difference from which direction the wind is blowing, the ship can turn into it.

Now let's assume our airplane that needs 50 knots of wind is flying off the deck of an aircraft carrier. If the carrier is steaming at 20 knots (23 mph) and there isn't any prevailing wind (flat calm), then the airplane only has to accelerate to 30 knots (34.5 mph) to become airborne, and needs a much smaller airfield (or deck).

Now, if our ship is steaming at 20 knots into a 20-knot wind, which gives us 40 knots of wind across the deck, our airplane now only needs to get its speed up to 10 knots to get airborne, and a much shorter deck. What happens if our carrier is steaming at 20 knots into a 35-knot wind? Theoretically, our airplane would become airborne while it is sitting on the deck, which is one of the many reasons planes are tied down when they aren't being used.

World War II aircraft were relatively small compared to today's carrier aircraft. When designing the *Essex*-class carriers and the aircraft that would fly off them, the Navy knew that if the carrier could steam at 33 knots, even if there wasn't any prevailing wind, most aircraft could attain enough speed to take off using only about half the length of the Flight Deck, or about 420 feet. Of course, the addition of any prevailing wind would require even less runway.

The addition of a **CATAPULT** meant an aircraft could be launched from a very short portion of the Flight Deck without any forward motion of the ship or prevailing wind.

So, to recap, it's the combination of the forward motion of the ship, the prevailing wind and the length of the Flight Deck that will allow an aircraft to become airborne.

■ During World War II, *Hornet* had one catapult on the port side of the Flight Deck and another on the Hangar Deck that would allow the launching of an aircraft off the starboard side of the ship. Only a few of the *Essex*-class carriers had the Hangar Deck catapult, and only *Hornet* kept its catapult until after the war.

The Hangar Deck catapult track was mounted on top of the armored Hangar Deck. To set the catapult track into the deck itself would seriously weaken the armored deck. Since the catapult track sat on the deck, it also hindered the movement of aircraft on the Hangar Deck. The catapult was located just aft of the forward elevator and forward of the bomb elevator in Hangar Bay number one. The track across the Hangar Deck wasn't long enough to launch the airplane, so extending out both sides of the ship were track extenders that would fold up when not in use. The plane to be launched was pushed tail first onto the track extender, which meant the plane and pilot were hanging about 20 feet over the edge of the ship. When launched, the plane shot through the width of the Hangar Deck, out onto the track extender on the starboard side, and, hopefully, into the air. This was always a tricky launch because as soon as the plane exited the Hangar Deck, it was hit by a wind shear equal to the forward speed of the ship plus any prevailing wind. After World War II, the extenders and the track were one of the first things removed when *Hornet* went into the shipyard for maintenance.

■ World War II aircraft could fly off under their own power with the aid of the ships forward motion into the prevailing wind, or they could be launched using the catapult. Usually they were flown off. Catapults were not often used because it was faster to fly the planes off. However, with a full deck load of aircraft lined up forward of the island, there often wasn't enough Flight Deck length to fly the plane off. So at that time they would catapult enough aircraft off the deck to free up enough space for the rest to fly off.

A catapult is similar to a giant slingshot. *Hornet's* catapults are hydraulic powered (all later model *Essex*-class carriers and all modern carriers have steam-powered catapults.) The **LAUNCH BRIDLE**, a "V" shaped cable, is attached to the wings of an aircraft and to the traveling "SHUTTLE" located in the catapult track. The shoe is attached to a cable that runs the length of the track, and is attached at both ends to a giant ram down in the catapult room (it works on a system similar to the elevators (see *HOW IT WORKS:* The Forward Elevator.)

The pilot, with the aircraft's engine running and taking directions from the catapult officer, taxies his plane to the end of the catapult track. The launch bridle is attached to the plane and to the shoe. When ready to launch, the catapult ram is released, pulling the cable, shoe and aircraft down the length of the track. This works under so much pressure that an airplane can be launched from a stop to 160 knots in 2.2 seconds with 200 feet of deck space.

■ The normal World War II load for a carrier like *Hornet* was anywhere between 80 and 110 aircraft, usually about 80 for operations and the rest were aircraft in storage or the parts of aircraft. Spare aircraft – wings, fuselage, tail, engines, etc., could be hung from the overhead on the Hangar Deck, which is why the distance from the Hangar Deck to the Flight Deck is over 27 feet. Part of that was taken up by the gallery deck which is also hung below the Flight Deck, but the rest is storage for extra planes. When one was needed, the parts were gathered and it was assembled in Hangar Bay 3.

■ U.S. Navy doctrine during World War II called for a "deck load" strike, meaning all of the aircraft for a given mission would be located on the Flight Deck at the same time and flown off together as fast as they could be launched. Often, there would be extra aircraft on the Flight Deck after the aircraft needed for the mission were launched. These remained either because there wasn't room on the Hangar Deck for them or usually because the ship's captain wanted to make sure he still had fighter aircraft available for immediate take off if enemy aircraft were detected in the area.

Once the aircraft for a given mission were launched, the remaining aircraft were moved, either using a motorized cart called a **MULE** or by hand using the available crewmembers on the Flight Deck. They were moved far enough up the deck to clear the back end of the Flight Deck, but not far enough to prevent the fighter aircraft enough room to take off. Generally they were stored right around the island.

There wasn't any delay in getting the planes moved because with aircraft sitting on the aft end of the Flight Deck, there wasn't any way to land an airplane. If one of the aircraft that had just taken off had mechanical problems and had to return to the ship, and if the aft end of the Flight Deck was "fouled," or full of aircraft, the pilot couldn't land. He had to try to land on another carrier that had a clear deck, wait until the deck was cleared or he had to ditch into the water and hope he was picked up by an escort ship. This is one of the design shortcomings the carriers had and the reason the straight deck design of all aircraft carriers was not very practical. This shortcoming lasted until the angle deck was developed.

■ Now we've successfully launched our aircraft on their mission and we've moved the extra aircraft up to the vicinity of the island. It's now time for the aircraft to come home. The pilots are tired, the adrenaline is running high, the aircraft may have mechanical or combat damage and the pilot may be injured, but they have to land their airplane. What happens next is what the pilots generally refer to as a "controlled crash." Landing an aircraft on the deck of a carrier is a crash no matter how you look at it, and it is up to the pilot and the Landing Signal Officer to control it.

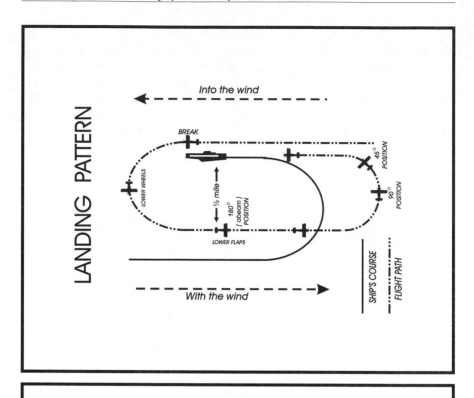

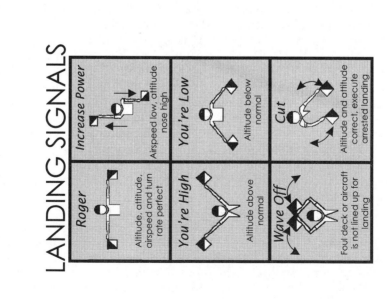

How to Land an Airplane

(Or, you gotta be kidding me. I'm going to land this airplane on that postage stamp?)

Carrier pilots like to refer to landing a plane on a small, moving and bouncing deck as a controlled crash. When you stop to think about it, that is a pretty appropriate description.

Hornet's Flight Deck is 108 feet wide and 846 feet long. The angle deck didn't exist until 1956. The deck may seem big when you stand on it, but landing an airplane approaching at over 75-knots (86 mph) eats up the deck very quickly. This is especially true when the forward half of the deck is loaded with parked and fueled airplanes. While catapults were used to launch an airplane, **ARRESTOR GEAR** was used to stop the plane on the Flight Deck.

Arrestor Gear

(Or, hook 'em if you can)

The arrestor gear consisted of a cable stretched across the deck and an energy absorption engine. During World War II there were sixteen arrestor cables stretched across the aft-end of the Flight Deck and eight more across the bow. The bow cables were added so planes could be landed on the bow of *Hornet*, but other than for training, they were never used and were removed the first time *Hornet* was sent to port for repairs. It was the sixteen stern cables that were used to stop planes that landed on the Flight Deck.

■ An arrestor cable was actually called a **CROSSDECK PENDANT**. It was 1 7/16 inches thick, 100 feet long and made of hemp and wire. It had a breaking strength of 180,000 pounds, was good for a maximum of 80 arrested landings and had to be replaced after that.

Attached to each end of the crossdeck pendant was a **PURCHASE CABLE,** also 1 7/16 inches thick and made of hemp and wire. It was good for 3,000 arrested landings. The other end of the purchase cable was attached to the energy absorption engine, which is located under the Flight Deck. There was one engine for each of the sixteen cables.

The crossdeck pendants were kept three inches above the Flight Deck by a series of springs. They were attached to the purchase cable, which then passed through the deck on both edges, **REEVED** around a series of **SHEAVES** and then attached to the engine. There was an 18 to 1 **REEVING RATIO**, meaning that for every foot of cable travel the sheaves would play out 18 feet of cable.

Each airplane had a retractable hook attached to the bottom of the plane's frame. When the pilot is ready to land, he drops the tailhook, which extends about 18 inches below the plane. Just before the wheels of the airplane strike the Flight Deck, the pilot drops the tail enough for the hook to catch one of the crossdeck pendants that are only three inches above the deck. The hook catches the pendant and the forward motion of the plane draws the pendant down the axis (length) of the deck. The cable end that is attached to the engine is connected to a **CYLINDER AND RAM ASSEMBLY**. As the cable is played out, the ram forces hydraulic fluid out of the cylinder at a metered rate, which forces the plane to stop. The metered rate is preset depending on the weight of the plane, (remaining fuel, armaments, etc.) and is adjusted for each plane as it lands.

Once the plane comes to a stop (a 25 ton plane traveling 105 knots (121 miles per hour) would stop in 228 feet) the tailhook is retracted by the pilot and the engine retracts the crossdeck pendant in about 15 seconds. The plane either taxies under its own power or is pushed forward to clear the deck for the next plane.

Davis Barrier

(Or, the Navy's version of the crash barrier)

Although there were sixteen cables for the tailhook to catch, any number of things can go wrong and the plane might not catch one of them. Once this happens, there has to be a way to stop the plane from crashing into the rest of the planes parked on the forward end of the Flight Deck. For this reason, the **DAVIS BARRIER** was developed.

Hornet had five of these barriers. They were made of heavy canvas or nylon and looked much like a tennis net stretched across the Flight Deck. The barrier was attached to a pole on each side of the deck and was 15 feet high. During World War II one of the barriers was always erected whenever a plane was landing because of the parked planes near the bow.

■ If the plane missed the crossdeck pendant, it would (hopefully) roll into the barrier and not bounce or fly over it. The barrier would snag the planes propeller and trap the plane, often dumping it upside down on the Flight Deck. The reason there were five barriers is because once a plane had been trapped, the barrier would have to be replaced. Then one of the remaining barriers would be set up for the planes still coming in to land.

The barriers were designed to be raised and lowered in 2-1/2 seconds with a 30 second cycle time. This allowed the barriers to be quickly lowered after a landing plane successfully snagged an arrestor cable. During the time the deck crew signaled the pilot to retract the tailhook, the barrier would be lowered so the plane could roll over it and continue toward the forward end of the Flight Deck. As soon as the plane crossed the lowered barrier, it would be raised in preparation for the next landing.

The Angle Deck

(Or, if all else fails, try it again)

After the **ANGLE DECK** was added in 1956, the number of cables was reduced to four and only one Davis Barrier remained. The angled deck is a great innovation because it allows:

- The simultaneous launching and recovery of aircraft. Aircraft can be launched off the forward end of the Flight Deck at the same time other aircraft are landing on the angle deck.
- Aircraft that are landing and miss the cables can fly off and go around for another attempt. Just prior to touching the Flight Deck, the pilot applies full power to his aircraft in anticipation of missing the cable. This allows him to have enough speed to take off if he needs it.
- Aircraft can be stored between the angle deck and the catapults.

■ The Davis Barrier is not set up unless there is an emergency, otherwise a pilot would not be able to try to go around for another attempt. If a pilot radios in he is having mechanical problems or the pilot is injured, the barrier is set up to catch the plane if it misses the cables.

■ During the course of Flight Operations there are as many as 350 crewmen on the Flight Deck, and they have to be aware of all of the actions taking place around them. Aircraft and vehicles are moving around, planes are landing or launching, fuel lines are out, ammunition and bombs are being moved about and all this is taking place on the pitching and rolling deck of a moving ship with a strong wind blowing across the deck. Is it any wonder that that the Flight Deck of an aircraft carrier is considered one of the world's most dangerous places to work?

Three dockside views of the Hornet Museum.

Chapter 16

A Self-Guided Tour of *Hornet*

Introduction

Most of the remainder of this book is designed as a fairly detailed self-guided tour of *Hornet* as it exists as a museum ship. It includes all of the areas that are open to the public as of the winter of 2003. Later editions of the book will incorporate areas that are opened in the future.

■ There are two areas that require a guide to visit, and two more that may or may not require a guide. All of the tour guides on *Hornet* are docents, or volunteer tour guides. These people come from a variety of backgrounds, but they go through many hours of formal training followed by many more hours of following other docents before they are allowed to conduct tours of their own. Although they come from diverse backgrounds, they all have one common trait—they devote their time and incur some personal expense because they love what they are doing and want to see *Hornet* preserved for future generations.

At the time this book was written, the two escorted tours are of the **FORWARD ENGINE ROOM** and the **COMBAT INFORMATION CENTER (CIC)**. These areas aren't always available for tours. If there aren't enough trained docents to conduct them or during special events when there are too many people on *Hornet*, these tours are not conducted. However, if tours are being offered, you may have to sign up for them. Any docent can tell you where the sign up sheets are, and there are a limited number of tours available on any given day.

Two other tours may require a docent or are sometimes self-guided (this again depends on the availability of docents and the size of the crowd.) These are tours of the **FORECASTLE (FO'C'SLE) DECK**, portions of the **THIRD DECK** and the **ISLAND** (the superstructure above the flight deck.) The remainder of the ship is strictly self-guided.

■ The self-guided tours in this book begin on the HANGAR DECK. They generally correspond to the museum's handout when you buy your ticket, and are listed on the accompanying maps. Subsequent chapters in this book contain the following tours:

- **HANGAR DECK**
- **FORECASTLE (FO'C'SLE)**, including the **5-INCH-GUN, CREWS QUARTERS, ANCHOR CHAINS** and **SECONDARY CONN.**

- **SECOND DECK,** including the **WARD ROOM, READY ROOMS, OFFICERS' QUARTERS, MEDICAL FACILITIES, CPO QUARTERS, MARINE QUARTERS, REPAIR LOCKER** and **CAPSTAN MACHINERY ROOM.**
- **ENGINE ROOM** (although this requires a guide, a detailed explanation of what happens in the engine and boiler rooms is included)
- **FLIGHT DECK**
- **ISLAND**
- **COMBAT INFORMATION CENTER (CIC)**

Other exhibits and displays are included where appropriate.

HOW IT WORKS!

Deck Numbering System and Nomenclature

Deck Numbering System

There are 18 **DECKS** (floors) on *Hornet*. To be technically correct, there are 8 decks and 10 **LEVELS**. As you go **DOWN** from the **HANGAR DECK,** the decks are called *decks*. As you go **UP** from the Hangar Deck, the decks are called **LEVELS.** There are seven decks below the Hangar Deck and 10 levels above it.

The **HANGAR DECK** is called the Main Deck or Deck Number 1. The next deck *down* is the **SECOND DECK** or Deck Number 2. Decks are as follows:

- Hangar Deck (Main Deck)   Deck Number 1
- Second Deck   Deck Number 2
- Third Deck   Deck Number 3
- Fourth Deck   Deck Number 4
- First Platform Deck   Deck Number 5
- Second Platform Deck   Deck Number 6
- Hold   Deck Number 7
- Third Bottom   Deck Number 8

There are also two unnumbered **BOTTOMS** below the Third Bottom. These are all fuel, oil and water storage areas or **VOID TANKS** to help with buoyancy.

Above the Hangar Deck the **LEVELS** are numbered 01, ("Oh one") 02, etc. as follows:

• Fo'c'sle	01 Level
• Gallery Deck	02 Level
• Flight Deck	03 Level
• Communications Deck	04 Level
• Flag Bridge	05 Level
• Bridge	06 Level
• Anti-Aircraft Control Deck	07 Level
• Pri-Fly	08 Level
•	09 Level
•	10 Level

Nomenclature

Hornet is a **SHIP** and not a **BOAT.** Ships carry boats, and *Hornet* had several boats used to transport personnel while in port. *Hornet* is also called **SHE,** a carryover from the days of the ancient mariners. While women on a fighting ship brought bad luck, man, by nature, is protective of woman. So the ship is referred to as SHE for his protection, something worth fighting for.

■ The front of the ship is the **BOW.** The back of the ship is the **STERN** or **FANTAIL.** If you are standing anywhere on the ship facing the bow you are facing **FORWARD.** Facing the stern you are facing **AFT.** If you face forward, the right side of the ship is the **STARBOARD** side and the left side is the **PORT** side. Compartments on the starboard side are odd-numbered and on the port side they are even-numbered.

The floors are called **DECKS,** the walls are **BULKHEADS** and the ceiling is the **OVERHEAD.** Rooms are **COMPARTMENTS,** connected by **PASSAGEWAYS**. You walk between compartments through **DOORS** and between decks on **LADDERS** through **HATCHES.** The openings on the side of the ship are called **PORTS**.

■ Food is prepared in the **GALLEY** and eaten in the **MESS.** Enlisted men sleep in **RACKS** in large **BERTHING COMPARTMENTS** while officers sleep in **BUNKS** in **STATEROOMS.** The restroom is called the **HEAD.** *(See other nomenclature in the* **GLOSSARY.***)*

■ Your tour of *Hornet* can be an all-day event. If you tour everything that is open by summer of 2004, you will climb about 24 sets of ladders (that is, 24 *UP* and 24 *DOWN*) and walk about 1-1/2 miles. There are several sets of **HEADS** (restrooms) available on board, located on the Hangar Deck and on the Second Deck. Other portable facilities may be available for special events.

There is a **GEDUNK** (vending area) on the Hangar Deck near the stern. Weather permitting, the **FANTAIL** is a great place to take a break. It provides a great view of San Francisco.

The **EXIT** is on the Hangar Deck, amidships, starboard side. The **LOST AND FOUND** is also located there. The **SHIP STORE** (gift shop) is located on the Hangar Deck and sells a great variety of items related to *Hornet* and the Navy.

■ The tours in this book are laid out in the order that will optimize your time and limit the number of ladders you have to climb. However, you don't have to take the tours in the order shown, and you don't have to visit all of the areas. The tours requiring a guide (**ENGINE ROOM** and **CIC**) may not be available. You can do the tours in reverse, but due to the nature of the confined areas, you should follow the self-guided tours in the direction listed.

■ Docents often get asked about how much of the ship crewmen were able to see. Crewmen (we aren't being sexist here as there were never any women assigned to *Hornet*. Some traveled as passengers during the Magic Carpet cruises, but that was all) were generally restricted to their **DUTY** (work), **BERTHING** (sleeping) and **MESS** (eating) areas. You weren't allowed to wander the ship or enter any area you weren't assigned to. Many former crewmen and current visitors to the museum have stated they saw more of the ship as a visitor than they ever did as a crewman.

Safety

The passageways you will walk through are very narrow and cluttered with equipment. The museum directors want the ship to remain this way so you can get a feel of what duty on board an *Essex*-class carrier was like. Consequently, there are a myriad of things that can happen. You can trip, fall or hit your head. You need to be extremely careful when moving around the ship.

An opening in a **BULKHEAD** (wall) is called a **DOOR** (believe it or not, the Navy actually calls a **DOOR** a **DOOR**!). Almost every door has a high **THRESHOLD** (or **KNEE-KNOCKER**) you have to step over. Some of these doors can be closed-off and some can't. The threshold is designed partly to keep water from passing from one compartment to another, but more importantly to improve the structural integrity of the ship. Watch your step when stepping over the Knee-Knockers.

Watch your head when going up and down **LADDERS** or through the doors, and always hold on to the side rails or chains when using the ladders. It might be easier to go **DOWN** the ladders backwards. Face the ladder like you do when you go **UP.** *(Docents have reported several instances where parents are carrying infants or small children in carriers strapped to the parents' back, and the parent has ducked to get through a low overhang and forgot about the child, who then has been hit full in the face. So PLEASE don't forget your child if he or she is riding in a carrier on your back!)*

Also, you need to have both hands free while using the ladders, so don't carry children or cameras while doing so. Also, **FOOD** and **DRINKS** are not allowed anywhere except on the Hangar Deck so you will have both hands free when using the ladders.

■ **DO NOT** enter any **COMPARTMENT** (room) that is closed or has a chain across it, as these are **OFF LIMITS.** *DO NOT* go *"EXPLORING"* on your own. Even if there is a closed door and it doesn't have a sign that says you can't enter, it is still off limits. No exceptions. A closed door or a chain means **STAY OUT!** There are over two thousand compartments on *Hornet*, many of them still sealed and containing bad or dead air. There are vast quantities of asbestos, carcinogens (poisons), oil, grease, etc. in these compartments. None are lighted and if you get lost, it may be a long time before someone finds you. *Anyone caught in any closed area will be subjected to removed from the ship.*

If you have children with you, make sure they **DON'T RUN** while on *Hornet.* The decks are all made of steel or covered with wood and the Hangar Deck has a non-skid coating that will take off skin if someone falls on it while running.

■ Remember, *Hornet* was built as a warship for 20-year old crewmen, and not for the convenience of the crew or visitors. As a museum, the directors are trying to maintain the ship as it was. Consequently, you have to be careful about what you do and where you go. Think about what you are doing and where you are.

The Tour

Elsewhere in this book is a **GLOSSARY** of terms. Throughout the tour portion, Navy terms will be used in **CAPITAL LETTERS** followed by the more common name in *parenthesis.*

There are several subsections called *HOW IT WORKS!* that are enclosed in a black box and with a background shade that explain how an object works, such as the **FORWARD ELEVATOR,** the **5-INCH GUN,** etc.

HOW IT WORKS!

Hull and Compartmentation

Hull

As the builders and owners of the RMS *Titanic* found out the hard way, there is no such thing as an unsinkable ship. However *Hornet* and the *Essex*-class aircraft carriers were built to be as unsinkable as the available technology allowed.

Hornet contains two hulls. The **INNER HULL** surrounds most of the vital machinery and the **OUTER HULL**, which consists of two parts—the **UNARMORED HULL** and the **ARMORED HULL**. The unarmored hull is above the **WATERLINE** and is built to withstand only the pressures and strains encountered by a loaded ship in heavy seas. The armored hull is the portion below the waterline made of extra plates of armor steel designed to minimize the impact of torpedoes. The only portions of the ship above the waterline that are armored are the Hangar Deck and the Fourth Deck.

Below the waterline, between the inner hull and the outer hull, are three more bulkheads. Between the bulkheads are **VOIDS**, (fresh water storage tanks and bunker fuel storage tanks.) This provides five layers of protection against damage from torpedoes. If a torpedo strikes the outer hull the resulting explosion may rupture the outer hull and even one or more of the interior bulkheads, but with five bulkheads, the damage will be confined and the ship will be able to function. If the ship were to take on a **LIST** to one side, then the voids on the other side of the ship can be filled with water to help reduce the list.

Keel

The **KEEL** is like the ship's backbone. It runs along the very bottom of the ship from the (stem) bow to the stern. **FRAMES** are then attached to the keel. Frames are spaced four feet apart and are numbered from stem to stern, starting with number 1 and ending with number 210. There are six frames lettered A through F (F is also number 1) in the very bow of the ship, not attached to the keel. **LONGITUDINAL FRAMES** run parallel to the keel to support the frames attached to the keel. **DECK BEAMS, BULKHEADS** and **PLATING** are used to complete the structure of the ship. When *Hornet* was built, all of the steel was **RIVETED,** but in future rebuilds

Compartmentation

The **THIRD DECK** is the lowest deck where you can walk from one end of the ship to the other end on the same deck. As you walk along the second deck, every time you come to a watertight door you are traveling between watertight compartments. In each compartment between every watertight door is a hatch going down to the **FOURTH DECK.** From the Fourth Deck down to the bottom of the ship, there are no doors in the bulkheads between watertight compartments. The only way to go between watertight compartments on the lower decks is through the hatch. This means that if you are on the Fourth Deck and want to get to an adjoining compartment on the same deck, you have to climb up to the Third Deck, walk through the watertight door, and go down another ladder to the Fourth Deck.

What these compartments do is prevent flooding by creating hundreds of watertight compartments. *Hornet* also has a **DOUBLE BOTTOM** divided into voids and tanks to help with the buoyancy of the ship. All tanks on the ship are interconnected so that fuel and water can be moved from tank to tank. Up near the fo'c'sle is a **COLLISION BULKHEAD** of reinforced steel. If *Hornet* should get into a collision with another ship, the area forward of the collision bulkhead is designed to absorb the impact.

The **WATERLINE** on the exterior of the hull is painted black, and this is how much water *Hornet* should draw if fully loaded. The distance from the waterline to the lowest part of the ship is called the **DRAFT** (or draught), which in *Hornet's* case is 29 1/2 feet. The distance from the waterline to the Hangar Deck is called the **FREEBOARD.** When the ship is balanced it is in **TRIM.** If out of trim, it is **DOWN BY THE HEAD** or **DOWN BY THE STERN,** or it is **LISTING** to port or starboard.

These are normally accompanied by one or more drawings that explain what happens. In some cases there are also photographs, but the drawings were added to explain what the photos can't.

■ You are now ready to begin your tour of the Hangar Deck. The **HANGAR DECK** tour begins at the top of the forward **BROW** (ramp) on the **QUARTERDECK** where you entered the ship. Return to the ramp to begin your tour.

■ Have fun and enjoy your visit. If you have any questions or comments about your tour, please feel free to contact any of the docents who will be happy to try to answer your questions.

HOW IT WORKS!

How Compartments are Numbered

Every compartment has an identification number stenciled on a bulkhead consisting of several numbers and letters, as follows:

A-0204-E
Fr15fr18
V1

To explain how this works requires knowledge of several things.

■ As explained earlier, **DECKS** are numbered one through eight, number one being the Hangar Deck. **LEVELS** are numbered 01 through 10. **FRAMES** are numbered 1 through 210, starting from the bow. All **COMPARTMENTS** are numbered from the **BOW** to the **STERN**. If you draw an imaginary line along the center of the ship from the bow to the stern, it would be called the **CENTERLINE**. All compartments on the starboard side of the centerline are **ODD** numbered and the port side are **EVEN** numbered. The forward bulkhead of any compartment is the **FRAME LOCATION NUMBER**.

From the centerline, compartments are numbered toward the sides of the ship, with compartments on the centerline being numbered 0, the second one to starboard is 1, then 3, 5 while the compartments on the port side are numbered 2, 4, 6, etc.

Furthermore, *Hornet* is divided into three **SECTIONS**. From the bow to the aft end of Hangar Bay 1 is **A SECTION,** followed by **B SECTION** (which extends back into Hangar Bay 3) and **C SECTION** (which extends to the fantail).

Each compartment is indicated by its primary use, as follows:

A	Stowage
AA	Cargo Hold
C	Control Space
E	Engineering or Equipment
F	Oil Stowage
G	Aviation Gasoline
K	Chemicals
L	Living Areas and Passageways
M	Ammunition
T	Vertical Access Trunks (Escape Trunk)
V	Voids
W	Water

The last part of the bulkhead number is the DIVISION that is responsible for it, as *E Division* indicates Electricians and *V1 Division* is the Flight Deck. (See *HOW IT WORKS:* LISTING OF DIVISIONS). Thus, if you see an identification number such as:

A-0204-E
Fr15fr18
V1

It would stand for:

A	forward section
02	second level
04	fourth space from the centerline
E	engineering space
Fr15fr18	is located between frame 15 and 18
V1	the division responsible is the flight deck

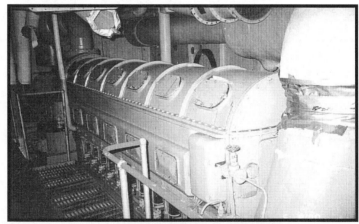

TOP: SHIPS BELL. MIDDLE: FORWARD 1000 KW DIESEL GENERATOR. BOTTOM: VIEW PORTS OF HANGAR BAY 1 FIRE CONTROL STATION. (AUTHOR)

Chapter 17

The Hangar Deck Tour

Hangar Deck Basics

The *Hornet's* **HANGAR DECK** was an extremely busy place as this was where aircraft were re-armed, refueled and repaired. This freed up the **FLIGHT DECK** so aircraft could be **LAUNCHED** (*take-off*) and **RECOVERED** (*land*). The Hangar Deck was protected from the weather, although huge access doors could be left open to allow air to circulate when aircraft engines were running or the weather demanded it.

The Hangar Deck is 654 feet long, 70 feet wide and 17 feet 5 inches high to the bottom of the Gallery Deck and 27 feet high to the bottom of the Flight Deck. Near the stern are numerous repair shops and spaces.

During World War II, when aircraft landed on the Flight Deck, they taxied under their own power or were pushed or pulled onto the forward **ELEVATOR.** They were then lowered to the Hangar Deck, and pushed or pulled down the length of the deck back toward the stern. They "worked" their way down the deck being rearmed, refueled or repaired as needed. Eventually they were taken back up to the Flight Deck via the portside deck edge (elevator #2) or rear inline elevator (elevator #3). The original elevator #3 no longer exists, having been closed off and replaced by the starboard side deck edge elevator in 1956. After the angled deck was added, aircraft generally went down to the Hangar Deck on elevator #2 since landing aircraft usually stopped either on it or very close to it.

■ The Hangar Deck is called the **MAIN** or **FIRST** or **NUMBER 1** deck. Most of the deck is also an armored deck, built from 2 1/2 inch thick Special Treatment Steel (STS). This is a nickel chrome steel alloy designed to prevent a bomb, kamikaze or other falling object that passed through the Flight Deck above from penetrating the Hangar Deck and passing into the spaces below. Below the armored portion of the Hangar Deck are stored all of the highly flammable items like aviation gasoline or jet fuel, bombs, rockets, gun ammunition, paint, etc. Also below the armored Hangar Deck are *Hornet's* engines, boilers and other critical machinery plus a large portion of the crew's quarters and **MESS** (dining) facilities.

The armored portion of the Hangar Deck extends from the edge of the forward elevator back to the edge of where the aft in-line elevator

HOW IT WORKS!

Readiness for Action and Material Conditions

Classifications

Throughout the ship you will notice doors, ports, hatches and other openings with the letters **X**, **Y** and **Z** placed on or next to them. These letters indicate when these openings should be closed and **DOGGED** while the ship is at sea. This is called **READINESS CONDITION**, and the opening must be closed as follows:

X—All openings marked **X** must be closed when the ship is in a well-protected harbor, except when undergoing repair or during the issue of **STORES** (supplies).

Y—All **X** and **Y** openings must be closed in unprotected ports.

Z—When the ship is at **GENERAL QUARTERS** (GQ), all **X**, **Y** and **Z** doors must be closed. Since General Quarters during combat might last for an extended period of time, condition **Z** can be modified to permit distribution of food, use of the HEAD or ventilation.

There are also several special conditions that apply:

Red Circle Z—These can be opened during long periods of General Quarters. When opened, they must be guarded so they can be immediately closed if necessary.

Black Circle X—These can be opened to give access to **BATTLE STATIONS**, for ammunition transfer, or the operation of vital systems.

Black Dog Z—A black **Z** enclosed by a larger black **D** are used for setting darkened ship condition.

Doors and Hatches

The strongest doors on *Hornet* are the **WATERTIGHT DOORS** (labeled WT). The handles on the doors are called **DOGS** and are **DOGGED DOWN** individually. Some watertight doors have **HAND WHEELS** which operate all of the dogs at once, and are called **QUICK ACTING WATERTIGHT DOORS** (QAWTD). All doors can be opened from either side although, during times of **GENERAL QUARTERS**, no watertight door can be opened without approval from damage control.

Doors that aren't watertight do not have dogs and are listed as **NON-WATERTIGHT DOORS** (NWTD). Other doors are: **AIRTIGHT DOORS** (ATD) that look similar to watertight doors; **SPRAYTIGHT DOORS** that are used on the bridge to keep rain and sea water out;

and **JOINER DOORS** that are used for privacy in staterooms, heads, etc. and that are similar to the doors in your home.

HATCHES are the heavy covers that cover openings between decks. When closed and dogged down, they cannot be opened except from the deck above. This means that during General Quarters crewmen in areas like the engine rooms and fire rooms can't open the hatch to escape. The hatches all have an **ESCAPE SCUTTLE,** which is a small round opening with quick-acting closures to permit escape. Most large sealed compartments also have **VERTICAL ACCESS TRUNKS** (escape trunks). These are small passageways going up several decks with a vertical ladder and an escape scuttle on the end.

was located. This is approximately even with the aft edge of where the starboard side deck edge elevator #3 is now located.

The Hangar Deck contains hundreds of **TIE DOWNS,** most of which have been removed or filled in to prevent tripping over them. The tie downs were used to tie down the aircraft so they wouldn't roll around the deck. The Hangar Deck is also covered with a very coarse surface to provide traction and prevent slipping. This surface is very rough and if you fall on it, you'll leave a piece of yourself behind for others to clean up.

■ About 17 feet above your head, as you tour most areas of the Hangar Deck, you will see the bottom of what is called the **GALLERY DECK.** On the Gallery Deck are located dozens of repair shops and workspaces, crew quarters and storage for thousands of spare parts. In those areas where the Gallery Deck doesn't exist, what you see about 27 feet above you is the bottom of the Flight Deck.

Two huge rolling **FIRE DIVISION DOORS** divide the Hangar Deck into three **HANGAR BAYS.** These doors are designed to prevent the spread of fire or explosions from one bay to the next. The hangar bay closest to the bow and forward elevator is called Hangar Bay 1. The second is Hangar Bay 2 and the last one near the stern is Hangar Bay 3.

The two fire division doors are located inside the **BULKHEADS** (walls) dividing the Hangar Deck. The doors no longer close because the pipes of the new fire control sprinkler system cross in front of the doors, but you can see the edges of the doors with the red and orange safety marks painted on them. The floor tracks for the doors still exist. The fire division doors were added during the 1952 rebuild because of the serious damage inflicted on other carriers by bombs and aircraft coming through the Flight Deck and exploding on the Hangar Deck. Fires quickly spread. Although no *Essex*-class carrier was ever lost, severe fires caused serious damage to several of them during World War II.

■ Throughout the Hangar Deck you will see hose reels, hose nozzles and pipes painted purple, red or green. Hose reels and pipes painted **PURPLE** were used to pump aviation gasoline into aircraft. **RED** nozzles are called **FIRE HOSE STATIONS** and are used for fire fighting with seawater pumped from outside the ship. The **GREEN** pipes and nozzles were used to dispense **AQUEOUS FILM FORMING FOAM (AFFF)** or **FOG/FOAM,** a chemical mixture under extreme pressure used to smother a fuel fire. Fog/foam making machinery is located one deck down on the **SECOND DECK**. Fires aboard an aircraft carrier were fast moving and generally of two types: fuel fed and/or caused by explosives. Remember, aircraft were being both refueled and rearmed on the Hangar Deck, so you would have highly volatile aviation gasoline or jet fuel and bombs, rockets and gun ammunition all located there. Any fire that got started could quickly ignite the fuel, which in turn would explode the bombs (also called **ORDNANCE**).

In the event of a fire, crewmen went to their assigned fire fighting stations and worked together to fight the fire. Water was used to cool the fires until the AFFF stations had been energized to make fog/foam. All crewmen were trained to fight fires, so if its normal crew didn't man one of the fog/foam or water stations, someone else could take over. The water hose used to fight a fire was either 1 1/2" or 2 1/2" in diameter.

If you remember your third grade science class, you know that you don't fight a fuel (gasoline, grease, solvent) fire with water because all the water does is spread the fire around. Most fires contained some sort of liquid fuel.You have to smother a liquid fuel fire with foam. One way to help fight a fire was to turn the ship hard to port or starboard to get the deck to slope in one direction enough for the fuel, water and foam to run out the large open doors along the edge of the deck. When not in use, fuel hoses were filled with carbon dioxide to prevent a fire.

■ To coordinate the efforts of the crews fighting a fire, there are three **CONFLAG STATIONS,** one located in each hangar bay. Each of the conflag stations is a fireproof blastproof room with several small view ports located high off the deck. If a fire got started on the Hangar Deck, the crewmen in the conflag stations would use sound-powered telephones and the public address (PA) system to communicate with the men fighting the fire on the deck. The conflag stations also controlled the fire division doors, and the conflag station in Hangar Bay 2 also controlled the other two conflag stations. All conflag stations were manned around the clock during flight operations. Conflag station 2 in Hangar Bay 2 is always manned when the ship is **UNDERWAY** or there are any aircraft on the ship.

Located around the Hangar Deck are **HATCHES** with **LADDERS** going down to the second deck. Around the hatches are 9-inch to 12-inch high steel **COAMINGS,** placed there to prevent water, or more importantly, burning fuel, foam or loose rolling objects, from falling down through the hatches.

High on the bulkheads all around the Hangar Deck are large gray boxes. These **LIFE JACKET LOCKERS** contained one-size-fits-all life preservers. The crew wouldn't normally wear them, however if needed, all someone had to do was pull on the release cord hanging from the bottom of each gray box. The bottom would swing open and all of the contents would tumble down to the deck. From there it was a scramble to get into one of the life preservers.

A Tour of the Hangar Deck

(Note: The USS Hornet Museum has several aircraft in various stages of restoration and more are being added. Although the purpose of Hornet and other aircraft carriers was to support its aircraft, the museum's aircraft won't be mentioned here. They have their own section in this book. They aren't included here because they tend to move around and on any given day some or all of them might be on the Flight Deck.)

■ When you enter the *Hornet* you enter through the **OFFICER'S QUARTERDECK** (STOP "A" on the Hangar Deck Tour Map on the following page) on the starboard side of Hangar Bay 1. This Quarterdeck is where officers and dignitaries entered the ship, and thus is considered a sacred area. Woe to the poor unfortunate enlisted man who walked on the quarterdeck. When tied up to a dock, you enter the ship when you walk up the forward **BROW** or **GANGWAY** (Navy term for a ramp). Only officers could enter through the forward brow. Enlisted personnel entered through the after brow (enlisted quarterdeck) located further back near the starboard side deck edge elevator.

When the ship wasn't tied up to a dock, there were ladders that hung down from the Hangar Deck and alongside the ship called **ACCOMMODATION LADDERS.** There was also a **JACOB'S LADDER,** a rope ladder that hung down from a **BOAT BOOM** (a long beam) that stuck out from the side of the ship. After a **MOTOR LAUNCH** (motorized boat) deposited its passengers at the accommodation ladder, the launch was tied up at the bottom of the Jacob's Ladder and the launch operator climbed the ladder to get back on the ship.

■ There was always a duty officer stationed at the entrance of the quarterdeck when personnel were leaving or entering the ship. There was a senior CPO (Chief Petty Officer) at the after-brow used by the enlisted men. When Navy personnel entered the ship they would stop on the top or last step, face the stern of the ship, come to attention and salute the **COLORS** (*United States flag*) flying at the stern of the ship. (Even if it couldn't be seen, it was still saluted.) Then the new arrival would step onto the deck of the ship, face the duty officer or CPO, salute again and announce *"Request Permission to Come Aboard, SIR!"* Permission would be granted and the person would enter the ship.

HANGAR DECK TOUR

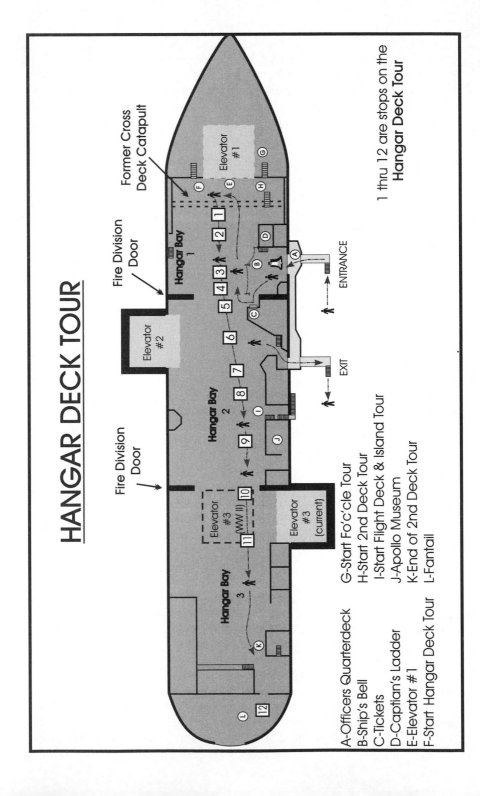

Former Cross Deck Catapult

Fire Division Door

Fire Division Door

Elevator #1

Elevator #2

Elevator #3 (WW II)

Elevator #3 (current)

Hangar Bay 1

Hangar Bay 2

Hangar Bay 3

ENTRANCE

EXIT

1 thru 12 are stops on the **Hangar Deck Tour**

A-Officers Quarterdeck
B-Ship's Bell
C-Tickets
D-Captian's Ladder
E-Elevator #1
F-Start Hangar Deck Tour

G-Start Fo'c'cle Tour
H-Start 2nd Deck Tour
I-Start Flight Deck & Island Tour
J-Apollo Museum
K-End of 2nd Deck Tour
L-Fantail

When departing the ship, this formality was conducted in reverse, with *"Request Permission to Go Ashore, SIR!"* being the announcement.

*(Note: If you are beginning the **HANGAR DECK** tour from inside the ship, your tour starts at STOP A, so return there. STOP "C" is where you pay your admission fee.)*

As you enter the ship you will see the huge **SHIP'S BELL** (STOP "B") mounted on a pedestal. At one time the bell had been mounted on one of the vertical supports in the **FO'C'SLE**. A shipfitter removed the bell while *Hornet* was in mothballs in Bremerton, Washington, and trucked it down to San Diego and placed it in his yard. When *Hornet* was being saved from the wreckers and developed as a museum, one of the volunteers tracked down the bell and bought it, then placed it on permanent loan to the USS Hornet Museum.

■ If you look toward the forward bulkhead on the quarterdeck, you will see a large shield. This was the ship's shield and matches the uniform patches worn by crewmen while *Hornet* was a CVS (anti-submarine carrier). To the left of the shield you will see a ladder along the side of the forward bulkhead going up to the gallery deck. On the ladder is a banner with the words CAPTAIN C. J. SEIBERLICH, COMMANDING OFFICER. This ladder was used by the ship's captain to get to his **IN-PORT** cabin (large cabin) on the gallery deck.

The captain had an inport cabin on the Gallery Deck and a **SEA CABIN** next to the **BRIDGE** up on the **ISLAND**. The in-port cabin was used to entertain Very Important People (VIP's), higher-ranking officers, the President of the United States, heads of foreign countries and even movie stars. The in-port cabin has its own **GALLEY** (kitchen) and **SECRET ROOM** where confidential publications, maps, reports, etc., were stored. Eventually the inport cabin will be open to visitors.

The Captain usually didn't use the in-port cabin while at sea because he spent most of his time in the sea cabin, but when in port, he had his quarters in the cabin directly at the top of the ladder. Captain Seiberlich was the last of *Hornet's* 23 commanding officers.

■ The walking tour starts at the **BOW** (forward) end of the Hangar Deck at the edge of the huge well (or hole) of the forward elevator **(ELEVATOR NUMBER 1**, STOP "E"). Walk up to the elevator well, and assuming the elevator is parked on the Flight Deck, you can peer down into the well. As you face the elevator well, look down and you will see two sets of three cables coming out of the deck and passing over a set of wheels. These are six of the twelve cables used to raise and lower the elevator (see *HOW IT WORKS: FORWARD ELEVATOR*.) The other two sets are visible along the back wall.

HOW IT WORKS!

Forward Elevator

The **FORWARD ELEVATOR** (elevator number 1) is located ahead of the armored portion of the Hangar Deck. It is used during the recovery process to take aircraft off the flight deck and down into the Hangar Deck for rearming, refueling, repair or storage.

Operation

The elevator platform (#1 on the Elevator Diagram on the following page) is suspended on twelve cables (2) grouped one set of three cables at each corner of the elevator, whose travel is controlled by a hydraulic piston (3).

When lowering the platform, gravity forces the piston inward when the hydraulic cylinder (4) is vented via the control valve (5) to the high pressure (HP) tank (6).

The control valve is operated either electrically or manually. When operated electrically the platform rate of descent is controlled by the residual air pressure in the low pressure (LP) tank (7). When operated manually, the rate of descent is controlled by the hand wheel (8) located on the Hangar Deck level.

The platform may be stopped at any position when manually operated. When operated electrically it will only stop at the flight deck or the Hangar Deck.

When raising the platform, hydraulic oil which was previously stored in the high pressure (HP) tank is introduced through the control valve back to the hydraulic cylinder which forces the piston out. This, in turn, pulls down on the cables, forcing the elevator upward.

At the same time four 150 horsepower electrically operated pumps (9) are transferring previously vented hydraulic oil from the low pressure (LP) tank to the high pressure (HP) tank, readying the system for the NEXT raise operation.

This stored high pressure (HP) oil also allows the elevator to be returned to the flight deck using the manually operated hand wheel in case of an electrical power failure. In an emergency, the platform can also be slowly raised to the flight deck utilizing a pair of 20 horsepower sump pumps (10) after sufficient oil has been transferred from the low pressure (LP) tank to the sump.

Specifications

Platform
size:	44' wide x 58' long
weight:	142,000 pounds or 71 tons
travel: (height)	27' 2.5"
maximum speed:	140' per minute
rate of descent:	11 seconds
rate of ascent:	14 seconds
normal cycle time:	(time to load aircraft on platform,

lower platform, remove aircraft and raise platform:
45 seconds)

manual raise:	nine minutes
load capacity:	46,000 pounds or 23 tons

Mechanical

Cable diameter:	1 1/4"
Number of cables:	12
Piston diameter:	30"
Hydraulic oil in system:	3310 gallons
Main pump horsepower:	four at 150 or 600 total
Sump pump horsepower:	two at 20 or 40 total hp
High Pressure system:	1000 PSI
Low Pressure system:	300 PSI

Safety Stanchions

Around the elevator on the flight deck are a series of poles with a heavy cable running between them. These were placed there as a safety measure to keep personnel from falling into the elevator shaft when the elevator is down. These poles are normally stored in the down position, and you can see the bottom of them when you look up into the elevator shaft when standing on the Hangar Deck.

These stanchions would always remain in the down position even during normal operations since the elevator would normally be in the up or flight deck position. However, when the elevator was going to be in the down position for any length of time, the stanchions would be raised.

Under the lip of the flight deck are a series of motors, one for each side. These motors are geared to a shaft, which turns a screw mechanism on the bottom of each of the poles. When you want the stanchions to go up, you turn the motor, which turns the shaft, which in turn runs the stanchions up. All the motors are tied together so all the stanchions work at the same time. Since there is already a cable between them (The cable is stored in a track on the flight deck—you can see it there) once the stanchions go up, you have a ready-made safety barrier.

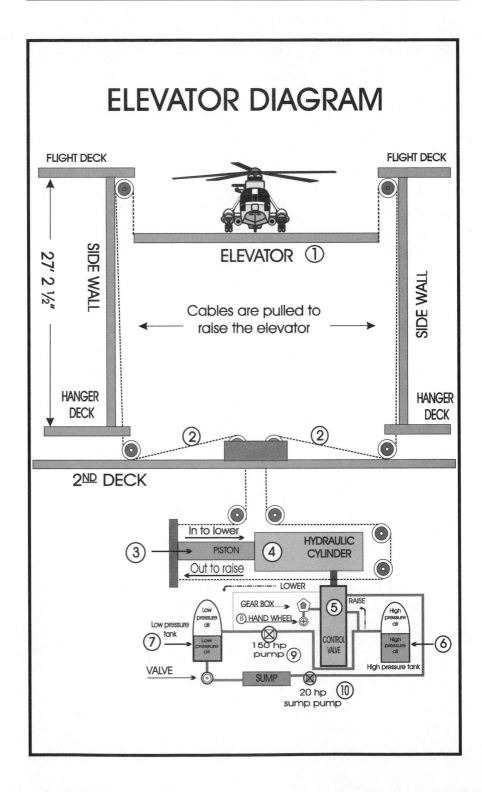

■ Half way up the back wall you see a faded "NO SMOKING" sign. For future reference purposes, on the 02 Level directly behind that sign is the **HEAD** (restroom) for the **FO'C'SLE CREW BERTHING COMPARTMENT**. Later, when you are touring that compartment, you'll have a good idea of where you are.

Still facing the "NO SMOKING SIGN," turn to your right. Located on the elevator sidewall are the controls for operating the elevator. The elevator can be operated hydraulically under full power or reserve power, or by hand by turning a small crank. Believe it or not, the 72-ton elevator is so well balanced it can be raised and lowered by hand!

Facing the "NO SMOKING" sign again, now turn left and look up. You'll see a painted sign that says **GAS REPAIR STA NO. 7** and you'll see five small rectangular view ports. Behind this bulkhead is the **CONFLAG STATION** for Hangar Bay 1. Whenever there was any refueling or arming going on in the hangar bay, the conflag station would be manned by personnel who could direct firefighting if a fire got started.

Look straight up and you will see a series of pipes with sprinkler heads. These are **WATER CURTAINS** that, in case of a fire on the Hangar Deck, could be turned on providing a solid wall of water that would help prevent the flames from entering the elevator well. There are seven of these on the Hangar Deck, one here, one on each side of the large **FIRE DIVISION DOORS** and one each in the middle of Hangar Bay 2 and 3.

If you look up high and around the edge of the elevator, you'll see a series of motors, faded orange painted rods and gears. These are connected to a series of vertical poles that fit through the Flight Deck. Connecting the poles on the Flight Deck is a cable. When the elevator is lowered, the motors turn the rods and gears, which raise the poles and cables on the Flight Deck creating a safety barrier. This will prevent personnel from falling through the open elevator shaft on the Flight Deck. Later, when you walk around the Flight Deck, you can see where the poles and cables are recessed into the deck.

On either side of the elevator well there is a ladder going up to the 01 Level. You will take the ladder to your right when you finish the Hangar Deck tour to go up to the **5-INCH GUN MOUNT, FO'C'SLE** (STOP "F") and the crew's quarters. You can either take that tour now or you can finish up the Hangar Deck tour. In either case, you will end up back where you are now standing. If the **FO'C'SLE** is open and there are no Docent-led guided tours of the fo'c'sle available and you want to do the fo'c'sle tour on your own at this time, go to the next chapter. When you finish that tour, come back to this spot.

(Note: Check with the Docent in the area or at the orientation area for fo'c'sle tours. There are times the fo'c'sle is closed to self-guided tours and you HAVE to take a guided tour!)

To Continue Your Tour of the Hangar Deck

As you face the faded "NO SMOKING" sign in the elevator well, you are facing the **BOW** of the ship. If you turn around and look down the length of the Hangar Deck, you will be facing the **STERN.** Depending on how many airplanes are parked on the Hangar Deck, and if there are any displays, you may or may not be able to see the other end of the Hangar Deck. You might see a small area of light coming in low on the back wall. That is the passageway out to the fantail. While doing the tour, you may have to move around aircraft or other items to see things that are pointed out, but always return to the place where you last made a stop. (*Stops on all tours are keyed to the map accompanying the tour.*)

■ We'll start our tour facing the stern. You should still be close to the safety fence at the edge of the well for elevator #1 and near the center of the deck. Facing the stern, walk about 14 paces and stop. This is your first stop (STOP "1"). You will be standing about where the track for the Hangar Deck side-launch catapult was located during World War II. Most of the early *Essex*-class carriers had the catapult, but *Hornet* is the only one that ever launched an airplane using it. It wasn't very safe for the pilot, and the track was on top of the armored deck which interfered with moving aircraft from the elevator into the Hangar Bay. The track across the deck also wasn't long enough to launch a plane, so there were large track extensions on both sides of the Hangar Deck that hung out over the side of the ship and were folded up when not in use. By the end of World War II all *Essex*-class carriers had given up their Hangar Deck catapult except *Hornet*, which hadn't gone back into port for 18 months and still carried hers at the end of the war.

Aircraft were launched off the starboard side (now to your left) through the huge rollup doors. How, you ask, did they ever get the wings through the upright stanchions? If you walk over to look at the doors, you'll see that the portions between the upright stanchions roll up, and then the stanchions roll to the right to create one large opening for the plane to be launched through. The same holds true for the large opening on the opposite side of the Hangar Deck. If you walked over to the rollup doors, then return to where you were when you made your first stop. Now face the stern of the ship.

As you look to your left again you will see a hatch that goes down to the second deck with a coaming surrounding it. You will use that hatch later when you do the tour of the **SECOND DECK.** (STOP "H").

■ Facing the stern, walk another 12 paces and stop. This is STOP "2." To your left you will see the green nozzle of one of the **FOG/FOAM FIRE FIGHTING STATIONS,** and to the right of it you will see the purple **AVIATION GASOLINE PUMPING STATION**. Facing the stern again, turn to your right and you'll see a basketball hoop. The crew used the Hangar Deck for recreational purposes whenever possible and basketball was one of several types of recreation you could do here. If you removed the aircraft from the Hangar Bay you have a large area where you could set up chairs. Chair storage was in the racks above the basketball hoop and other similar areas. Below and to the left of the basketball hoop is a red nozzle and pipes. This is a **FIRE HOSE STATION** used for fighting fire with seawater.

Facing the stern again, look up and to your left at about 11:00. You will see a flat wall just above the quarterdeck with four small hatch covers. Behind this bulkhead is the projection room. Movie projectors (there were no VCR's when *Hornet* was in service) located there could show movies on a screen that rolled down in front of the **CONFLAG** station to your rear, near the forward elevator. A large portion of the crew could see the movie, and it wasn't uncommon for crewmen to hang chairs from the bottom of the gallery deck and other locations to get a good view of the screen.

At other times, the elevator could be lowered to within a few feet from the Hangar Deck and used as a stage. Guest entertainment, crew productions, volleyball and the ships' band would perform from the stage. It was also used during religious services.

■ Facing the stern again, walk 12 paces and stop. This is STOP "3." Now look to your left to the large "black hole." This is the large **BOMB ELEVATOR** that travels between the Flight Deck, Hangar Deck and the Third Deck **READY SERVICE MAGAZINE** where bombs are stored. The Bomb Elevator is large enough to handle a **NUCLEAR WEAPON.** Although the Bomb Elevator was designed to allow arming of aircraft on the Hangar Deck, after several serious and tragic accidents on other aircraft carriers, re-arming was banned on the Hangar Deck after World War II and took place only on the Flight Deck.

Above the Bomb Elevator is *Hornet's* **SCOREBOARD.** This is a hand-made exact replica of the board that *Hornet* carried throughout its post-war career. The original is located in a museum in Pensacola, Florida. One of the *Hornet* Museum's volunteers made the scoreboard and hand painted all of the symbols.

■ Once again facing the stern, to your right you will see the large round hose reels and the purple pipes. This is another aviation refueling point. Aviation gasoline was pumped from storage tanks located far down below the waterline, through the pipes and hoses into the aircraft. Once refueling was completed or during an emergency, carbon dioxide was pumped into the hoses and pipes to prevent the gasoline fumes from igniting.

To the right of the fueling station is a ladder with stainless-steel siding that goes up to the Gallery Deck. At the top of this ladder was the

ADMIRAL'S IN-PORT CABIN. *Hornet* was often the flagship of a fleet, task group or task force of other ships, and as such there would often be an admiral and his staff on board. His in-port cabin was smaller than the Captains In-port Cabin. Like the captain, the admiral had a sea cabin in the flag bridge up in the island just below the captain's bridge. When there was no admiral on board, the Admiral's In-port Cabin was used by VIP's or as a conference room. Above the fueling station is another large shield depicting the patch worn by crewmen and pilots when *Hornet* was a CVA (Attack) carrier.

■ Facing the stern again, walk 14 steps and stop. This is STOP "4." To the right is another green-painted fog/foam unit. Above the fog/foam nozzle, on the bulkhead which divides Hangar Bay #1 and #2, are two of the gray life-preserver boxes. On the deck in front of the wall is an **AMMUNITION HOIST** that used to load 5-inch gun ammunition into the magazines down below the waterline. Look back at the quarterdeck to your left. Hanging down from the **OVERHEAD** (ceiling) is the remains of a large pulley. This was used to load pallets of ammunition or equipment from the side of the ship to the Hangar Deck. Ammunition pallets were moved to the ammunition hoist and the shells were fed down the hoist, by hand, one shell at a time.

The white bulkhead dividing Hangar Bay #1 and #2 contains one half of the rolling fire door that could be closed in case of a fire. The other half of the door is in the wall on the opposite side of the Hangar Bay. The edge of the door is painted with a red and orange checkerboard pattern. The doors roll in the raised track that runs on the floor between the two doors. Directly above the track is another set of sprinkler heads to provide a wall of water in case of a fire. Crossing in front of the doors is a large pipe. The pipe didn't exist when *Hornet* was an active ship. It was placed there as part of the modern firefighting equipment. The doors can no longer be rolled shut.

Hangar Bay 2

Walk toward the stern and stand directly on top of the raised track. This is STOP "5." If you look straight up you will see the pulley system used to close the doors. To your right is another set of purple fuel lines. To the left of the fuel lines is a tall metal shaft with four large cables entering from the deck above. This is one of the cable sets used to raise and lower the port side deck edge elevator which is located outside the long wall of roll up doors and rolling stanchions.

■ Now facing the stern again, walk 20 paces and stop. This is STOP "6." To your left is the exit from *Hornet's* Hangar Deck and the exit from the ship. Above that is the **CONFLAG** station for Hangar Bay #2. To the right of the exit is a long slanted bulkhead. Behind this are the uptakes that pull smoke and fumes from the fire rooms up to and through the island and out the funnel on top of the island. Facing the stern, to your right are roll up doors going out to the port side deck edge elevator.

■ Walk another 20 paces toward the stern and make STOP "7." To the left and below the NO SMOKING sign is a door that leads you to the bottom of the escalator (STOP "H"). A common question is if the escalator was added on after the *Hornet* became a museum. The answer is no. The escalator was added in 1956. It was placed there to help the pilots, whose ready rooms are located the next deck down, get up to the Flight Deck, three decks above, with all of their gear. Pilots found it almost impossible to climb four sets of ladders to the Flight Deck with their parachute, weapons, maps, charts and everything else.

Mounted on the uptake bulkhead to the left of the escalator door is a board with the word **"CRUNCH"** on it. This was used to remind the crew how many plane moves had been made on the Hangar Deck without a "CRUNCH," or airplanes colliding with one another while being moved. Obviously, CRUNCH'S were to be avoided because they meant some sort of damage had probably occurred.

Facing the stern, to your right is another purple aviation fuel line and the other set of cables for the elevator. Above this and to the left is a small compartment hanging out over the deck with big windows. This is the **HANGAR DECK CONTROL STATION.** Inside is a table with a scale drawing of the entire Hangar Deck and small model airplanes, one for each plane on the ship. These models were pushed around on the drawing to figure out how to move aircraft around the deck so the ones needed at a given time could be moved to the elevators. The models show how the planes would fit and which ones had to be moved. The Hangar Deck was very crowded with dozens of airplanes being worked on at any one time, and it was like trying to fit a jigsaw puzzle together.

■ Walk about 35 paces toward the stern and stop. This is STOP "8." On the deck to your left is a carpet that outlines the Mobile Quarantine Facility where the astronauts from Apollo 11 and 12 were quartered. (Depending on when you read this, there might even be an Airstream trailer parked there that was used on one of the Apollo missions.)

■ Walk another 10 paces and stop. This is STOP "9." On the deck in front of you are Neil Armstrong's first footsteps on earth after landing on the moon. Astronauts Armstrong, Aldrin and Collins were brought aboard *Hornet* in a helicopter that landed on the Flight Deck. The helicopter was brought down to the Hangar Deck on the port side deck edge elevator and towed to where the first footprint is painted. The astronauts walked from the helicopter to the trailer, and then were locked inside the trailer for their trip back to Houston. To the right of the carpet/trailer is a door to the **APOLLO EXHIBIT,** (STOP "J") and to the right of that is a small bomb elevator that extends up to the **FLIGHT DECK** and down to the Magazine.

■ Facing the stern, to your right is another fog/foam and aviation gasoline station. Walk toward the stern and stand on top of the track the doors rolled on that separate Hangar Bay 2 and Hangar Bay 3. You can see the doors on either side of the deck. This is STOP "10."

Hangar Bay 3

To your right, through the door marked **WEATHER,** is the *Hornet's* **THEATRE** where continuously running videos are shown. Next to that is the **PLANKOWNERS WALL**, listing all of the individuals who donated funds to help start the museum.

■ Walk 20 paces toward the stern and stop. This is STOP "11." You will be standing almost directly under the original elevator number 3. To your left is the new elevator number three that was added in 1956. This elevator folds up to allow passage through confined areas. (*Although the World War II version of Hornet could pass through the Panama Canal, after all of the rebuilds, Hornet is now too large to fit*). The large weather doors roll to one side, unlike the rollup doors in Hangar Bay 1. To your right is the **FLIGHT SIMULATOR** that you can ride for an additional cost.

Hangar Bay 3 is the largest of the three hangar bays. This is where all of the aircraft maintenance was conducted, and it is surrounded by repair shops and contains several overhead hoists. During World War II seriously damaged aircraft that made it back to the ship were pushed overboard instead of trying to repair them because it wasn't cost effective to keep them.

■ Throughout your tour of *Hornet* you will notice red light fixtures in most of the compartments. These were used at night because white light affects night vision, and it also can be seen at long distances. Red light doesn't affect night vision. Most compartments down inside the ship used white light if it didn't show outside.

Overhead lighting in Hangar Bay 3 was usually bright white instead of red light because of the repair work going on. The hangar bay could be secured so no light would show outside and the mechanics could work. Also, spilled hydraulic fluid is red and invisible under red light.

The **CONFLAG STATION** is to your right front near the back bulkhead. Below that and all around the back of the deck are shops. To your left front is the access door to the **FANTAIL**. To your left are the men's **HEAD** (restroom) and the women's **HEAD**. To the right of the women's head is what looks like a windowless room extending from the bulkhead. On the backside of this room is the ladder down to the **CPO**

MESS (Chief Petty Officers dining room). This is the **EXIT** from the **SECOND DECK** tour (STOP "K").

■ If you walk through the passageway to your left front out to the **FANTAIL,** you will have a great view of San Francisco. Located on the fantail are **BITTS** (cleats) that the **MOORING LINES** are attached to. There are also **CAPSTANS** that pull the mooring lines tight. To the left near the rail is a large reel and next to it, bolted to the deck is a small tripod. This is the **FANFARE UNIT**, a small **DROPPED SOUND AND ECHO ACOUSTICAL DECOY,** STOP "12." If an enemy submarine was tracking *Hornet*, the decoy would be dropped overboard and pulled behind *Hornet* at about 600 feet. The decoy was actually a better target for a **HOMING TORPEDO** then the ship itself!

Far above the fantail is the overhang for the Flight Deck and the **SAFETY NET** that is designed to catch anyone blown off the Flight Deck. The tall vertical pole running from the Flight Deck down below the fantail was covered in lights and is a visual extension of the centerline on the Flight Deck. It was used by the pilots to maintain visual orientation between the ship and the landing deck.

Because of its exposed location, the fantail was off limits to all personnel whenever aircraft were landing. If a plane came in too low and crashed into the end of the deck, debris could scatter all over the fantail, killing or injuring anyone on the deck.

■ This concludes the **HANGAR DECK** tour. If you haven't completed the **FO'C'SLE TOUR,** then return to the area of elevator number 1 to begin that tour. If you have already completed the fo'c'sle tour, return to the **HATCH** going down to the second deck back, by Stop "H", to take the **SECOND DECK TOUR.**

HOW IT WORKS!

Department Organization

The **COMMANDING OFFICER** of *Hornet*, referred to as **CAPTAIN**, was a Captain in rank (equal to a full Colonel in the other services). As **CAPTAIN**, he was in command of the ship and the Air Group(s) attached to it. He was ultimately responsible for everything the ship and the crew did or failed to do. It was for this reason the Captain seldom left the **BRIDGE** while *Hornet* was at sea.

Assisting the Captain and the Number Two man in charge of *Hornet*, always ready to assume command if something happened to the Captain, was the **EXECUTIVE OFFICER**. During time of **GENERAL QUARTERS** and during other times of distress, the Executive Officer, (also called the **XO**), would remain in **SECONDARY CONN,** just below the forward end of the Flight Deck. During normal operations, the Executive Officer is responsible for all matters relating to the personnel, routing and discipline of the ship.

■ Like any large, formal organization, *Hornet* was divided into **DEPARTMENTS** and **DIVISIONS** to manage operations and provide a chain of command. Following is a list of the principle departments on *Hornet*.

Operations Department

The **OPERATIONS OFFICER**, who is responsible for collecting, evaluating and disseminating combat, tactical and operational information, commanded this Department. Divisions reporting to the Operations Officer are:

Electronics (**OE DIVISION**): these men had to operate and maintain *Hornet's* vast network of over 2,000 electronics devices needed to operate all of the radio, radar and navigation equipment.

Meteorological or Weather (**OA DIVISION**): performed all the functions of a weather office. Collected, evaluated and disseminated weather information for all ships and aircraft in the task group and provided weather forecasts.

Combat Information Center (**CIC**, or **OI DIVISION**): see *HOW IT WORKS:* COMBAT INFORMATION CENTER.

Carrier Air Traffic Control Center (CATCC, or OC DIVISION): coordinated and scheduled *Hornet's* flights and missions, provided information to launch and recover aircraft, and controlled aircraft on their departure and approach for landing.

Photographic or *Air Intelligence* (**OP DIVISION**): was responsible for the Photo Lab, which included all official photography, photo developing and printing of photographs. Air Intelligence coordinated all intelligence functions required for *Hornet* and the air groups.

Communications Department

The **COMMUNICATIONS OFFICER** commands the Communications Department. He has charge of visual and electronic communications and of classified publications and devices. Divisions reporting to the Communications Officer are:

Signal (**CS DIVISION**): managed visual means of communications via flags, signal light or semaphore.

Radio and Crypto Security (**CR DIVISION**): managed all of *Hornet's* radio communication, including classified or crypto communications.

Air Department

The **AIR OFFICER**, also referred to as the **AIR BOSS**, commands the Air Department. The Air Boss is responsible for aircraft launching, landing and handling operations. He is also responsible for service, maintenance and repair of aircraft, and handling of aviation fuels and explosives. Divisions reporting to the Air Boss are:

V1 DIVISION, or the Flight Deck Crew: these men managed the movement and security of aircraft on the Flight Deck.

V2 DIVISION: maintained the Catapults and the Arresting Gear machinery needed to launch and recover aircraft.

V3 DIVISION, or the Hangar Deck Crew: was responsible for the movement and security of aircraft on the Hangar Deck. They also handled maintenance of aircraft on the Hangar Deck.

V4 DIVISION, or Aviation Fuels: these men were responsible for receipt and stowage of aviation fuel and fueling and defueling of aircraft on the Flight Deck and Hangar Deck.

V5 DIVISION: maintained all helicopters on *Hornet.*

V6 DIVISION: maintenance of various aircraft support material such as fork-lifts, power carts, tractors, starting jets, etc.

Navigation Department

The head of this department is the **NAVIGATOR**, who is responsible for the safe navigation and piloting of the ship.

Gunnery Department

The **WEAPONS OFFICER** commands the Weapons Department and is responsible for all of the various bombs, rockets, torpedoes, shells and machine gun ammunition that were carried on *Hornet*.

1st DIVISION: maintained the forward "A Section" spaces on the ship and operated Mount 53, a 5-inch gun on the port side forward.

2nd DIVISION: maintained the middle "B Section" spaces and operated Mount 54, a 5-inch gun on the port side aft. Also manned the LIBERTY BOATS.

3rd DIVISION: maintained the aft or "C Section" spaces and operated Mount 56, a 5-inch gun on the starboard side aft.

5th DIVISION: responsible for the maintenance of the 5-inch guns, Ammunition Hoists and Magazines.

7th DIVISION: the **MARINE DETACHMENT** (see *HOW IT WORKS:* THE MARINE DETACHMENT.)

BOAT DIVISION: maintained and managed all of the ship's small boats.

F DIVISION: these were the Fire Control personnel who maintained and operated the Fire Control Directors.

G DIVISION: maintained and managed the nine bomb elevators and all of the ammunition magazines.

W DIVISION: maintained the Special Weapons spaces and Torpedo Shop.

Engineering Department

The **ENGINEERING OFFICER** commands the Engineering Department, which is responsible for the operation and maintenance of all propulsion and auxiliary machinery. **DAMAGE CONTROL** and **DAMAGE REPAIR** also fell under the Engineering Department, as did the **ELECTRICAL OFFICER** and the **ELECTRICAL DEPARTMENT.**

A DIVISION: machinery repairmen were responsible for air compressors, laundry equipment, refrigeration, steam heat, and generators.

B DIVISION: Boiler Room or Boiler Division personnel whose responsibility was to operate and maintain the boilers to generate steam for power, heating, galleys and the distillation of water.

E DIVISION: the ship's electricians maintained dozens of shops to supply electrical service throughout the ship.

M DIVISION: maintained the ships steam turbine engines and other equipment in the Engine Rooms.

R DIVISION: ship's service personnel maintained the Carpenter Shop, Damage Control, Metal Shop and ventilation.

Supply Department

Commanded by the **SUPPLY OFFICER**, the Supply Department is responsible for the procurement, receipt, stowage and issue of all equipment, repair parts and consumable supplies, including food. The Supply Officer is responsible for payment of the crew.

S1 DIVISION: tens of thousands of supply items and spare parts are maintained and stored on board *Hornet* and the S1 Division is responsible for them.

S2 DIVISION: over 125 cooks and helpers served four meals per day to the crew, and during World War II that meant as many as 12,000 meals per day. The division was responsible for the preparation and serving of these meals in three galleys. It also managed the butcher shop, bakery and scullery.

S3 DIVISION: the division managed the Barber Shops, Tailor Shop, Cobbler Shop, and Laundries. It also maintained an inventory of almost 2,000 items of material for the ship's crew.

S4 DIVISION: was responsible for disbursing (fund accountability) and safekeeping of all money and payroll for the ship.

S5 DIVISION: ship's stewards maintained "officers country," the Ward Room, officer's pantry and officer's staterooms.

S6: DIVISION: was responsible for Aviation Supplies.

Medical Department

The **SENIOR MEDICAL OFFICER** commands this department. He is responsible for maintaining the health of the officers and crew. (See *HOW IT WORKS:* THE MEDICAL DEPARTMENT.)

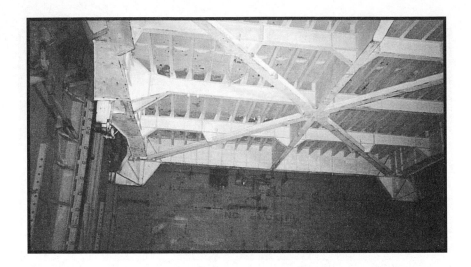

TOP: THE UNDERSIDE OF THE NUMBER 1 (FORWARD) ELEVATOR. THIS ELEVATOR IS STILL IN OPERATION, AS SHOWN IN THE PHOTO BELOW.
BOTTOM: WITH THE ELEVATOR IN THE DOWN POSITION, YOU CAN SEE THE SAFETY BARRIER IN THE UP POSITION (THE POLES AROUND THE EDGE OF THE HOLE.) PHOTOS BY THE AUTHOR.

Top: The forward elevator in the down position and Hornet's F8U positioned for a ride up the Flight Deck. Bottom: a primary duty on the Hangar Deck is moving aircraft around. Confined spaces, expensive aircraft and a volatile mixture of fuel and ordnance make this a very demanding job. Aircraft are moved around the deck with motorized "mules" (left). During World War II, aircraft were also moved by hand. (Author photos)

TOP: DETAIL VIEW OF THE ROLL-UP DOOR MECHANISM.
BOTTOM: ONE OF THE PURPLE COLORED FUEL STATIONS. THIS
ONE IS LOCATED NEXT TO THE FIRE DOOR SEPARATING HANGAR
BAY 2 AND HANGAR BAY 3. (AUTHOR PHOTOS)

Chapter 18

A Tour of the Fo'c'sle

The naval term **"fo'c'sle"** (pronounced fok-sel) derives from the word "forecastle" which is an ancient term for that part of a ship (castle) that is between the front of the ship (bow) and the foremast. Early ships literally had one or more "castles" build upon the upper deck. Ideally, crewmen could stand on top of the "castle" and shoot their arrows down into the enemy on a lower deck.

Hornet's fo'c'sle is the area in front of elevator number 1 and above the main, or Hangar Deck. A tour of the fo'c'sle will take you up and down three sets of ladders, and you will visit four main areas of the ship.

■ You begin your tour on the forward end of the Hangar Deck, near the forward elevator and facing the elevator. To your right, behind the edge of the elevator shaft and inside the small corridor, you will see a ladder going up to the 01 Level. Behind the ladder is a door leading into an area of several private rooms. This is where some of the officers had their staterooms. It is closed to the public at this time. Also located

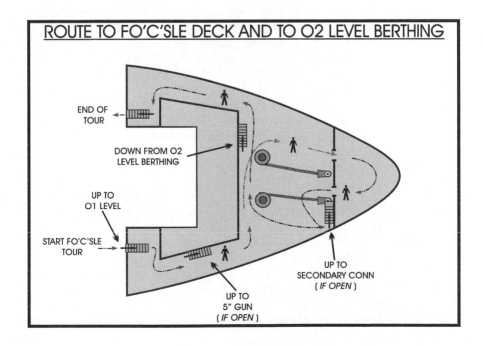

ROUTE TO FO'C'SLE DECK AND TO O2 LEVEL BERTHING

END OF TOUR

DOWN FROM O2 LEVEL BERTHING

UP TO O1 LEVEL

START FO'C'SLE TOUR

UP TO SECONDARY CONN (*IF OPEN*)

UP TO 5" GUN (*IF OPEN*)

down this passageway is the forward 1000KW diesel generator. This may be open for tours, check with a docent.

If you go up the ladder, the door at the top of the ladder goes into the berthing (quarters) areas for the junior officers, and it is also closed off. However, turn right at the top of the ladder, then make a left after you step outside. As you walk down the corridor, on you right are storage areas. Note the portholes on your left. When *Hornet* was built in 1943, the portholes faced the outside of the ship. The corridor you are walking through and the storage areas to your right didn't exist then as they were added in 1956.

After you've crossed through three of the little compartments, you'll come to a ladder on your left that goes up to the gallery deck. Take this ladder at the top of which sits a 5-inch gun mount. Do not go up to the gun mount if there is a chain across the ladder.

Five-Inch Gun Mount

The **5-INCH/38 (5"/38) DUAL-PURPOSE** gun you see behind you as you come up the ladder was not part of the original ship. When *Hornet* was built she carried twelve 5-inch guns. Eight of the guns were located in four turrets (two guns per turret) with two turrets located in front of the island and two behind it (the island is the big structure sitting on top of the flight deck). The remaining four 5-inch guns were located on the gallery deck on the port side of the ship in two gun tubs, similar to the gun tub you are standing in. The four port side guns could cover that side of the ship while the 8 guns in turrets could cover the starboard side, port side, forward or aft, and could shoot almost vertically.

During the rebuild in 1953 the four turrets were removed and two gun tubs holding two 5-inch guns each were added on the starboard side of the ship, one of which you are standing in. The other one is aft of the starboard side deck edge elevator number 3. Then, in 1965 four of the 5-inch guns were removed, leaving only one in each of the four gun tubs. (See *HOW IT WORKS:* 5-INCH/38 CALIBER GUN MARK 24.)

■ What was the purpose on an aircraft carrier for the 5-inch gun that could throw a shell over ten miles? If you answered to shoot at other ships, you would only be about 5 percent correct. The 5-inch gun is not very large as far as warship guns are concerned. *Hornet* and other aircraft carriers are very vulnerable, and they always steam as part of a **TASK GROUP** with several escort ships. If an enemy warship ever got close enough for *Hornet* to shoot at it with its own 5-inch guns, chances are *Hornet* wouldn't be here. In only one instance in World War II did enemy battleships and cruisers get within shooting distance of American carriers, and that was during the Battle of Leyte Gulf. The carriers were small escort carriers carrying only one 5-inch gun. The enemy ships fired at the carriers from so far away that the carrier's puny 5-inch guns were useless. One of the escort carriers was sunk, and several severely damaged before the enemy fleet withdrew. *The purpose of the 5-inch gun was primarily anti-aircraft defense,* and they were very effective against dive-bombing aircraft.

The question is then, could you see a standard World War II Japanese airplane that was ten miles away, the normal range for the 5-inch guns. And if you could see it, could you hit it? Chances are that at extreme ranges without some sort of help, the answer would be no. However, with the addition of two items, the radar and the exploding proximity fuse, the 5-inch gun could be very lethal to aircraft.

■ An aircraft carrier's first line of defense against enemy aircraft is its own fighter aircraft, which can be vectored out to intercept the incoming enemy. Until World War II, and before the invention of radar, even its own aircraft were pretty much useless as an anti-aircraft defense because by the time inbound aircraft were detected, it was generally too late to launch your own. Radar solved that. The ability to detect incoming aircraft 20 to 30 minutes before they arrived near your fleet gave the defending aircraft carrier time to launch fighters and for them to gain enough altitude to be able to do combat with the enemy.

During World War II *Hornet* had several types of **RADAR** and **FIRE DIRECTION CONTROL** (FDC) radar, all of them located on the **MAST**, and none of them currently exist.

HOW IT WORKS!

5-Inch/38 Caliber Gun Mount Mark 24

There were 12-5-inch guns on *Hornet* during World War II, and during its career all but four were removed. There were four turrets with two guns each located on the flight deck, two turrets in front of and two behind the island. The remaining four guns were located on the port side Gallery Deck. There were no 5-inch guns on the starboard side Gallery Deck because the guns in the four turrets covered that side of the ship. The 5-inch gun you now see on the tour was added in 1953.

The 5-inch guns, along with almost 100 smaller guns, were used for anti-aircraft defense. During the war there was a **GUN FIRE DIRECTOR** located up on the island that controlled all of the 5-inch guns. In 1953 the **MARK 56 GUN FIRE DIRECTOR** was added which helped improve accuracy because its radar was tied directly to the 5-inch Mark 24 guns.

Specifications

The gun barrel is 190" or 15.8 feet long, and the total weight of the mount (barrel, carriage and platform) is 38,000 pounds (19 tons). Ammunition came in two parts: a **PROJECTILE** (or the "bullet") that weighed about 54 pounds, and a brass **POWDER CASE** that weighed 28 pounds. Each 5-inch gun required a 14-man crew to operate it and a highly trained crew could fire 8 to 12 rounds a minute.

The 5-inch Mark 24 gun had a range of 18,000 yards (or 10.2 miles), a maximum altitude of 37,000 feet and it has a maximum **ELEVATION** (the direction you can aim the barrel) of 85 degrees, or almost straight up. The Rounds traveled 2,700 feet per second, or it took about 20 seconds to travel 10 miles. They were very effective against dive-bombing aircraft because of the altitude they were able to shoot.

Operation

The gun can be operated in any one of three ways: **AUTOMATIC, LOCAL OR MANUAL CONTROL:**

1) Automatic Control: accomplished with the use of the Mark 56 Gunfire Director, the gun was aimed using an electric-hydraulic system. Once the Mark 56 Director "locks on" a target, it supplies electrical signals to the gun's hydraulic system which, in turn, automatically moves the platform left or right and the gun barrel up or down as it tracks the target. (See *HOW IT WORKS*: GUNFIRE CONTROL SYSTEM MARK 56.)

2) Local Control: this is a manual-hydraulic system. If the Mark 56 Director is out of action, the gun crew can use a series of hand wheels and the optics mounted on the gun platform to track a target, using the hydraulics to help with the movement of the gun.

3) Manual Control: this is strictly a manual operation to be used if both the Mark 56 Director and the hydraulic system are down. Once again, the gun crew can use the hand wheels and optics to control the gun, but this is extremely slow and only used as a last resort.

■ Both manual and local control require the operations of several crewmen. The **POINTER** sits on a seat on the platform to the left of the gun. He operates a hand wheel that raises and lowers the gun barrel while looking through a set of optical sights. He also has a **TRIGGER,** which he can use to fire the gun. Meanwhile, the **TRAINER,** sitting on the right side of the gun and using another set of optical sights, turns a hand wheel, which turns the whole gun platform. Assisting the pointer and trainer are two **SIGHTSETTERS** who operate the **SIGHT ANGLE** and **DEFLECTION** hand cranks to match the orders given the pointer and trainer. In manual operation, both the pointer and his sightsetter and the trainer and his sightsetter must set their sights to match. This provides a redundant fire control system in the manual operation.

Ammunition

Regardless of what method is used to control the gun, fuzes had to be set, and ammunition loaded manually by hand. Before a projectile could be fired, it had to be retrieved from the **MAGAZINE** or **AMMUNITION READY SERVICE ROOM,** have its **FUZE** set and then be manually loaded into the breech of the gun.

The Magazine

Ammunition, both the projectile and the powder case, is stored in a magazine located down on the 5th deck near the bottom of the ship and below the water line. Each component is stored in a separate compartment, and there are compartments for each type of gun ammunition, bomb and torpedo used on the ship. Access to the magazines by crewmen is through a watertight hatch, which is closed and sealed during General Quarters. Because of the danger of having all of these explosives on board, the magazines can be quickly flooded by seawater. Flooding a magazine is only done in the most extreme cases because it usually means the loss of the crewmen in the magazine who won't be able to escape.

Ammunition for the 5-inch gun is loaded one projectile or powder case at a time into the **AMMUNITION HOIST** down in the magazine. The projectile/powder case travels along the ammunition hoist and exits in the **AMMUNITION READY SERVICE ROOM** near the gun. During a time of potential combat, some ammunition is stored in the ammunition ready service room, but when combat isn't anticipated, everything is stored in the magazine.

Ammunition Service

Ready service projectiles, stored in the ammunition ready service room, are manually passed out through the **AMMUNITION PORTS** to one of the three **PROJECTILEMEN** who are part of the gun crew. Projectiles are manually placed nose down into one of the three **SOCKET FUZE SETTERS** located on the left side of the gun platform.

Meanwhile, the powder case is passed through the ammunition port to the **SECOND POWDERMAN**, who in turn hands it off to the **FIRST POWDERMAN,** who loads the powder case into the **GUN LOADING TRAY.**

Fuze Setters

Fuzes are set one of three ways: 1) to explode when the projectile strikes a target, 2) explodes by timed (distance) setting or 3) explodes when the projectile comes within about 20 feet of the target (proximity fuze). The **FUZE SETTER** sits on a chair on the gun platform, facing the rear. Taking his instructions from either the **MOUNT CAPTAIN** or from information passed from the **GUN DIRECTOR,** he sets the fuzes of each projectile as it is placed nose-down in the socket fuze setters. The **PROJECTILE LOADER** then places each projectile into the gun loading tray and operates the ram that forces the projectile with the powder case behind it, into the **BREECH** of the gun. Remember, this is being done from eight to twelve times per minute.

Firing the Gun

Once the projectile and powder case have been rammed into the breech, the gun is ready to fire. If the gun is being aimed by automatic control, the platform will turn and the gun barrel will elevate as it tracks the target. If either manual or local control is being used, the pointer and trainer will turn and elevate the gun using hand wheels.

The gun can be fired from the **RADAR ROOM COMPLEX,** part of the **GUN FIRE CONTROL SYSTEM MARK 56,** or by the gun pointer.

Once the gun is fired, the brass powder case is ejected and drops onto the deck, where it is pushed aside or tossed overboard, and the whole cycle is repeated.

Personnel and their Duties

The gun crew consists of 14 members (or 15 in a training mode, see the accompanying chart) as follows:

1) Mount Captain—directs the rest of the gun crew.

2) Gunner's Mate—assists the mount captain and makes emergency gun repairs.

3) Pointer—elevates and depresses the gun barrel and fires gun under manual control.

4) Trainer—turns gun platform when under local control.

5) Sightsetter—operates the sight angle and deflection hand cranks.

6) Shell Guard—supervises loading, operates shell guard.

7) Second Powderman—retrieves powder case from the ammunition loading ports and passes it off to the First Powderman.

8) First Powderman—manually loads the powder case into the loading tray.

9) Hoistman—using a pair of steel tongs, retrieves the brass shell casing after it falls to the deck and tosses it overboard so other crewmen will not trip over it.

10) Projectile Loader—manually loads projectile from fuze setting sockets into gun tray and operates lever that rams the projectile and powder case into the breech.

11) Fuze Setter—verifies fuze settings when in automatic mode and dials in fuze settings manually when in local mode.

12) Projectilemen (three of them)—pick up shells from the ammunition loading ports and place them nose down into the fuze setting sockets.

13) Sightchecker (training only)—does a double-check on the sights to make sure the gun is aimed properly.

Gun Director Mark 56

The **GUN FIRE CONTROL SYSTEM MARK 56** fire direction control radar located behind and up three steps from the 5-inch gun was added in 1953 when the starboard side guns were added. This director tracks incoming aircraft far enough away to allow the **RADAR ROOM COMPLEX** directly behind the radar to provide what is called a "firing solution" or "firing setup" for the guns.

■ The **PROXIMITY FUSE** was one of the great secret weapons of World War II. Designed in the early 1940's and introduced in 1942, the proximity fuse was far and away superior to the other principle type of anti-aircraft ammunition, the **PERCUSSION** (contact) and the **TIMED** fuse.

■ Prior to the invention of the proximity fuse, the only way to shoot down an airplane was to hit it, much like shooting a bird. This was very impractical, and most hits were due to either good luck on the part of the shooter or the aircraft was so close that it was hard to miss, as in a torpedo bomber flying low and slow.

The proximity fuse was a tiny radio transmitter fitted into the nose of an explosive **ROUND** (bullet) that was designed to detect an object (airplane, and it didn't make any difference whose airplane it was). When the round got within 20 feet of the object, the round would explode, causing a large burst of **SHRAPNEL** into which the airplane (hopefully) would fly. If the shrapnel hit the plane, it would damage the plane, kill or wound the pilot or both. (See HOW TO TARGET AN AIRPLANE portion of *HOW IT WORKS:* GUN FIRE CONTROL SYSTEM MARK 56.) If the round missed a target, it would explode at a pre-determined distance so it wouldn't come down and strike another ship.

■ The 5-inch gun was very effective against **DIVE BOMBING** airplanes since the gun could shoot almost straight up. Dive bombing aircraft were coming in on a fairly straight, fast approach, and if the 5-inch gun crew had the opportunity to shoot at it, there was a good chance for a hit. A 5-inch round would destroy an aircraft.

Gun Fire Control System Mark 56

Walk up the three steps between the 5-inch gun and the fire director. Walk a few feet toward the next ladder. Just before it, turn right. If the **RADAR ROOM COMPLEX** is open (and sometimes it will not be: if not, return to the 5-inch gun and go to the next section) then walk through the first door and turn right into the next door. You are in the gunfire control room that controls the two forward starboard 5-inch gun mounts.

This room was added in 1953 when the 5-inch guns were added. The computer technology is ancient, but the system does an outstanding job of doing exactly what it was designed to do: target aircraft.

As you enter the room, to your right is the electrical control panel. Across the room are two power supply **BANKS** (columns), one for the computer and one for the guns. The large panel along the back wall is the **GUN FIRE CONTROL SYSTEM MK 56**. Check out the gauges and dials. It looks really old, and it is.

Along the left side wall in front of the big panel is the low cabinet that contains the **MK30, MOD 40** computer used to determine the **TRAIN** (direction) and **ELEVATION** of the fire direction control radar and the guns themselves. There are four gauges on top of the computer. On the bulkhead above this computer is the **WIND TRANSMITTER** and the **TRAIN PARALLAX CORRECTOR** (used to compensate for the difference between the line of site of the gun and the director). (See *HOW IT WORKS:* THE GUN FIRE CONTROL SYSTEM MARK 56.)

Ammunition Ready Service Room

Walk back past the 5-inch gun to the door in the bulkhead to your left. Walk into the small room. To your left up three steps is the **AMMUNITION READY SERVICE ROOM** (ammunition handling room), one of four on the *Hornet*. Go into the room if it is open.

As you enter the room you will see the four **AMMUNITION PORTS** to your left. Along the right bulkhead are several stainless steel racks. These are the storage racks where ammunition was placed for ready storage prior to passing it out to the guns.

HOW IT WORKS!

Gun Fire Control System Mark 56

The **GUN FIRE CONTROL SYSTEM (GFCS)** is a series of integrated subsystems that combine the following to compute a **GUN ORDER** (fire order or fire mission) for air, surface or shore targets:

1) ship movement data (*Hornet's* movement)
2) wind data
3) target data (enemy movement)
4) projectile (the round or "bullet") data

The primary purpose of the 5-inch/38 caliber gun is for anti-aircraft defense and this is what the **GFCS** system was designed to facilitate. There are four of these systems on *Hornet*, one for each of the guns (or two guns when there were two to a position) and they were added in 1953, replacing an earlier system that had been located on the island.

How to Target an Aircraft

As any hunter can tell you, shooting and hitting a flying object (such as a bird) is at best an uncertain procedure. Even then, the hunter at least has several factors working in his favor: the bird doesn't know it is being shot at; the bird isn't shooting back and the hunter is standing on solid ground.

Even if you can see it, an airplane is not an easy target to hit. There are many factors to consider when shooting at an airplane:

1)   speed of the target.

2)   elevation of the target (flying level, climbing or descending?)

3)   direction it is traveling (toward you, away from you or parallel to you in any of 360 degrees of direction.)

4)   the platform (ship) the shooter is standing on is not stable: the ship is going up and down with the wave action, the ship is moving and may be zig-zagging or making sudden course changes

5)   time, which you don't have much of (an airplane flying directly at a target at 240 miles per hour allows the target less than three minutes to shoot at it starting at 12 miles out.)

6)   condition of the gun tube (barrel—every time you fire a round out of a gun, it creates more wear on the barrel, which has to be compensated for.)

It is for all of the above reasons that the Gun Fire Control System Mark 56 was developed. Although there were various earlier models of the GFCS, the Mark 56 was the most advanced model available when it was added to *Hornet* in 1953.

■ Basically, when preparing to shoot any large gun you have to aim **IN FRONT OF** and **ABOVE** or **BELOW** the target in order to have the projectile either hit the target or arrive close enough to it to cause the proximity fuze to explode the projectile. Aiming in front of a target is called "leading" the target. This is required because from the time the projectile leaves the gun until it travels out several miles, the target will have flown some distance, and the projectile will pass behind the target. Theoretically, if you "lead" the target correctly, the projectile and the target will meet.

It's not all that easy, however, as two other events occur which have to be compensated for: gravity and spin. When the gun is fired, there are grooves in the barrel that cause the projectile to spin. This causes the projectile to immediately gain altitude (elevation), which means that if you aim directly at a target too close to the gun, the projectile will pass **OVER** the target. To compensate, you have to fire **BELOW** the target. However, a target usually isn't that close, so gravity takes effect. As the projectile travels away from the gun, it flies in a large arc, eventually falling back to earth. It is for this reason that you have to aim the gun above the target, depending on how far away it is, and you have to lead the target, depending on its speed and distance from you.

If all of this doesn't complicate matters enough, you have to add in the speed of the ship, its stability due to wave action, the prevailing wind and wear of the gun barrel.

Gun Fire Control System Mark 56

The GFCS Mark 56 (the radar located next to the 5-inch gun) can track and compute gun orders (firing solutions) for aircraft targets up to 640 knots (736 mph), and provides automatic tracking out to a range of 30,000 yards (17 miles). Total time from target acquisition (or "locking on" the target) to providing a gun order is two to three seconds. The system can be operated in automatic or manual mode.

The GFCS supplies range, bearing and elevation data to the computer located in the **RADAR ROOM COMPLEX** behind the Director. The computer develops tracking signals and passes them onto the electric drives that turn the **GUN MOUNT** (platform) and elevates or depresses the gun barrel. The tracking signals account for all movements of the target, *Hornet*, wind and gun barrel wear and provides the correct firing solution to place a projectile to within 10 yards of the target.

The Computer Mark 30, Computer Mark 42, Wind Transmitter Mark 5 and the Train Parallax Corrector Mark 6 all reside in the radar room. These systems take tracking information from the Gun Director Mark 56, determine the rate of change of position, and elevation of the target and the ship, to determine train (direction) and elevation lead angles. A separate system determines the projectile fuze setting. This information is fed electrically to the hydraulic systems that turn and elevate the gun.

Five personnel operate the Gun Director Mark 56 and the Radar Room Complex: one Director Officer and a Director Operator in the Director itself plus 2 Console Operators and one Radar Computer Technician in the Radar Room.

In the center of the room are two gray boxes. These are **AMMUNITION HOISTS** used to transport the shells and powder canisters up from the **MAGAZINE** located down near the bottom of the ship.

The hoists consist of a continuous chain with brackets at 90 degrees and runs at a continuous speed. Down in the magazine almost 100 feet away, a crewman standing next to the hoist is passed a shell from another crewman and then places it on the bracket. The shell moves along the chain and eventually appears at the top of the ammunition hoist, where it is removed and either placed in a storage rack or passed out through the ports to the guns.

At the end of the firing mission, all ammunition is sent back down the ammunition hoist to the magazine where it goes back into storage. No live ammunition is stored in the ammunition ready service room.

Now go back down the three steps. Directly ahead of you, IF IT IS OPEN, is a large **BERTHING COMPARTMENT** (crew sleeping area). Since this compartment is used for the *Hornet's* Youth Liveaboard Program, it may not be open. If not, go back outside, turn left, go down the ladder you came up, turn left 180 degrees and walk forward to the fo'c'sle where the **ANCHOR CHAINS** are located. Then skip the next section of this book and pick up where the **"FO'C'SLE DECK"** section starts.

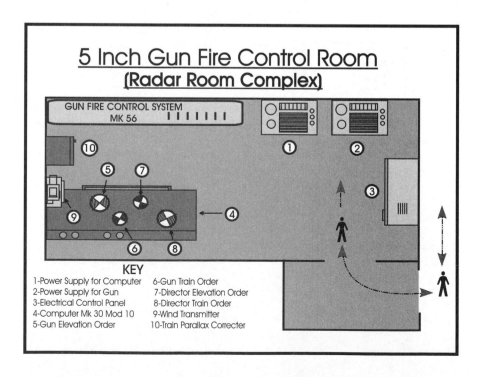

Fo'c'sle Berthing Compartment

This **BERTHING COMPARTMENT** on the 02 Level is one of the largest on *Hornet*. Primarily the **QUARTERS** (sleeping area) for the catapult operators, plane handlers and 1st Division bos'n's mates, it is located directly under the forward edge of the flight deck. As you enter the room, you see the large triangular shaped object hanging from the overhead. This is part of the catapult mechanism.

There are three berthing compartments here: the small one you are currently standing in, another similar in size on the port side and a large one in the center. Walk past the row of **RACKS** (beds), turn left and pass through the door into the large center berthing compartment.

Within the three compartments were 257 racks, either three or four high (the top rack has been removed so they can't be used by the liveaboards). As an active Navy ship, the racks would fold up against their center poles to create more deck space. They are currently bolted in the down position as a safety precaution. The racks have a canvas bottom and a mattress.

Usually the junior members of the crew had the bottom bunk, for two reasons: the crewman in the top bunk had to step on the bottom bunk to get into the top one and, too put it nicely, if someone on an upper bunk got seasick the person in the bottom bunk might get wet.

Typical of all of the berthing compartments, this one was very noisy. Crewmen were coming on and off duty at all hours, talking, slamming lockers and making other noises. The forward elevator is directly behind the **HEAD,** and the two catapults are on the flight deck directly overhead. It was never a quiet room, but if you are tired enough, you'll shut out the noise.

■ After you walk through the door from the small berthing compartment, go straight ahead toward the middle of the room and turn left at the bunks. Directly ahead is the HEAD. This is the only head for the 257 crewmen in these three compartments.

Taking a shower on *Hornet* was always a challenge. Fresh water for showers got the last priority, the boilers getting first and then the mess halls. Certain times of the day were designated for showers, and everyone had to get it done quickly. You would jump in, get wet, jump out with your soap (this is where soap-on-a-rope came from) while the next guy jumped in and got wet. When you were done soaping, you jumped back in and got about 60 seconds to rinse off. Assuming of course that the water hadn't been turned off, in which case you rinsed with cold salt water or maybe you didn't rinse at all if all the water had been turned off. If there were any indication that the boilers were going to run short of water, all fresh water on the ship would be turned off in the boiler rooms.

■ If the noise wasn't bad enough, consider that you are about 60 feet above the waterline. Movement of the ship, rocking side-to-side and fore-and-aft, is amplified the higher above the waterline you are.

Each crewman got one of the aluminum lockers for his personal gear. Only about 24-inches tall, 24-inches wide and 12-inches deep, everything of a personal nature, clothing, uniforms, writing material, letters from home, books; all had to fit in one of these lockers. Dress uniforms were turned inside out with seams laid flat, then placed under the mattress so as you slept, you also pressed your uniform.

■ Now wind your way around the racks and exit the berthing compartment through the door to the **FO'C'SLE.** After you go through the door, go down the ladder to your left. WATCH YOUR HEAD. There is a low overhead as you go down the ladder.

Fo'c'sle Deck

The focal point of the fo'c'sle are the two **ANCHOR CHAINS,** which are attached to the **ANCHORS** hanging off the side of *Hornet*. You saw one of the anchors on the very bow of the ship. This is called a **STOCKLESS** anchor. There were two anchors on *Hornet*. When it was built, there was one on each side of the bow, but during the FRAM II conversion in 1965 the port anchor was moved to the bow where it now resides. This had to be moved so it would clear the **SONAR** dome added to the bottom of the ship.

Each of the anchors weighs 15 tons (30,000 pounds). Each chain is over 1,100 feet long, and is made up of hundreds of **LINKS**, which weigh an average of 129 pounds. One end is attached to the anchor and the other is attached to a reinforced bulkhead far down inside the **CHAIN LOCKER** several decks below. The chain wraps around the large brass-covered **WILDCAT** and drops down through the deck. The wildcat is connected to the **ANCHOR WINDLASS** (winch) motor which moves the anchor chain up or down. Also connected to this motor is a **CAPSTAN,** the vertical drums for handling the **LINES** (chains).

Next to the chains are two hand wheels. One is the **WILDCAT BRAKE** and the other is the **CONTROL HANDWHEEL.** Connected to each chain are two short chains called **STOPPERS** that has one end secured to the deck and the other to a **PELICAN HOOK** which secures the anchor chain. These secure the raised anchor and take the stress off the **ANCHOR ENGINE** that powers the wildcat. To drop the anchor, a crewman removes the retaining pin from the pelican hook and then strikes the lever on top with a sledgehammer, making sure he stays clear as the anchor falls into the water, pulling the chain and creating a huge cloud of rust. The anchor's free fall is stopped by the wildcat brake.

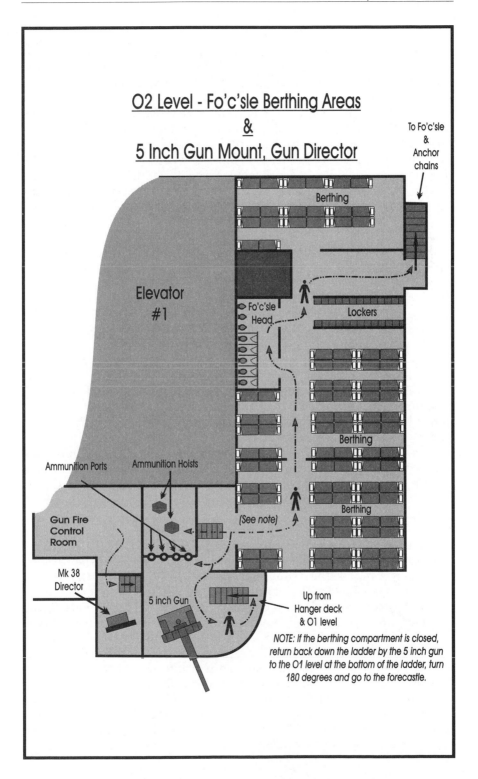

O2 Level - Fo'c'sle Berthing Areas
&
5 Inch Gun Mount, Gun Director

To Fo'c'sle
&
Anchor
chains

Berthing

Elevator
#1

Fo'c'sle
Head

Lockers

Berthing

Ammunition Ports   Ammunition Hoists

Berthing

Gun Fire
Control
Room

(See note)

Berthing

Mk 38
Director

5 inch Gun

Up from
Hanger deck
& O1 level

NOTE: If the berthing compartment is closed,
return back down the ladder by the 5 inch gun
to the O1 level at the bottom of the ladder, turn
180 degrees and go to the forecastle.

Near the top of the first vertical column between the chains (the one with the black ladder and on the other side of the column) is where the huge ship's bell hung, the one you saw on the Quarterdeck as you came aboard.

On either side of the deck is a large **HAWSER REEL** containing **MOORING LINES** (large ropes). Above the starboard side capstan is a large storage rack hanging from the overhead, containing what look like slats for a large picket fence. This is the **PROTECTIVE PALISADE** that is stretched like a fence across the flight deck during rough weather to help break-up waves that break over the forward end of the flight deck. It protects stored aircraft and personnel.

■ Facing the bow, you'll see a bulkhead with two arched doors. That bulkhead existed when *Hornet* was built, but none of the bulkheads on the sides of the fo'c'sle deck did because the deck was open to the weather. In May 1945 *Hornet* steamed into a typhoon and a wave broke over the flight deck collapsing 24-feet of the deck. It was for this reason *Hornet* left the war and had to go back to Hunters Point for repair. In 1956 this area was enclosed in what the Navy calls a **HURRICANE BOW.** To the right of the doors is a ladder that goes up to **SECONDARY CONN.**

On the other side of the arched doors is the **BULLNOSE,** or the very front of the ship. During World War II there was a **GUN TUB** hanging out over the bow with a **QUAD 40-MILLIMETER ANTI-AIRCRAFT GUN** that could shoot straight up in front of the flight deck. In 1953 the single gun tub was replaced by two, each containing a quad 40. These were removed when the bow was enclosed.

On the starboard side of the bullnose is what looks like a mount for a 5-inch gun. That is exactly what it is, a **TRAINING AID** to train crewmen on how to load the 5-inch gun without having to work on the real thing.

Secondary Conn

If it is open, go up the ladder into **SECONDARY CONN.** This large compartment has most of the equipment found on the bridge. Secondary conn is the redundant system for operating the ship if something happened to the Captain, crew or machinery on the bridge.

During combat or General Quarters the **EXECUTIVE OFFICER** (the number two officer in charge of the ship) and a group of officers and men maintained station in the secondary conn, which is about as far from the bridge as you can get. If something should happen to the island, bridge or Captain so the ship could not be operated, the Executive Officer and his crew could run the ship.

You enter the compartment by passing through the door. On the bulkhead in front of you are seven **PORTS** (or portholes to landlubbers.) After you leave the *Hornet*, you can see these from the parking lot to get an idea where you were standing.

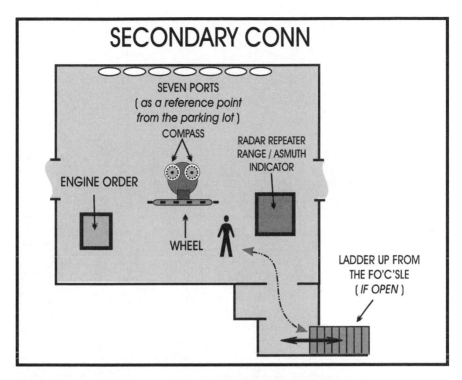

SECONDARY CONN

SEVEN PORTS
(*as a reference point
from the parking lot*)

COMPASS

RADAR REPEATER
RANGE / ASMUTH
INDICATOR

ENGINE ORDER

WHEEL

LADDER UP FROM
THE FO'C'SLE
(*IF OPEN*)

Closest to the door is the **RADAR REPEATER.** Next to it is the **WHEEL** which is used to steer the ship (at the time of this writing, the wheel is gone, but it is exactly like the one you will see on the bridge). On top of the wheel mount are two **GYRO REPEATERS,** and next to it is the **ENGINE ORDER TELEGRAPH**.

■ Leave Secondary Conn the way you entered. Go back down to the fo'c'sle deck and face the long bulkhead with the ladder to the berthing compartment you recently left. On the lower portion of the bulkhead are three doors. Inside is **OFFICERS COUNTRY** (officers quarters). In the days before the fo'c'sle was closed in and waves broke over the deck, woe be the poor enlisted man who happened to open one of the doors at the wrong time and flooded officers country. One could spend the rest of one's enlistment mopping up the flood!

■ This ends your fo'c'sle tour. Walk to the bulkhead with the doors, turn right and follow the passageway along the port side to the down ladder that will deposit you back on the Hangar Deck.

ABOVE: TWO VIEWS OF A 5-INCH GUN. TOP: THE GUN TRAINER SITS ON THE BICYCLE STYLE SEAT WHILE THE SIGHTSETTER STANDS BEHIND HIM. MIDDLE: THE BREECH MECHANISM. THE SHELL GUARD STANDS WITH HIS BACK TO THE BRACE AT LOWER RIGHT WHILE THE POINTER SITS IN THE BICYCLE SEAT. THE PROJECTILE LOADER AND FIRST POWDERMAN STAND TO THE LEFT OF THE BREECH. BELOW: GUN DIRECTOR MARK 56. TWO CREWMEN WORK INSIDE THE DIRECTOR.

ABOVE: GUN FIRE CONTROL SYSTEM MARK 56 (LEFT). BASICALLY, THE COMPUTER THAT CONTROLS THE 5-INCH GUN.

ABOVE: THE TOP OF AN AMMUNITION HOIST USED TO TRANSPORT 5-INCH GUN AMMUNITION FROM THE MAGAZINE LOCATED BELOW THE WATERLINE NEAR THE BOTTOM OF THE SHIP. BELOW: TYPICAL MAGAZINE, THIS ONE USED TO STORE MISSILES.

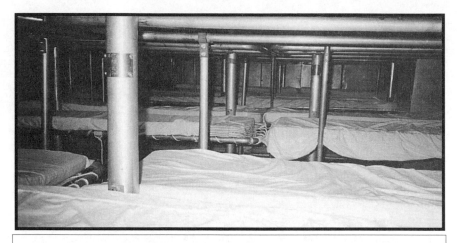

A MAZE OF RACKS IN THE FO'C'SLE BERTHING COMPARTMENT.

ABOVE: FO'C'SLE AND ANCHOR CHAINS. LADDER AT RIGHT GOES UP TO THE SECONDARY CONN. BELOW: SEC CONN WITH COMPASS PLATFORM AND (MISSING) WHEEL. THE RADAR REPEATER IS TO RIGHT.

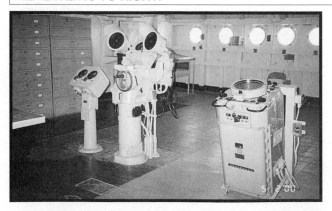

Chapter 19

The Second Deck

The majority of *Hornet's* **SECOND DECK** is devoted to **OFFICERS COUNTRY, OFFICERS MESS FACILITIES, PILOT READY ROOMS, MARINE QUARTERS** and **MEDICAL FACILITIES**. *(See "HOW IT WORKS:* THE DECK NUMBERING SYSTEM.)

Begin your tour of the Second Deck at the DOWN ladder located next to the large roll up doors on the forward end of the starboard side of Hangar Bay 1. As you go down this very narrow ladder, WATCH YOUR HEAD. This is one of the worst overhangs you will encounter, and the steel deck is 2-1/2 inches thick. You don't want to hammer the deck with your head.

At the bottom of the ladder, you go right about 10 feet to the bulkhead. The **PASSAGEWAY** (hall, corridor) to your right is closed. It goes to some of the officers quarters. Turn left and watch that you don't fall over the large **HATCH** on the floor. You are walking toward the **STERN**.

The bulkhead to your right is the **INNER HULL** of *Hornet*. All openings and doors in this hull are watertight. From this deck to the very bottom of the ship, all of the ships vital components are inside the inner hull. When you are in the **ENGINE ROOM**, the bulkheads on the sides of the compartment are part of this inner hull. This protects the ship in case the **OUTER** or **ARMORED HULL** is breached by a bomb, torpedo or rocket.

Along this bulkhead are a series of levers and gauges that were used to flood the **MAGAZINES** (ammunition storage areas) with seawater if they were in danger of a fire. A few feet further down the passageway on the right are another set of levers and gauges that drain water from the **BILGES**.

■ Walk forward a couple of paces. To your left is a small compartment that contains the machinery used to make the **FOG/FOAM** used on the Hangar Deck to fight fuel fires. Directly above this room is the green FOG/FOAM station located next to the roll up doors on the Hangar Deck. *(Fog/foam is a protein-based product made out of animal by-products and salt water.)*

Walk up to the bulkhead with the RED door with the letter "Z" on it. To the right of the red door is a small round object painted red-white-black. Each color has three holes drilled into the face and either one, two or three notches on each edge. These round objects are electrical connections for the heavy-duty black cables you see on the bulkhead to your right. They serve the same function as the electrical

2nd DECK TOUR

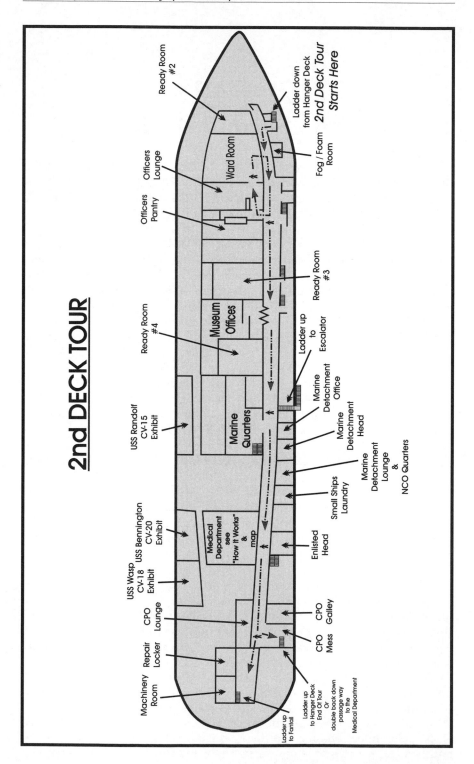

Ready Room #2

Ladder down from Hanger Deck
2nd Deck Tour Starts Here

Officers Lounge

Fog / Foam Room

Ward Room

Officers Pantry

Ready Room #3

Museum Offices

Ladder up to Escalator

Ready Room #4

Marine Detachment Office

USS Randolf CV-15 Exhibit

Marine Quarters

Marine Detachment Head

Marine Detachment Lounge & NCO Quarters

USS Wasp CV-18 Exhibit

USS Bennington CV-20 Exhibit

Medical Department see "How It Works" & map

Small Ships Laundry

CPO Lounge

Enlisted Head

Repair Locker

Machinery Room

CPO Galley

CPO Mess

Ladder up to Hanger Deck End of Tour
Or
double back down passage way to the Medical Department

Ladder up to Fantail

outlets in your home, only they are 440 volts. The ends of each cable have one, two or three ribs around the cable. Three ribs goes with three notches, two ribs with two notches, etc. If there is light available, one end of the cable would go into the red holes, the other end into the red holes on another plug. If there isn't any available light, this can be done in the dark by matching up the ribs and notches. This is how emergency power was routed throughout the ship.

After you pass through the red door, continue straight down the passageway and past the entrance to the **OFFICERS WARDROOM** on your right. *(On this tour you will continue down the passageway and enter the wardroom from the OFFICERS PANTRY.)*

Past the wardroom door there are numerous levers and gauges on the bulkhead to your right. This is one of several **VOID TANK CONTROL STATIONS** you'll see on this deck. *(Void tanks are empty tanks located near the bottom of the ship that can be filled with water to help counter-balance a list.)* There are also several levers used to control the sprinkler valves on the Hangar Deck.

Continue down the passageway and pass through the next two bulkheads. After the second bulkhead, turn left. You are entering **OFFICERS QUARTERS** number 223 and 225. **FLIGHT OFFICERS** used these compartments. There are several of them along this passageway and the passageway on the port side.

The compartments were for two officers. Each had a bunk and a large locker for uniforms and clothing. Each compartment had a desk, a safe and a washbasin. Note that the partitions don't go all the way to the **OVERHEAD** (ceiling). They were somewhat private, but they weren't quiet!

■ Return to the passageway, turn left toward the stern, and continue walking. The next room to the left is another of the officers quarters. Continue down the passageway toward the stern and enter the next door to your right. This is the **OFFICERS PANTRY.** Food was prepared in the galley several decks down and sent up to the pantry via dumbwaiters. In the pantry it was kept heated and served to the officers. This pantry was manned around the clock so anyone could eat a meal or a snack before or after his watch or flight mission.

As you enter the pantry, to your right front is a down ladder that goes one level to the **OFFICERS SHIPS STORE** and the **FLIGHT SUIT MESS** on the third deck. *(This is currently closed to the public).* Pilot officers who were wearing their flight suits during meal times ate down there. At the bottom of the ladder was the **MARINE GUARD POST.** One deck down from that (fourth deck) was the **NUCLEAR WEAPONS MAGAZINE**, and there was always an armed Marine guard on duty on both decks.

To your right is another compartment with a brick tile floor, this is the **OFFICERS LOUNGE**. This room was for the officers to sit and play

HOW IT WORKS!

Pilot Ready Rooms

Each aircraft **SQUADRON** on *Hornet* had its own **READY ROOM,** where squadron members met and received their orders for upcoming operations. During World War II there were five Ready Rooms, one for each of the five squadrons (two fighter, one bomber, one dive-bomber and one torpedo), all located on the **GALLERY DECK** just below the Flight Deck.

That location turned out to be inappropriate when many pilots, while waiting in their Ready Rooms, were killed or injured when bombs or kamikaze aircraft penetrated the Flight Deck. After World War II three of the Ready Rooms were moved to the Second Deck under the Hangar Deck to provide more protection for the pilots.

Once the Ready Rooms had moved to the Second Deck, it was discovered that pilots couldn't easily navigate the four levels of ladders up to the Flight Deck with all of their uniforms, survival gear, parachute, maps, weapons, etc. Consequently, the **ESCALATOR** was added to the outside of the Island that would take pilots from the Second Deck up to the Flight Deck.

■ Pilots spent many hours in the Ready Rooms. Once they were on duty and on call, they remained in or around the Ready Room, sometimes for hours, awaiting orders. Like most of the military, it was "Hurry-up and Wait."

The Ready Room was equipped with fairly comfortable chairs. Each pilot had his own permanent seat assignment. Squadron officers would brief pilots prior to each mission. Status boards near the front of the room listed the status of each aircraft and pilot. Other boards listed the current weather conditions and the current radio frequencies and call signs. There was always a pot of coffee and freshly baked doughnuts available. Once the pilots returned from their mission, they all met in the Ready Room and were de-briefed prior to being assigned a new mission or being released to eat or return to their rooms.

■ Currently three ready rooms are open for tours: READY ROOM 2, located next to and ahead of the Ward Room, READY ROOM 3 and READY ROOM 4 located off the long starboard side passageway on the Second Deck. All contain interesting displays, and Ready Room 3 has a continuous showing of the movie *The Ship That Would Not Die, USS Franklin.*

cards, games, etc. while off duty. It was heated and air-conditioned. Plenty of hot coffee, soft drinks, snacks and donuts were kept available around the clock. Donuts were baked in the bakery two levels down. Note the large photographs on the bulkheads around the room. They are World War II vintage, in approximate chronological (time) order, starting with the photo behind the wall to your left and continuing clockwise around the room to the big double door to your front.

After you have looked at the photos, go through the big double door into the next room. This is the **WARDROOM** where officers ate their meals, getting their food from the pantry. **MESS STEWARDS** served officers their meals. *(Up until the mid-50's the U.S. Navy was segregated. Mess stewards were almost always of African American or Philippine descent and could not hold any rating above that of mess steward. During General Quarters the stewards worked as ammunition handlers and fire fighters.)*

The photographs around the Wardroom bulkheads are post-World War II, again starting from the photo on your left as you enter the room. On the forward bulkhead is a door into **PILOT READY ROOM #2.** After you complete the photographs, go back through the pantry, turn left, go through the door into the passageway and turn right, facing the stern, and continue to walk.

■ The ladder on your left goes up to the Quarterdeck. After you pass through the next door, you'll find **READY ROOM #3** on your right. (See *"HOW IT WORKS:* PILOT READY ROOM.)

Continue down the passageway through the next door. To the right is the museum office. Continue walking aft, pass through the next door, and the ladder to your left takes you up to the EXIT, Hangar Deck or Flight Deck. To your right is a **FIRE MAIN.**

Pass through the next door and the following red door. **READY ROOM 4** is on your right. The ladder to your left goes up to the Hangar Deck and up to the **ESCALATOR** to the Flight Deck. The first door on your left is the **MARINE STORES** (supply room), and the next door on your left is the **MARINE DETACHMENT OFFICE.** (See *HOW IT WORKS:* MARINE DETACHMENT.) The Marine Detachment Commander used this office.

Through the next door to your right is the **MARINE BERTHING** area with 24 bunks and lockers. Directly inside the door is the double set of ladders going DOWN to the forward engine room. There is also a large bank of **VOID TANK CONTROL** valves in this compartment. *(This is also the access to the ENGINE ROOM. It is not open for self-guided tours. To take a tour of the engine room, see a docent at the reception area on the Hangar Deck. See HOW IT WORKS: THE ENGINE ROOM.)*

While in the passageway facing the stern, turn left into the **MARINE'S HEAD,** with its red floor and highly polished fixtures. Continue down the passageway through the next door. This is another

HOW IT WORKS!

The Marine Detachment (MARDET)

Hornet had a **MARINE DETACHMENT,** also referred to as the Seventh Division of the Gunnery Department, consisting of approximately 52 officers and men who were assigned the task of maintaining internal security. Their quarters are on the starboard side of the Second Deck near the base of the Escalator. Members of the **MARDET** were the only personnel on *Hornet* who were allowed to carry weapons.

An armed escort always accompanied the *Hornet's* Captain and Executive Officer. Other Marine guards were posted outside the **MAGAZINES** (where bombs, rockets and ammunition is stored), and they were in charge of the **BRIG,** or the ships jail.

On the Third Deck below the Ward Room is a Marine Guard Station, provided to guard against access to the nuclear weapons shops and Magazines.   During combat, the Marine Detachment manned Mount 57, the 5-inch gun located on the starboard side, aft of the Number 3 deck edge elevator, which is called the **MARINE GUN.**

Other duties included providing ceremonial units for special occasions, the daily color guard and conducting training for Marine landing forces embarked on *Hornet*.

MARINE BERTHING area and their lounge. This is also the Marine **NON-COMMISSIONED OFFICERS** (NCO) quarters. Along the bulkhead to your right are the ready racks to hold weapons.

Through the next door is another ladder going up to the Hangar Deck. Pass through the next door, walk about 15 paces, and at the end of the long wall on your left is the entrance to a small **AUXILIARY LAUNDRY.** This small laundry was primarily used by the **MEDICAL DEPARTMENT** located down the passageway, or for overload for the regular ship's laundry. In the laundry, note the large press on the right, and two large dryers and the washer on your left.

(The main laundry is down two decks. It contains several large industrial size washers, dryers, clothes presses, dry cleaner, shirt folders, etc., enough to do the daily laundry of almost 3,000 men. This will eventually be opened for tours.)

■ Continue on down the passageway toward the stern and pass through the next door. To your right is the entrance to *Hornet's* **HOSPITAL / MEDICAL FACILITY.** *(If the medical facility is open, it is one way only and will deposit you on the Hangar Deck on the other side of the ship. It is recommended that you continue the Second Deck tour and come back later to tour the Medical Facility. The Medical Facility and Operating Rooms tour is at the end of this chapter.)*

Continue down the passageway to the sign that says **"AIR CONDITIONING OFFICE"** on the left and another fog/foam station on the right. Through the door by the sign is the **ELEVATOR MACHINERY** for the starboard deck edge elevator. Continue down the passageway through two doors and walk around another ladder to the Hangar Deck. You are in another of the many **CREW BERTHING** compartments.

Hornet was built using rivets, and all of the subsequent rebuilds used welds. As you enter this compartment, along the bulkhead to your left, hidden behind the racks is a small 12" wide extension that runs from the deck to the overhead. This used to be the outside hull before the blisters were added in 1956. At the bottom of the extension is part of the original ship, and you can still see the rivets.

As you pass through another door, to your left is a large **HEAD.** Pass through two more doors. To your left through the door is the **CREW'S RECEPTION ROOM, LADIES WAITING ROOM** and **LIBRARY.** Next to the door is a double set of ladders. A number of marriages were performed on *Hornet*, most of them on these ladders. The loud humming noises you hear in the passageway and at other locations around the ship are the electrical transformers.

■ Pass through the next door into another crew berthing compartment, then through another door into the **CPO MESS.** The **CHIEF PETTY OFFICER (CPO) MESS** is where *Hornet's* CPO's (senior enlisted men) ate their meals. Once again, the meals were prepared in the GALLEY and brought here to eat. The CPO Mess is currently used by the museum for catered meals on busy weekends, and can be reserved by tour groups or organizations for meals or meetings. If the door to the right is open, go into that room. This is the **CPO LOUNGE.** The bulkheads on either side are the inner hull, which shows how narrow the inner hull is this far back on the ship. In the center of the room is the **RUDDER CENTERING DEVICE,** used to center the rudder and lock it into position if the steering mechanism is out of order and the rudder can't be used. The ship could be steered with just the propellers if necessary. Return back out to the CPO Mess.

■ Now you have a three-option decision to make. You can end the Second Deck tour here by taking the ladder in the center of the room up to the Hangar Deck. Your second option, if it is open, you can continue the tour through the door on the aft bulkhead. This will take you to the

CPO QUARTERS, REPAIR LOCKER and **MACHINERY ROOM** before and a ladder that will take you up to the fantail, which will also end the tour. Your third option is to check out the CPO QUARTERS and then return to where you are now standing, then go back down the passageway to the **MEDICAL FACILITY.**

■ This concludes the Self-Guided Tour of the Second Deck. Once you've gone up the ladder to the Hangar Deck via any of the ladders, you can return to the forward elevator to start the **HANGAR DECK TOUR, FO'C'SLE TOUR** or the **ENGINE ROOM TOUR.** If you've already completed those tours, then you are ready to start the **FLIGHT DECK** tour. To start the Flight Deck Tour, go forward on the Hanger Deck to the door leading to the escalator on the starboard side in the middle of HANGAR BAY 2.

The Medical Facility or Sickbay

The **MEDICAL FACILITY** is run by the **MEDICAL DEPARTMENT** and commanded by the **MEDICAL OFFICER.** The Medical Facility is located on the Second Deck, aft of the **MARINE DETACHMENT,** and consists of 20 rooms and offices. There were usually four medical doctors and 15 to 18 **HOSPITAL CORPSMEN** attached to the Medical Department.

The Medical Department is responsible for all aspects of the health and welfare of the crew, including daily inspections of fresh water supplies and all food. The Medical Officer was usually a Captain in rank, and there were two or three junior officers who did the hands-on medical procedures. The enlisted men served as Hospital Corpsmen and nurses.

There is a **PHARMACY,** stocked with medications, which were dispensed by prescription. **PHARMACIST MATES** were in charge of this area. The **LABORATORY** performed various tests, chemistries, cultures and blood cross matching. There is a simple **X-RAY** table, x-ray machine and shielding panels. A separate **HEARING TEST** chamber is provided in order to perform hearing tests on the pilots.

■ The **OPERATING ROOM** consisted of one surgery table, and it was well stocked with surgical and burn supplies. All types of minor surgery and some major surgeries were performed, however highly technical operations on the heart, chest and brain weren't usually done as the facility didn't have the proper equipment. Because there were surgeons on board, *Hornet* also served as a receiving station for seriously injured or sick crewmen from the escorting destroyers because these small ships only had a Pharmacist Mate and no hospital.

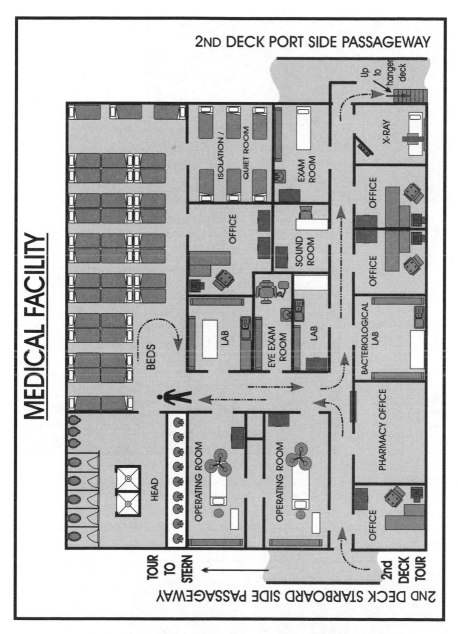

In the **HOSPITAL WARD** are three beds for surgical patients, where they were monitored while they recuperated. The remaining hospital beds were reserved for the medically ill and for minor injuries.

■ At the end of the tour of the Medical Department, you will exit to the port side passageway, where a ladder will take you up to the Hangar Deck, just behind the **FLIGHT SIMULATOR**.

ABOVE: A VOID TANK CONTROL STATION ON THE SECOND DECK.

ABOVE: THE OFFICERS PANTRY. FOOD WAS PREPARED IN THE GALLEY AND TRANSPORTED HERE TO BE SERVED. JUNIOR OFFICERS SERVED THEMSELVES, WHILE SENIOR OFFICERS WERE SERVED BY STEWARDS. BELOW: THE OFFICERS WARD ROOM WHERE OFFICERS ATE THEIR MEALS.

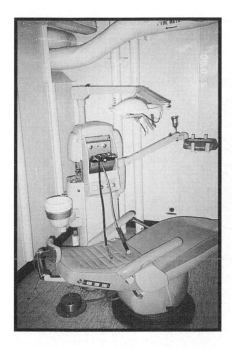

ABOVE LEFT: 1960'S DENTAL TECHNOLOGY. ONE OF THE CHAIRS IN THE DENTAL OFFICE. ABOVE RIGHT: ELECTRICIAN'S NIGHTMARE. TELEPHONE CABLES FROM HORNET'S INTERNAL TELEPHONE SYSTEM. BELOW: THE MAIN GALLEY WHERE UP TO 16,000 MEALS PER DAY WERE PREPARED.

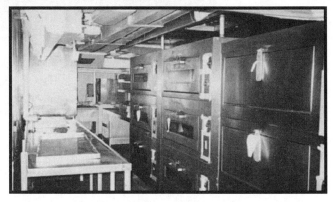

TOP: MIXING KETTLES IN THE GALLEY. MIDDLE: SOME OF THE OVENS IN THE BAKERY. BELOW: STEAM IRONS IN THE LAUNDRY. THE GALLEY, BAKERY AND THE LAUNDRY ARE NOT YET OPEN TO THE PUBLIC.

Chapter 20

THE ENGINE ROOM

Hornet has four Westinghouse steam-powered gear-turbine engines located in two engine rooms. Each engine turns one of the four propellers that drive *Hornet* through the water at a standard speed of 25 knots (almost 29 miles per hour), with a maximum speed of 33 knots (almost 40 miles per hour). Combined, the four engines generate 150,000 shaft horsepower.

Steam is generated in one of the four fire (boiler) rooms. There is one boiler for each engine, and all of the boilers are interconnected so that the boiler for engine 1 can be used for engine 2 if engine 2's boiler is down for repair or is damaged, etc.

Currently, *Hornet's* Engine Room #1 is open for tours. It is the furthest forward of the two engine rooms. Between it and the bow of the ship are two fire rooms with the boilers for the two engines in Engine Room #1. Behind Engine Room #1 are two more fire rooms, and then the second engine room. The four fire rooms and the second engine room aren't open to the public.

Hornet's Engine Room #1, the one open for tours, operates the two outside propeller shafts, and the extreme end of the shafts can be viewed as part of the tour. Tours are docent-led only. From the Hangar Deck, it is four decks down to the engine room, and the ladders on the last two decks are very steep. There are numerous open decks and platforms in the engine room, consequently, children under 12 are not allowed on the tour for safety reasons.

How Steam Is Made

Steam needed to run the engines is not like the steam created by boiling water on your stove or your clothes iron which boils around 212 degrees. Steam used to run *Hornet's* steam engines is super-clean, super heated to 850 degrees, and is under 750 psi (pounds per square inch) of pressure.

Seawater is first pumped into ballast tanks and is then pumped into the **DESALINATION TANK** where it is evaporated by heat to .05 grains of salt per volume, which is almost pure H20 (water) and is much more pure than what you can buy at the store. This water is then stored in tanks and used by the crew for drinking, showers, and cooking. However, the boilers use the majority of the water, and the boilers have first call on all fresh water on the ship.

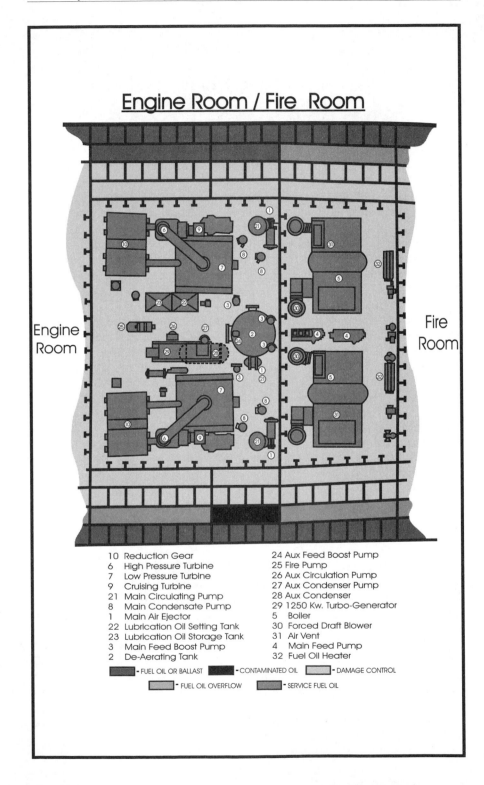

Engine Room / Fire Room

Engine Room

Fire Room

10	Reduction Gear	24	Aux Feed Boost Pump
6	High Pressure Turbine	25	Fire Pump
7	Low Pressure Turbine	26	Aux Circulation Pump
9	Cruising Turbine	27	Aux Condenser Pump
21	Main Circulating Pump	28	Aux Condenser
8	Main Condensate Pump	29	1250 Kw. Turbo-Generator
1	Main Air Ejector	5	Boiler
22	Lubrication Oil Setting Tank	30	Forced Draft Blower
23	Lubrication Oil Storage Tank	31	Air Vent
3	Main Feed Boost Pump	4	Main Feed Pump
2	De-Aerating Tank	32	Fuel Oil Heater

- FUEL OIL OR BALLAST   - CONTAMINATED OIL   - DAMAGE CONTROL

- FUEL OIL OVERFLOW   - SERVICE FUEL OIL

The water then goes into the **MAIN CONDENSER**, where the **MAIN CONDENSATION PUMP** sucks the water, under vacuum, out of the Condenser at the same time the **AIR EJECTOR** sucks the air out of the Condenser. The water is then pumped into the **DEAERATING FEED TANK** where the water is heated, and the remaining oxygen is removed, and then flows into the **BOOSTER PUMP**, which raises the pressure and maintains it at 15 psi. Then, the **MAIN FEED PUMP** boosts the water to 500 psi prior to pushing the water into the **BOILER**.

The Boiler contains hundreds of tubes that the water passes through. At the base of the boiler is a firebox, fed by bunker oil that is sprayed under high pressure, which heats the water in the tubes to about 500-degrees and creates saturated steam. At this point, the steam has neither the heat nor the pressure needed to drive the engine, and there is still moisture in the steam. This 500-degree steam is then passed back through the boiler in another set of pipes, which raises the temperature to 850 degrees and it expands to 600 psi, at which point all of the remaining moisture is removed. This is called **SUPERHEATING**. When the saturated steam is removed from direct contact with the water in the boiler, its temperature will rise if more heat is added.

The Engines

The superheated steam is then pumped into the main, or **HIGH PRESSURE TURBINE (HP)** engine. The HP Turbine contains dozens of steam-tight sealed chambers. Through each chamber runs a shaft that has one end that goes into the **REDUCTION GEAR**, which is used to turn the shaft that turns the propeller. Attached to the shaft in each chamber is a set of blades, like a fan. As the steam, at 600 psi, is forced into the first chamber, it causes the blades to turn the shaft. The steam then passes from one chamber into the next chamber, but as it is doing so, it passes through a set of fixed blades attached to the chamber wall that forces the steam into another direction, into the face of the next set of blades. So, as the steam passes through all of the chambers, one set of blades in the chambers turn the shaft while the set between the chambers redirects the steam into the next set of turning blades.

Eventually, the steam will leave the HP Turbine and enter the **LOW PRESSURE TURBINE (LP)**. In the LP Turbine is another shaft passing through another series of sealed chambers similar to the HP Turbine. This shaft also goes into another set of Reduction Gears. As the steam passes through the LP Turbine, it eventually loses both pressure and heat. With all the energy gone from the steam, it reverts back to water. It is then pumped by the Main Condensation Pump back into the Deaerating Feed Tank, where the entire process is repeated.

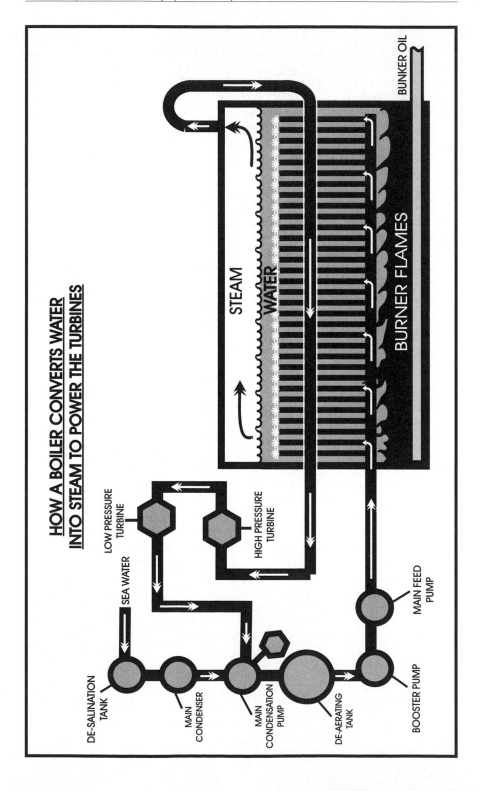

HOW A BOILER CONVERTS WATER INTO STEAM TO POWER THE TURBINES

STEAM

WATER

BURNER FLAMES

BUNKER OIL

LOW PRESSURE TURBINE

HIGH PRESSURE TURBINE

SEA WATER

MAIN FEED PUMP

DE-SALINATION TANK

MAIN CONDENSER

MAIN CONDENSATION PUMP

DE-AERATING TANK

BOOSTER PUMP

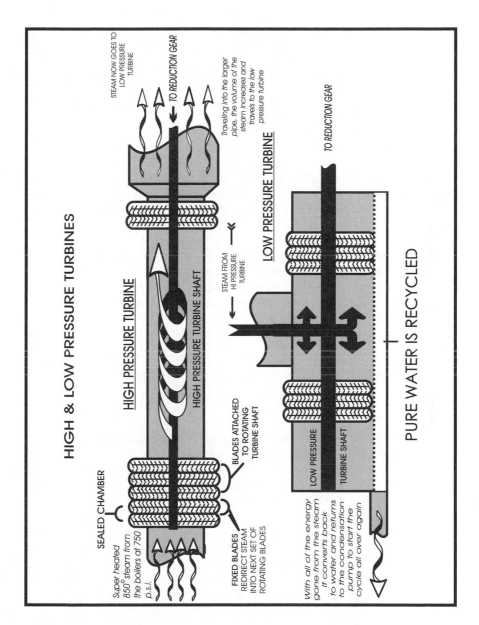

HIGH & LOW PRESSURE TURBINES

STEAM NOW GOES TO LOW PRESSURE TURBINE

TO REDUCTION GEAR

Traveling into the larger pipe, the volume of the steam increases and travels to the low pressure turbine

LOW PRESSURE TURBINE

TO REDUCTION GEAR

HIGH PRESSURE TURBINE

HIGH PRESSURE TURBINE SHAFT

STEAM FROM HI PRESSURE TURBINE

SEALED CHAMBER

BLADES ATTACHED TO ROTATING TURBINE SHAFT

LOW PRESSURE

TURBINE SHAFT

PURE WATER IS RECYCLED

Super heated 850° steam from the boilers at 750 p.s.i.

FIXED BLADES REDIRECT STEAM INTO NEXT SET OF ROTATING BLADES

With all of the energy gone from the steam it converts back to water and returns to the condensation pump to start the cycle all over again

Reduction Gear

REDUCTION GEARS connect the turbines to the propeller shafts. There are two sets per shaft, one off the HP Turbine and one off the LP Turbine. The Reduction Gear housing reflects the size difference between the two sets of gears: the HP Turbine turns a set of smaller gears while the LP Turbine turns a set of larger gears. Within the Reduction Gear housing are dozens of gears of different sizes.

As the steam passes through the turbines, it causes the shaft supporting the blades to turn at thousands of revolutions-per-minute (RPM). This is much too fast for the ships propeller to turn, and in fact, the propeller would disintegrate at that speed. The Reduction Gear then slows the speed of the shaft down to less than 300 rpm, fast enough to push *Hornet* through the water at up to 33 knots.

Propellers

Hornet's four **PROPELLERS** are four-bladed, made of solid manganese bronze, 15 feet in diameter and weigh 27,000 pounds. They are attached to the **PROPELLER SHAFT**, the other end of which is located in the housing of the Reduction Gear. The shafts are 20 inches in diameter, made of solid steel. The two outside shafts, the ones powered by the engines in the Forward Engine Room, are almost 260 feet long! As they pass through the ship to the propellers, they travel in long watertight compartments called **SHAFT ALLEYS** located at the bottom of the ship. They then pass through the hull and are attached to the propellers. The port side propellers turn clockwise (inboard), the starboard propellers turn counterclockwise. Also, the shafts make 1-1/2 turns between the engine and the propeller. *(NOTE: you can walk through Shaft Alley and watch the shaft turn if you visit the* Jeremiah O'Brien, *a World War II Liberty Ship docked in San Francisco.)*

Rudder

A **RUDDER** is used to steer the ship, and *Hornet* has one Rudder with 429 square feet of surface area. To change course (direction), the Helmsman turns the Wheel up in the Pilot House, which sends a series of electrical impulses to the **STEERING ENGINE**, located deep inside the ship near the stern. The Steering Engine then turns the Rudder.

A Rudder works by the effect of the water pushing against one side of it. To steer straight ahead, the rudder needs to be in the centered position. Turning the Wheel to port causes the Steering Engine to turn the Rudder to port, which works as a drag by forcing water against one side of the rudder. Since the propellers are still turning, the forward motion of the propellers on the starboard side will push the ship forward, while the effect of the port side propellers will be reduced by the drag on the Rudder.

Because *Hornet* has four propellers, it can be steered without the rudder. When the rudder is in the center position, the ship will turn to port if the propellers on the starboard side turn faster than the port side propellers. *Hornet* can even turn in its own length if the port propellers are run in reverse while the starboard propellers are run forward. If the rudder is damaged, the propellers can still steer the ship by alternating the port and the starboard propellers.

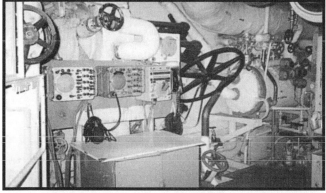

TOP: THE FACE OF A BOILER (CURRENTLY CLOSED TO THE PUBLIC.)
MIDDLE: CONTROL PANEL FOR THE FORWARD STARBOARD
ENGINE.
BELOW: LOW PRESSURE TURBINE TO CENTER LEFT. THE HIGH
PRESSURE TURBINE IS AT THE BOTTOM OF THE LARGE
CROSS-OVER PIPE BELOW THE SHORT LADDER. THE FLAT SURFACE
IN THE FOREGROUND IS THE TOP OF THE REDUCTION GEAR.

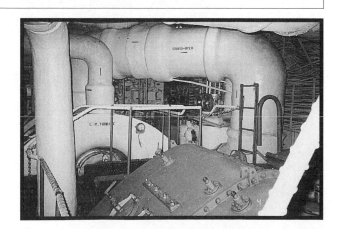

TOP: ANOTHER VIEW OF THE HIGH PRESSURE TURBINE JUST
BELOW THE LARGE PIPE. THE REDUCTION GEAR IS IN FRONT AND
MILES OF ELECTRICAL CABLE ALONG THE BULKHEAD IN THE REAR.
BELOW: THE END OF THE STARBOARD OUTSIDE (NUMBER 1)
SHAFT. BOTTOM: THE NUMBER 2 SHAFT PASSES THROUGH A
MACHINERY ROOM AT THE STERN OF THE SHIP AND THROUGH THE
BULKHEAD AT THE RIGHT. BEYOND THE BULKHEAD IS THE
PROPELLER.

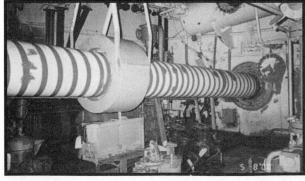

Chapter 21

The Flight Deck

Take the **ESCALATOR** that runs from the **HANGAR DECK** to the **FLIGHT DECK.** The escalator may or may not be working. Although it hasn't worked for years, the museum is trying to get it operational. You can access the Flight Deck via the escalator or one of the two ladders that go from the Hangar Deck to the Flight Deck. If possible, take the escalator even if it isn't working.

In any event, once you have arrived at the Flight Deck, you will be on the **03 LEVEL** at the base of the **ISLAND.** (It's called the ISLAND, not "the building," "house" or "superstructure.") Walk out the door to the Flight Deck. You are now standing on the key component of this or any aircraft carrier. This is where all the aircraft, either fixed-wing or rotary (helicopters) were launched or landed. During *Hornet's* 26-year active career, over 155,000 fixed-wing aircraft landed on this deck.

As you exit the door from the Island onto the Flight Deck, almost directly across from you is the port side deck edge elevator and the angle deck. This is the elevator that transported the Apollo astronauts and their helicopter down to the Hangar Deck after the recovery of Apollo 11 and Apollo 12. Keep in mind that when *Hornet* was built, the angle deck didn't exist—*Hornet* was built as a straight-deck aircraft carrier.

(For a description of what happens on *Hornet's* Flight Deck, see *Chapter 15, AIRCRAFT CARRIER 101.*)

■ The Flight Deck is made of wood, actually a 3/16-inch thick steel plate base covered with 3 inches of wood. Currently, there is also a metal cover over part of the deck, added to protect the wood from jet blast, which tended to set the wooden deck on fire. The deck is very uneven, so watch where you are stepping so you don't step into a hole. As you walk out of the island, turn right. Your Flight Deck tour will take you around the deck in a counter-clockwise direction. Walk to the front of the island. Inside the island you will pass by the **FLIGHT DECK CREW SHELTER** and the **FLIGHT DECK CONTROL ROOM.** These are currently closed. (See *HOW IT WORKS*: RAINBOW JERSEYS.)

■ At the front of the island you will see a long chain fence running up to the bow. Walk forward a few feet and stand at the near end of the long fence (STOP 1). To your right rear the fence goes along the deck that goes around the island. This portion of the deck was added in 1956 and wasn't part of the original ship.

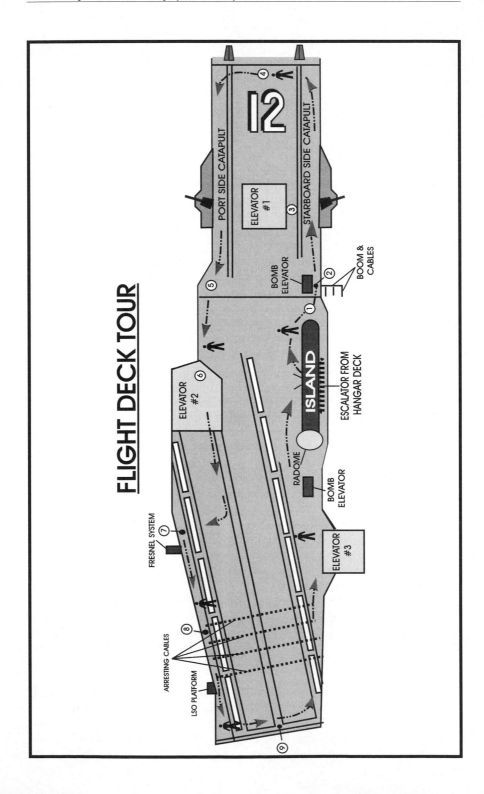

FLIGHT DECK TOUR

Standing next to the fence and looking over the edge, you see the **GALLERY DECK CATWALK.** During World War II this catwalk contained almost a continuous line of 20-millimeter anti-aircraft guns. The large baskets hanging on the edge of the platform contained inflatable life rafts.

■ Starting at the end of the fence, walk forward toward the **BOW** about 22 paces to the long metal plate running across the deck, and stop (STOP 2). This is an **EXPANSION JOINT**. To the right is a long boom hanging off the edge with three cables running up to a similar boom near the top of the island. On top of the boom and running along it is a thin rod. This is actually a handrail! There was a cable running along the bottom of the boom that a crewman could stand on, using the thin rod to hold onto. This way, repairs could be made to the booms or cables.

To your left is the hatch cover for the top of the large bomb elevator you saw on the Hangar Deck. In front of that to your left front is the track for the starboard catapult.

Now walk toward the bow about 40 paces and stop (STOP 3). To your left is the forward or **NUMBER ONE ELEVATOR** you saw the bottom of on the Hangar Deck. Walk up to the edge of the elevator. At your feet you will see the posts and cable for the safety barrier that can be raised or lowered whenever the elevator is down. You saw the mechanism for this on the Hangar Deck.

■ Now walk back to the fence. Look over the edge and you will see the top of the gun director and 5-inch gun mount you saw during the **FO'C'SLE** tour.

Notice the nine long poles alongside the catwalk. They may be in the upright position or in the 90 degree down position, hanging off the side of the ship. Docents always get asked what these poles are for, and they like to tell visitors they are either fishing poles (great for the children—you have to have some way to catch fresh fish) or, *(and if you remember this, you've been around awhile)* that they are curb feelers!

But, in reality, they are **RADIO ANTENNAS** used to communicate with aircraft. They can be used in either the up or down position, but they are always in the down position during any flight operations. The wings of aircraft often overhang the deck and could foul the antennas. During World War II there were actually four large steel cage masts located on the edge of the Flight Deck, but these too were on hinges and could be lowered during flight operations.

■ Now walk to the forward edge of the Flight Deck. Watch your head so you don't hit the overhead signaling cable that runs to the forward edge of the deck. At the bow, turn left and walk to the **JACKSTAFF** (flagpole, STOP 4). You are now standing right over the **SECONDARY CONN** you may have visited during the FO'C'SLE tour.

HOW IT WORKS!

The Landing Signal Officer (LSO)

and

Fresnel Lens Optical Landing System (OLS)

Recovery of aircraft on *Hornet* is the responsibility of the **LANDING SIGNAL OFFICER** (LSO) who stands on a small platform, aft on the port side of the Flight Deck. However, during World War II, the LSO stood at the aft end of the Flight Deck.

The LSO watched each plane as it made its approach to land, and using one small paddle in each hand, gave visual directions to the pilot. He would signal the pilot to fly higher, lower, left or right. The pilot followed the LSO's commands, and eventually, if the LSO deemed the pilot was going to make a good landing, he signaled the pilot to land. If the LSO felt something was wrong, he would give a **WAVE-OFF** and the pilot was expected to go around and try it again. It was all done visually with the small paddles. This method worked well when using the relatively slow aircraft of the World War II era. With the development of jet aircraft, a new system had to be developed.

Fresnel Lens Optical Landing System

About half way down the port side of the angled Flight Deck is a platform extending off the side of the ship and containing a series of lights. This platform contains the **FRESNEL LENS OPTICAL LANDING SYSTEM,** which is a **GYRO-STABILIZED** optical system designed to aid pilots when landing on the Flight Deck.

With the advent of the jet age, the LSO standing next to the deck waving paddles was found to be pretty much useless since the human eye could only see them about one-half mile away. The British Navy came up with a solution using a series of mirrors and lights that would project the glide-path of the landing aircraft off the mirror. A series of lights told the pilot if he was too high or too low. The gyro-stabilizer allows the lens to always remain stable even if the ship is pitching and rolling.

■ The Fresnel Lens Optical Landing System was developed as an improvement of the mirror system. Five vertical lenses are surrounded by reference lights set in such a way that if a pilot is on the correct glide-path, the middle light lens will be illuminated. Running horizontally on both sides of the middle lens is a series of six green lights, and running vertically on either side of the middle lens is a series of five red lights.

As the pilot approached the Flight Deck, and about a mile from it, he **CALLED THE BALL,** which meant he can see the lens. He is going to try to line up the center lens (the ball) with the green horizontal lights. If he is too high, he loses the "ball,": if he is too low, he will see red lights. If the LSO feels he won't make the landing, the red vertical lights come on, which indicate a **WAVE OFF,** and the pilot is expected to go around. The pilot needs to fly over the edge of the Flight Deck and about 10 feet above it in order for the **HOOK** on the bottom of the plane to catch one of the four **CROSSDECK PENDANTS** (or arrestor wires). To assist the pilot with side–to-side references, the deck is painted with lines showing the centerline of the deck and the right and left limit lines. These are all lit up at night. Extending down from the centerline and the Flight Deck is the **DROPLINE**, which contains a series of yellow lights that help the pilot line up the centerline. The Dropline is the vertical pole you see when standing on the Fantail.

■ Working with the LSO are several people, including squadron personnel, **RADIO LISTENERS** and **RADIO TALKERS**. The LSO tries to get the plane to land and snag the number two or three Crossdeck Pendant. If the pilot misses the pendants, he is called a **BOLTER** and the aircraft continues to fly off the **ANGLE DECK** and makes another attempt at landing.

Look over the edge of the deck and you will see a wire net running along the very forward end of the deck. That net and the others at various locations are placed there to catch anyone falling off, or more likely being blown off the edge of the deck. The safety fence you have been following was not in place when *Hornet* was at sea because it would interfere with the aircraft. Consequently it was an all too common occurrence for someone to get blown overboard. Remember, if *Hornet* was steaming at 33 knots into a 30-knot wind, the wind across the deck was 63 knots (72.5 miles per hour) so it was difficult to even stand on the deck. Add in **PROP WASH** or **JET BLAST** and you can see why something was needed to prevent anyone from falling into the water.

Now face **AFT** down the length of the Flight Deck. Looks pretty big, doesn't it? The pilots can tell you it doesn't look all that big from a few thousand feet.

■ Now look at the **ISLAND.** The row of windows on the front of the island two levels up is the **FLAG BRIDGE** (the admiral's bridge or 05 Level). Directly above that is the **NAVIGATION BRIDGE** or the **CAPTAIN'S BRIDGE** (06 Level). Hanging over the Flight Deck with the

HOW IT WORKS!

Rainbow Jerseys

The launching and recovery of aircraft requires hundreds of personnel who work on the Flight Deck. Each person has a specific job and, much like a well-choreographed ballet, he must do his job in a prescribed sequence. At the same time, he must be vigilant about everything that goes on around him. It isn't an overstatement that the Flight Deck of an aircraft carrier is one of the most dangerous places in the world for the hundreds of personnel working there.

Flight Deck personnel have to be easily identifiable, and for that reason everyone on the deck is required to wear a colored JERSEY that signifies what it is that person is supposed to be doing. Following are the colors of the jerseys and what they represent.

- PURPLE JERSEY: Aviation Fuels: responsible
        for re-fueling aircraft
- BLUE JERSEY: Plane Handlers, Aircraft Elevator
        Operators, Tractor (Mule) Drivers,
        Messengers, Hangar Deck workers and
        Phone Talkers
- GREEN JERSEY: Catapult and Arresting Gear
        Crews, Air Wing Maintenance Personnel,
        Cargo Handling Personnel, Hook Runners
        and Helicopter Landing Signal Personnel
- YELLOW JERSEY: Aircraft Handling Officers,
        Catapult and Arresting Gear Officers and
        Plane Directors
- RED JERSEY: Ordnance Handlers, Crash and Salvage
        Crews, Explosive Ordnance Disposal (EOD)
- BROWN JERSEY: Air Wing Plane Captains
- WHITE JERSEY: Squadron Plane Inspectors,
        Landing Signal Officer (LSO), Air Transfer
        Officers (ATO), Safety Observers, Medical
        Personnel

green windows on the 08 Level is **PRIMARY FLIGHT CONTROL** (PRI-FLY). On the tall **MAST** are two huge **RADARS**: the big square one (also known as a bed-spring radar) is the **AN/SPS-30** Height-Finding Radar to detect the height of aircraft, and the big black thing that looks like a satellite dish is the **AN/SPS-43** Air-Search Radar. These were added to *Hornet* in 1956, and in reality, the two you see were never part of *Hornet*. *Hornet's* two radars were removed when it was decommissioned and used elsewhere. The two you see came from *Oriskany*, CV-34, before it was sold and scrapped.

■ Turn right and walk to the port side edge of the Flight Deck, then, turn left and walk up to where the fence makes a short jog to the right. Over the edge is the port forward 5-inch gun. Off to your left front is the end of the port side catapult. Continue to follow the fence as it makes a jog to the left, and walk to the metal expansion plate running across the deck (STOP 5). To your left front is port catapult **BLAST DEFLECTOR.** This can be raised and lowered as needed whenever a plane is launched, and is designed to protect aircraft and crewmen standing on the deck from jet blast.

■ Now walk along the fence toward the stern to where the fence makes a 90-degree turn to the right. Take a few more steps and you will be standing on top of the port deck-edge elevator, or elevator number 2. Follow the fence about ten paces and stop on the center of the wide white line (STOP 6). Look toward the stern. This is the **LANDING CENTERLINE** for the pilots to guide on when they landed.

Walk down the white line and keep walking when it turns yellow. Just before it turns white again, look down and you will see a raised steel dome. There is a small glass window facing the stern. There is another one about 50 feet down the white line. Below the deck is a room and a post where a video camera is mounted that records every landing (haven't you always wondered how they get those great landing shots you see in the movies?)

From the dome, turn right, go to the fence and turn left and start walking. Walk over another steel plate and just beyond, hanging off the edge, is the **FRESNEL OPTICAL LANDING SYSTEM** (OLS), (STOP 7). (See *HOW IT WORKS:* FRESNEL LENS OPTICAL LANDING SYSTEM.)

■ As you walk aft along the fence, you will have to walk around five low square metal boxes. Inside these boxes is the pulley assembly for the **ARRESTOR GEAR CROSSDECK PENDANT** (STOP 8). *(See Chapter 15, AIRCRAFT CARRIER 101.)*

■ After you pass the last of the low boxes, the aft 5-inch gun is located on the catwalk, still in its protective cover where it has resided for over 30 years.

Halfway between the gun and the stern, hanging off the edge of the deck is the **CANTILEVERED PLATFORM** or the **LANDING SIGNAL OFFICER** (LSO) platform. This is where the LSO would stand when he was directing landing aircraft. Note the large net around the platform. This is the LSO's safety net that he could jump into if an aircraft made a bad landing. (See *HOW IT WORKS:* LANDING SIGNAL OFFICER.)

■ Walk down the fence to the stern, turn left and walk to the **FLAGSTAFF** (STOP 9). For obvious reasons, this was only used while in port. Face San Francisco. Somewhere between where you are standing and the city, the cruiser USS *Pennsylvania* was anchored in 1911 when Eugene Ely made the first ever airplane landing on a ship.

■ Looking aft, between the fence and the net is a short curved portion of the deck known as the **RUNDOWN.** Designed to lessen the impact of an airplane that settled too low while landing, any plane striking it generally resulted in the total destruction of the aircraft and a huge fire on the Flight Deck.

■ Now walk toward the starboard fence, turn left and face the island and the bow. On the back of the island just below Pri-Fly is a large round dome. This is the **RADOME,** with an **SPN-35** radar inside that enabled pilots to make a carrier controlled approach for landing (similar to an instrument approach where the carrier provides the instructions). On top of the Radome is the top of the large square black **FUNNEL** (It's not called a smokestack!) where smoke and gasses from the boilers and engine rooms were vented.

■ As you walk toward the bow, you will cross over the large double white line. There is one on the port side too. This is the **LANDING BORDERLINE,** which indicates a safe landing area. The smaller red and white line is the safety line, and aircraft could be parked behind it during landing operations.

As you are walking, you will pass the five starboard arrestor cable boxes and the last 5-inch gun mount off the edge of the deck. Still walking forward, you will pass the starboard deck-edge or number 3 elevator. This elevator can fold into a vertical position to allow for passage through narrow waters.

Just past the elevator is the hatch for the small bomb elevator that goes down to the **MAGAZINE.**

Although it's hard to see, on the starboard side of the tall mast is an open ladder going all the way to the top. Not something most people would want to climb!

As you walk back past the Island on your right side, look up and you will get a good view of the bottom of Pri-Fly. Just below it is the **PHOTO PLATFORM** used to photograph all landings.

You have now completed the Flight Deck tour and are ready to begin the **ISLAND** tour.

The Island

TOP LEFT; THE LOWER SET OF WINDOWS BELONG TO THE FLAG BRIDGE WHERE THE ADMIRAL AND HIS STAFF WORK. THE UPPER SET IS THE NAVIGATION BRIDGE WHERE HORNET'S CAPTAIN AND THOSE REPSONSIBLE FOR RUNNING THE SHIP WORK. HIS CHAIR IS BEHIND THE TWO LARGE WINDOWS ON THE RIGHT. TOWERING ABOVE ALL IS THE MAST WITH ITS ARRAY OF ANTENNA'S AND RADARS. AT THE BOTTOM OF THE PHOTO IS THE END OF THE STARBOARD CATAPULT.

TOP RIGHT; CLOSEUP OF THE ISLAND. THE GLASSED-IN AREA IS PRI-FLY, AND BELOW THAT IS THE PLAT, OR PHOTO PLATFORM. BELOW THE NUMBER 12 AND NEXT TO THE RIBBON BOARD IS VULTURES ROW WHERE OBSERVERS CAN WATCH FLIGHT OPERATIONS.

BOTTOM RIGHT: ANOTHER VIEW OF THE AFT END OF THE ISLAND, SHOWING THE MAST, THE TOP OF THE FUNNEL (THE LARGE BLACK SQUARE), THE FLIGHT DECK LIGHTS BELOW THAT, THEN THE WINDOWS OF PRI-FLY. THE LARGE ROUND OBJECT IS THE RADOME HOUSING THE CATCC APPROACH/LANDING RADAR.

TOP AND MIDDLE: ALTHOUGH NOT ON THE FLIGHT DECK AND OPEN TO THE PUBLIC ON GUIDED TOURS ONLY, TWO VIEWS OF THE MACHINERY THAT OPERATES THE STARBOARD CATAPULT. THE CREW HAD A SENSE OF HUMOR. BOTTOM: THE ARRAY OF LIGHTS THAT MAKE UP THE FRENSNEL OPTICAL LANDING SYSTEM HANG OFF THE PORT EDGE OF THE FLIGHT DECK.

Chapter 22

Island Tour

Depending on the number of visitors and the availability of docents, there may be a guided tour of the Island, but if not, you may be able do the tour on your own. In any case, both tours start on the Flight Deck near the door facing the Flight Deck near the aft end of the Island.

There are two portions of the tour: the **NAVIGATION BRIDGE,** (the 06 LEVEL) and **PRIMARY FLIGHT CONTROL,** or **PRI-FLY** (the 08 LEVEL). Pri-Fly usually isn't open unless there is a docent available, but if it is open, go to Pri-Fly before you go to the navigation bridge. You get to Pri-Fly from the 06 Level. If the ladder going up to Pri-Fly is chained off, then Pri-Fly is closed.

■ The **ISLAND** is the Command and Control center of the ship. The Navigation Bridge is where the pilothouse, chart room, captain's sea cabin and the bridge are located. Located one deck below is the **FLAG BRIDGE** (05 Level) where the Task Group commander (normally an admiral), and his staff operated. Two decks above the Navigation Bridge is Pri-Fly. Hanging off the aft end of the Island is the **RADOME** used to assist pilots with instrument landings. Towering above

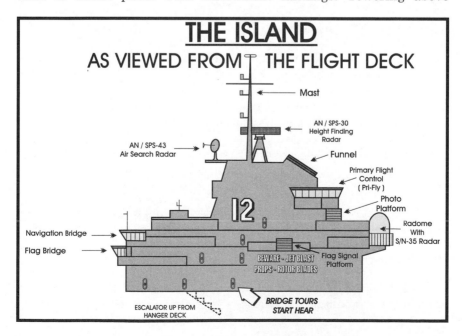

THE ISLAND
AS VIEWED FROM THE FLIGHT DECK

- Mast
- AN / SPS-30 Height Finding Radar
- AN / SPS-43 Air Search Radar
- Funnel
- Primary Flight Control (Pri-Fly)
- Photo Platform
- Radome With S/N-35 Radar
- Navigation Bridge
- Flag Bridge
- BEWARE - JET BLAST PROPS - ROTOR BLADES
- Flag Signal Platform
- 12
- ESCALATOR UP FROM HANGER DECK
- BRIDGE TOURS START HEAR

everything is the **MAST** that contains several radars and a myriad of communications equipment. Much of the physical space in the Island is devoted to the **UPTAKES** for the boilers in the fire rooms, meaning the Island serves as the ship's funnel (don't call it a smoke stack!).

■ The Flight Deck (03 level) of the Island contains several small compartments, including the **FLIGHT DECK CREW SHELTER** and the **FLIGHT DECK CONTROL ROOM,** both located in the forward portion of the Island. In the center of the Island is the passageway connecting the escalator, several sets of ladders and the Flight Deck. As you exit the Island, turn left and walk to the next door. This door is the entrance to the Island tour.

■ You begin the tour by climbing three sets of ladders up to the 06 Level, then turn 180 degrees around the ladder and pass through the door into the **CHART ROOM.** If Pri-Fly is open, you would continue up the ladder by the Chart Room door two more levels. Otherwise, continue your tour in the Chart Room. If you are going up to Pri-Fly, the next level up is the **ANTI-AIRCRAFT CONTROL DECK.**

Anti-Aircraft Control Deck

On the 07 Level, one level above the Navigation Deck, is the Anti-Aircraft Control Deck. Inside the Island is the **ANTI-AIRCRAFT CONTROL ROOM**, the **WEATHER OFFICE** and the **PLAT (PHOTO) PLATFORM.**

Anti-Aircraft Control Room

This room is the **GUN BOSS'** battle station and takes input from the four Fire Control Directors located next to the 5-inch guns. The information is shown on two radarscopes, and is then processed. That information is used to assign a director and gun to fire at the target, and when the target is in range, the gun is fired by remote control. Also in the room is a large plotting board to record the location of all incoming aircraft, and the status of weather variables, such as wind and rain.

Weather Office

All weather related information passed through this office and was disseminated to all locations needing accurate weather information.

Plat Platform

This is a film camera and later a video camera station. All aircraft launchings or landings, from the very first aircraft on *Langley,* CV-1, up through aircraft carriers today, are recorded. This provides a visual record for review and analysis of any problems during flight operations.

Primary Flight Control

Once you climb the last ladder and turn right, you will enter Pri-Fly. You are located in what is basically the control tower of an airport, or in this case *Hornet*, with a spectacular view of the Flight Deck. Personnel working in Pri-Fly are responsible for the operation of the Flight Deck and all air traffic within a five mile radius of the ship.

The **AIR BOSS** and several other crewmen working in Pri-Fly monitor all aspects of the air group when operating on or near the carrier. The Air Boss sat in the chair overlooking the Flight Deck and directed all of the air operations on the deck. He was in constant communication with the Captain or the Officer of the Deck to make sure the ship was in the correct position to launch or recover aircraft.

Several sets of switches located next to the Air Boss controlled the two catapults, and he could flip the switch to shut down either catapult if a safety issue arose. Another set of switches controlled the landing lights on the deck. Located between the Air Boss and his chief assistant, known as the Mini-Boss, are the controls for the optical landing system.

All of the **ARRESTER ENGINES** are controlled here. The weight of an approaching aircraft will show in the small window by each engine. Buttons located here adjust the tension on the Arrester Engines so an aircraft isn't damaged by too much tension or allowed to slide off the deck due to too little tension.

On the bulkhead next to the **ENGINE ROOM UPTAKE** is the **STATUS BOARD** listing the weight and condition of all aircraft on the ship and in the air. The remainder of Pri-Fly is devoted to

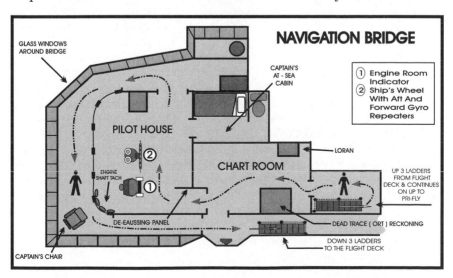

GLASS WINDOWS
AROUND BRIDGE

NAVIGATION BRIDGE

CAPTAIN'S
AT - SEA
CABIN

① Engine Room
Indicator
② Ship's Wheel
With Aft And
Forward Gyro
Repeaters

PILOT HOUSE

LORAN

CHART ROOM

UP 3 LADDERS
FROM FLIGHT
DECK & CONTINUES
ON UP TO
PRI-FLY

ENGINE
SHAFT TACH

DE-EAUSSING PANEL

DEAD TRACE (ORT) RECKONING

DOWN 3 LADDERS
TO THE FLIGHT DECK

CAPTAIN'S CHAIR

communication equipment that connects Pri-Fly to the rest of the ship, the aircraft, and all of *Hornet's* escorts.

■ Now retrace your steps and go back down three levels to the Navigation Bridge (06 Level) and enter the **CHART ROOM** at the bottom of the ladder.

Chart Room

The Chart Room was always a very busy place. It was here that the **NAVIGATION OFFICER** and his staff of Quartermasters determined where, exactly, the ship was located at any given time. Navigating your automobile is a piece of cake when you have roads and landmarks to follow.

Ocean navigation from the time of the ancient mariners until the late 1900's hadn't changed very much until orbiting satellites were introduced. Basically, you took a position fix, which you recorded on a chart, of the stars and sun using a sextant. Then you tracked the course and speed you were steaming and logged them on the chart. Theoretically, if all calculations worked out correctly, when you took your next position fix, you should be where the chart says you are. Theoretically.

If you have an accurate position fix, and if you steam at a constant speed and never change course, you will be out of position the next time you do a fix because you didn't account for wind and water currents. Now throw in the movements of a combat vessel, which, during combat will be changing both course and speed, or zigzagging, or there is a typhoon or you haven't seen the stars in a few nights, then you can see the complexity of tracking the location of the ship.

Thus, you have the Chart Room. Located in front of you as you enter the room is the **DEAD RECKONING TRACER** (DRT). This is a mechanical device that tracks the ship's movement starting from a navigational (position) fix by calculating the ship's speed and course, (with automatic heading and speed inputs.) The Precision Analog Computer located to the right of the DRT performs the calculations. The ships position is then shown on the chart via a light beam projecting up through the chart. There is another DRT located down in the **COMBAT INFORMATION CENTER** that does the same thing. The two DRTs must match so the crew knows its exact location on the ocean. Daily at dawn, noon and dusk the Navigator or his assistant goes outside with a **SEXTANT,** takes a sighting and using the ships master clock and a set of printed tables calculates the longitude and latitude of the ship. This is the information used to reset the DRT.

Several other pieces of equipment are located in the Chart Room, including:

1) **LO**ng **RA**nge radio **N**avigation system (**LORAN,** which is a long-range radio navigation position-fixing system), is used to track the location of the ship. It consists of an array of fixed stations that transmit precisely synchronized signals to mobile receivers. By contacting at least two of the known stations and determining their direction, two lines can be drawn from them, and where they intersect is your location.

2) A **RADAR REPEATER** for detecting landmarks such as mountain peaks.

3) **CHRONOMETERS** which are used to indicate the correct time.

4) **FATHOMETER** to record ocean depths.

Walk on through the forward door into the **PILOT HOUSE**. Just before going through the door you cross the **NAVIGATORS OFFICE**. If at any time the Captain wanted workspace but didn't want to leave the bridge, he would take over this area and close it off with the sliding curtain. The rest of the Captain's staff and their office was located on the 02 Gallery Deck level.

Pilot House

The Pilot House is where *Hornet* was controlled from. Basically, the ship was steered from here. It is one of five places that you can steer *Hornet.* (**SECONDARY CONN** below the forward end of the Flight Deck and the **AFTER STEERING** located way down inside the ship, just above the rudder, are two other locations.) It isn't very large considering the number of crewmen who worked here. During World War II the **BRIDGE,** located in front of the Pilot House, wasn't enclosed, meaning it was open to the weather. Consequently, the Pilot House ports had blast shields on them. You can still see the shields when you go out onto the Bridge.

As you enter the Pilot House, to your immediate right is the control panel for the **DEGAUSSING** equipment. Degaussing controls the ship's magnetic signature (influence) to minimize the effectiveness of magnetic mines or torpedoes.

■ In front of you as you enter is the **ENGINE ORDER TELEGRAPH** (STOP 1 on the Navigation Bridge Map) that was used to tell the engine room how fast (forward or backward) the ship should be steaming. The Engine Order Telegraph was operated by first pulling it through several stations (stops) to ring the bells, and stopped on the command you sent to the throttle man in the **ENGINE ROOM.** There, an identical telegraph is used to send the same signal back up to the Pilot House to confirm the order. Above the Engine Room Telegraph are four **ENGINE SHAFT TACHOMETERS,** which show how fast the four shafts attached to the propellers are turning.

HOW IT WORKS!

Sound-Powered Telephones

SOUND-POWERED TELEPHONES are a major component of communications aboard *Hornet* and all navy ships. They are still used today. Sound-Powered is exactly what powers them: the vibrations of speech against a plate in the mouthpiece. No batteries or outside electrical power is needed. If the ship's power goes out or the normal phone lines are disrupted, Sound-Powered phones are the only way to communicate. Generally **PHONE-TALKERS**, crewmen picked because of their ability to speak clearly and loudly, are assigned to the Sound-Powered phones and are given information they pass to the Talker at the other end of the line. Each phone contains a **HANDSET** and a **HEADSET.**

Sound-Powered Telephone **CIRCUITS** aboard *Hornet* fall into three categories:

- **PRIMARY:** includes all circuits necessary for controlling armament, engineering, damage control, maneuvering and surveillance functions during battle.
- **AUXILIARY:** duplicates many of the primary circuits for the purpose of maintaining vital communications in the event of damage to the primary system. Auxiliary circuits are separated as much as possible from primary circuits.
- **SUPPLEMENTARY:** consisting of many short, direct circuits, such as the Bridge to the Quarterdeck, Quarterdeck to the Ward Room, etc.

Close to all of the Primary and Auxiliary phones is a mechanical switchbox that can route calls to various locations.

Voice and Speaking Tubes

Another method of communicating aboard *Hornet* is by use of **VOICE TUBES,** metal tubes about 3-1/2 inches in diameter that pass between key compartments, primarily in the Island.

To the right of the Engine Room Indicator is the ships **WHEEL** (STOP 2). This is used by the **HELMSMAN** to turn the rudder to steer the ship. *Hornet* has power steering. When the Wheel is turned a signal is sent to one of two steering engines that turn the rudder. The Helmsman is usually a Second or Third Class Petty Officer. The Helmsman gets his instructions from the **OFFICER OF THE DECK** (OOD). Course changes are given in **DIRECTIONS,** (left or right) and **COURSE HEADINGS** (in degrees) and the **HELMSMAN** turns the Wheel to the new course. In the center of the Wheel stand, called the **HELM,** is the **RUDDER ANGLE INDICATOR** which tells the Helmsman how the rudder is placed in relation to the ship. On either side of the Rudder Angle Indicator are the **AFT GYRO REPEATER** and the **FORWARD GYRO REPEATER.** These are tied by electrical signal into the **GYROCOMPASSES** located below decks that show the course the ship is headed.

Also working in the Pilot House is the **LEE HELMSMAN**, usually a Third Class Petty Officer or seaman who manages the Engine Order Indicator.

■ The Engine Order could be either a standard increment such as "all ahead standard" or "all ahead standard, indicate 150 rpm". Engine orders could be "port engines ahead 2/3, starboard engines back full, etc." The four engines could be independently controlled, as pairs or all four together.

■ Also working in the Pilot House was the **QUARTERMASTER OF THE WATCH**, responsible for maintaining the ship's **DAILY LOG.** The **BOATSWAIN'S MATE OF THE WATCH** does the announcing over the Public Address **(1MC)** system. There were also several **SOUND POWER PHONE TALKERS** who are responsible for passing orders and information around the ship via the **SOUND POWER TELEPHONES.**

As you head out the door to the right, you will see the captain's **SEA CABIN** on your right. When at sea, this is where the captain spent most of his time if he wasn't on the bridge. It is small, but it does allow the captain to be close to the bridge if he is needed in an emergency. It contains a bunk, desk and a combination shower/toilet. Now walk through the door from the Pilot House out to the Bridge.

Bridge

During World War II the Bridge was not enclosed, so life could be cold and wet. As you exit the Pilot House you will be facing the **AUXILIARY CONNING STATION** (AUX CONN). From this area, you can look directly down the side of the ship. This is where most of the **BRIDGE WATCH TEAM,** and always the Captain, would be during underway replenishment and when approaching a pier to dock. During **UNDERWAY REPLENISHMENTS** (UN-REP) a resupply ship or a ship being resupplied would steam about 80 to 120 feet away, about the distance to the center of the pier *Hornet* is tied to. It would be the responsibility of the OOD to make sure proper spacing was maintained.

HOW IT WORKS!

Replenishment at Sea or

Underway Replenishment

During World War II *Hornet* went 18 months without ever tying up to a dock, and only had to then because of damage to the Flight Deck caused by a typhoon off Okinawa in May 1945. No ship could carry enough food, fuel or ammunition to sustain itself at sea that long. Steaming at a standard 25 knots, *Hornet* carried only about ten days worth of fuel and during combat operations could burn through a full load of fuel in four days.

Between campaigns or combat operations, *Hornet*, and the rest of its Task Group, would retire to one of the forward supply bases established by the navy, such as Eniwetok or Ulithi. There the ships would take on board everything needed to sustain them for the next operation: fuel, gasoline, oil, food, spare parts, replacement personnel, even the mail. Without the availability of a dock, all this material would be transferred between *Hornet* and the numerous supply ships by a **LIGHTER**, or small boat. The supply ships (during the height of the war there were hundreds of them, each usually carrying only one commodity, like bulk dry goods (wheat for making bread), frozen meat, ammunition, mail, etc.) would load material onto the lighters, and this material would be loaded, by crane, onto *Hornet.* There was usually enough food and ammunition on board to sustain the ship for several weeks. Fuel and aviation gasoline, however, was a different matter.

■ Once *Hornet* went to sea with its group of escorting destroyers and cruisers, *Hornet* not only had to manage its own supply of fuel oil, it also had to serve as a floating service station for its escorts. Not counting the days *Hornet* was at anchor at a supply base, during its 18 months at sea *Hornet* was either being refueled or refueling its escorts on an almost daily basis. In fact, on 270 occasions it was transferring fuel to its escorts and on another 1,262 occasions it was transferring spare parts, personnel, mail, etc. to the destroyers. Additionally, on an average of every five days it was, in turn, being refueled by fleet oilers who supplied the bunker oil to run the ship and the aviation gasoline for the aircraft.

■ **UNDERWAY REPLENISHMENT,** or **UN-REP** as the navy calls it, is a very demanding process because supply ships have to approach within 80 to 120 feet (the current distance from the *Hornet* and the center of the pier it is tied to) and steam an exact parallel course and exact speed. Lines (cables) are passed between the two ships, normally from *Hornet's* starboard side, and then fuel hoses, up to five inches wide, are run along the lines and attached to the other ship. Fuel oil or gasoline is then pumped through the hoses. Meanwhile, other lines are passed between the ships to transfer other material or personnel. Standing next to each cable and hose is a crewman with an axe, ready to cut the connections in an emergency. Once the UN-REP is completed, hoses and lines are retrieved and the process is repeated for the next ship in line.

■ The Bridge Team, or the officers who would always be on the bridge, included the following officers who rotate the positions with other officers, four hours per shift. The Captain usually be on the bridge or in his Sea Cabin.

OFFICER OF THE DECK (OOD), usually a senior Lieutenant (equal in rank to a captain or an 03 in the other service branches). He is responsible for the ship's overall operation, including navigation and the sequence of events to support flight operations. He is also responsible for ship handling, communications, routine tests and inspections, reports, and carrying out the plan of the day (POD).

JUNIOR OFFICER OF THE DECK (JOOD), The JOOD is the principle assistant to the OOD and is training to become the OOD. At the direction of the OOD, he CONNS or navigates the ship, sharing the job with the JOOW.

JUNIOR OFFICER OF THE WATCH (JOOW), the assistant to the JOOD.

■ As you walk forward from the AUX CONN and around the front of the Pilot House, you'll pass several radios, a **SURFACE RADAR** repeater, and various switches and controls. To your left you'll see the round port covers that would be closed to protect the Pilot House. Probably the most prominent item on the Bridge is the **CAPTAIN'S CHAIR,** located on the port side of the Bridge above the Flight Deck. No one, EVER, sat in this chair except the Captain. The Captain has direct communications to all vital areas of the ship via the telephones along the bulkhead.

To the left of the chair is a black communication console connected by loud speaker to key areas of the ship. There is also a red phone that allows secure communication to the President and other command authorities. Finally, there is a toggle switch that controls the Flight Deck conditions (Red Light indicates a **FOUL** deck, Green Light indicates a **CLEAR** deck.)

Next to the red phone is a black intercom box that connects with the **COMBAT INFORMATION CENTER** and the **AVIATION CONTROL**

CENTER. There are also two intercoms, the **1 MC** (MAIN COMMUNICATIONS) allows the Captain to speak to the entire ship, and the **5 MC** addresses the Flight Deck. Below the box is a button to summon the Captain's **MARINE ORDERLY.**

Above the Captain's chair is a TV monitor to view both launch and recovery operations, an **ANEMOMETER** to record wind speed and direction and the ship's steering gyro compass. Now walk past the Captain's chair out the door onto the **FLAG SIGNAL PLATFORM.**

Flag Signal Platform

The oldest form of sending signals between ships at sea, still used today despite modern communications, is the signal flag. Signalmen composed messages and ran up flag messages on the lines above the flag board. Individual flags were used for the alphabet, numbers or commands. Some flags represented entire messages, and groups of flags were used to send messages by code. The Flag Signal Platform is where the flag messages were sent from.

■ This concludes the Island Tour, and you return down to the Flight Deck via the ladder on the Flag Signal Platform.

HOW IT WORKS!

Combat Information Center (CIC)

Air Intercept Center (AIC)

Carrier Air Traffic Control Center (CATCC)

Air Operations Center (AOC)Carrier Controlled Approach (CCA)

Anti-Submarine Warfare Command and Control Center (ASWCCC)

On the Gallery Deck, just below the Flight Deck, and located between the Island and the port side deck-edge elevator are the **COMBAT INFORMATION CENTER (CIC),** the **CARRIER AIR TRAFFIC CONTROL CENTER (CATCC), AIR OPERATIONS (AOC)** and the **CARRIER CONTROLLED APPROACH (CCA)** compartments. Presently, only the CIC (and not the other two compartments) is open for *guided* tours. Due to the design of the

CIC, the hundreds of lights, knobs and dials and the lack of light, self-guided tours are not feasible. However, in case CIC tours aren't available during your visit, a description of CIC is included.

Combat Information Center, Air Intercept Center

The purpose of the CIC is to collect, evaluate and disseminate information about the status of both friendly and enemy forces. The room contains eight **RADAR REPEATERS**, each of which can be switched to any of several radars. There is a **SURFACE TARGET PLOTTER**, a **DEAD RECKONING TRACE** (similar to the one on the Navigation Bridge) and several **PLOTTING BOARDS** where the information is written from the back side. You have probably seen something similar to the CIC in any of several motion pictures. Usually you see the person drawing lines backwards on a clear plastic board. Attached to the CIC is the **AIR INTERCEPT CENTER (AIC)**, which contains four more radar repeaters. In a room behind the CIC is the **ANTI-SUBMARINE WARFARE COMMAND AND CONTROL CENTER (ASWCCC)**, which currently contains displays of **ANTI-SUBMARINE WARFARE (ASW)** equipment.

The CIC operates around the clock and is commanded by the **CIC WATCH OFFICER**. Current information about all aircraft within range of *Hornet's* radars is tracked on the radar repeaters and plotted on one of the plastic plotting boards. One board lists the status of each of *Hornet's* aircraft; another lists the call sign and radio channel of each aircraft. Others are used for **ANTI-SUBMARINE WARFARE (ASW)** information, **SURFACE FORMATIONS**, etc.

Carrier Air Traffic Control Center and Carrier Controlled Approach

In two compartments directly behind the CIC, and not open to the public, are the **CATCC** and **CCA**. The CATCC has the same function as an FAA approach-control radar facility at a civilian airfield. It provides information for inbound aircraft, especially when the weather is too poor to locate the carrier visually. Basically, the CATCC works with a pilot until he is in the **CARRIER LANDING PATTERN**. The pilot is then handed off to the CCA, which works with the pilot in the final approach until he is lined up with the centerline on the flight deck and can "CALL THE BALL" on the **OPTICAL LANDING SYSTEM**. Once the pilot has visual on the ball, he is handed off to the **LANDING SIGNAL OFFICER (LSO)** who works the pilot down onto the deck.

Air Operations Center

Also located behind the CIC is the **AIR OPERATIONS CENTER.** This is where the planning and coordination for flight operations is conducted. Close contact is required with the Air Boss, CATCC, CIC, Flight Deck, Hangar Deck and all Ready Rooms. All aircraft, pilot and mission assignments are made here.

The Mast

Towering above the Island is *Hornet's* **MAST**. It is used to support numerous radars, navigation lights, signal lights, weather instruments, flags and various other electronic devices. Access to the top of the Mast is via a vertical ladder that runs up the starboard side. As you can well imagine, climbing that ladder is probably not something most people would care to do. Obviously, that portion of *Hornet* will never be open to the public.

■ This ends your walking tour of the USS Hornet Museum. New portions of the ship will be open in the future. Please come back often.

You exit the ship on the Hangar Deck near the gift shop. Thank you for visiting *Hornet!*

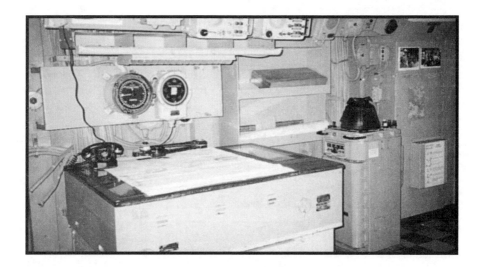

Top: Chart Room behind the Navigation Bridge. In the foreground is the Dead Reckoning Tracer (DRT). On the bulkhead is a Gyro Compass Repeater and Ditometer Log (i.e. Speedometer.) above that are several communications control panels. To the right of the DRT is a Radar Repeater.

Bottom: the Pilot House. Before the Navigation Bridge was enclosed, the ports (port holes) had to be kept closed during bad weather. The Hornet was steered using the wheel at right center. At left center is the Engine Room Telegraph.

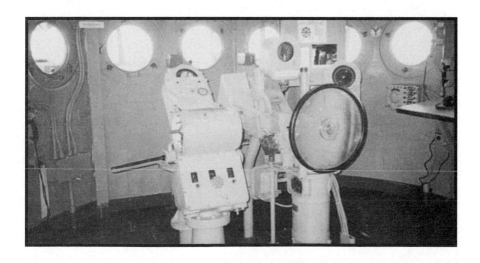

TOP: NAVIGATION BRIDGE WITH CAPTAIN'S CHAIR AND AN ARRAY
OF RADIO TELEPHONES.
MIDDLE: VULTURE'S ROW BEHIND THE NAVIGATION BRIDGE,
WHERE OBSERVERS COULD WATCH FLIGHT DECK OPERATIONS.
BELOW: THE COMBAT INFORMATION CENTER (CIC) LOCATED ON
THE GALLERY DECK BELOW THE ISLAND. THE STATUS OF ALL
FRIENDLY AND ENEMY FORCES ARE MONITORED HERE. THE ROOM
IS JAMMED WITH RADAR AND COMMUNICATIONS EQUIPMENT.

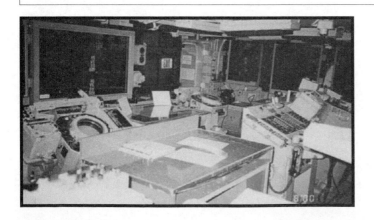

Appendices
& Glossary

Appendix 1

Hornet's Aircraft

During the 26 years of *Hornet's* service to America, about two dozen different types and sub types of aircraft were assigned to *Hornet's* eight air groups. For various reasons, dozens of other types of aircraft that weren't assigned landed aboard. In all, there were 115,445 arrested landings on *Hornet's* deck, the last one taking place on February 20, 1970.

On the following pages is a brief description of some of the more notable aircraft that were assigned to *Hornet* during her career.

ABOVE: GRUMMAN TBF IN FLIGHT (N.A.) BELOW: TWO VIEWS OF THE HORNET'S TBM-3 DURING THE RESTORATION PROCESS (AUTHOR).

Grumman TBF and Eastern TBM Avenger

(Torpedo Bomber)

In April 1940 Grumman Aircraft Company was ordered to develop a replacement for the Douglas TBD Devastator, which proved to be a wise move as early wartime events would prove. The first TBF was used at the Battle of Midway, flying off *Hornet*, CV-8. Five of the six aircraft were lost, the remaining one dumped over the side after limping back to *Hornet*. However, the Avenger proved to be a successful aircraft and remained in use in various roles until the mid-fifties.

The Avenger was designed to carry one torpedo or a 2,000-pound bomb in the weapons bay. There was a three-man crew, a pilot, a gunner in the dorsal (top) turret behind the pilot and a radar operator/gunner in the ventral (bottom rear) portion of the fuselage.

Grumman built 2,290 of the TBF-1 and several experimental and lend-lease versions until March 1944. The Eastern Aircraft division of General Motors built 7,546 of the TBM-2 and TBM-3 and various night, photo-reconnaissance, radar, searchlight and anti-submarine versions. Almost 1,000 were sold to Britain, Australia and New Zealand.

Technical Data (typical to TBM-3 versions)

Crew: three: pilot, gunner and radar operator
Engine: One 1,900 HP Wright (propeller)
Dimensions: Width: 54 feet 2 inches (16 feet 9 inches with wings folded); length: 40 feet; height: 16 feet 5 inches.
Weight: Empty 10,545 pounds; gross 17,900 pounds
Performance: max speed 275 mph at 16,000 feet; cruising speed 145 mph; service ceiling 30,100 feet; range 1,010 miles.
Armament: two fixed forward shooting .50-cal machine guns, one Dorsal (upper) .50-cal machine gun, one ventral (lower) .30-cal machine gun; up to 2,000 pounds of torpedoes or bombs in the weapons-bay.

■ The Hornet Museum's TBM-3 served with the carriers *San Jacinto, Wasp, Hancock* and *Hornet* before being modified as one of the Navy's first carrier on-board delivery (COD) aircraft in late 1945. From 1946 to 1951 it served with VR-2 in Hawaii before being transferred to VR-22 at Norfolk, Virginia. From 1953 until 1956 it served aboard the *Coral Sea,* then was sold to a private fire fighting company in Nevada in 1959.

It is worth noting that this aircraft flew off the *San Jacinto* during the same time frame that former President George Bush was a pilot on the same ship, flying this type of aircraft. President Bush was in a TBM-3 when he was shot down during the war. Although there is no way of knowing for sure, it is always fun to speculate that President Bush might have flown this exact plane at sometime during his career.

Grumman F6F Hellcat

(Fighter)

Grumman Aircraft Company was given the order in June, 1941 to develop a new fighter to replace the F4F Wildcat. This proved to be a wise decision, because six months later combat with Japan would show the Wildcat was inferior to the Japanese "Zero."

In only eighteen months the plane was designed, test units were built, it was tested and enough production copies were built to be delivered to the fleet in early January, 1943. *Hornet*, CV-8 carried the Wildcat, but by the time *Hornet* CV-12 was built, its air groups would carry the F6F Hellcat.

Several versions of the F6F were assigned to *Hornet's* air groups, mostly the F6F-3 which was the first large production design. Later the F6F-5 version was flown along with the F6F-3N or F6F–5N night fighter and the F6F–3P or F6F–5P photo-reconnaissance versions.

The Hellcat met or exceeded all of its requirements. It was the most successful carrier-based fighter aircraft ever built, and carrier-based Hellcats were credited with shooting down 4,947 enemy aircraft, almost 75% of all of the Navy's air-to-air victories.

By the end of the war, 12,275 F6F Hellcat's had been built, and they remained in use by the Navy as trainers and drones until mid-1961.

Technical Data (typical to all versions)

Crew: 1
Engine: one 2,000 HP Pratt & Whitney (propeller)
Dimensions: Width: 42 feet 10 inches (14 feet 8 inches with wings folded); length 33 feet 7 inches; height 13 feet 1 inch.
Weight: Empty 9,328 pounds; gross 15,415 pounds.
Performance: Max speed 380 mph at 23,400 feet; cruising speed 168 mph; service ceiling 37,300 feet; range 945 miles; carried a drop tank under the fuselage.
Armament: six fixed forward shooting .50-cal machine guns with 400 rounds of ammunition each.

Grumman F9F-2, F9F-5 Panther

(Jet Fighter)

Grumman started development of its first jet fighter in mid-1946, and the first operational units were delivered to the fleet in mid-1949. The Panther was a single engine fighter with the very noticeable addition of the wingtip fuel tanks.

The Panther only flew off *Hornet* for two years, mostly the F9F-5 version which went operational in late 1950. The Navy kept the various F9F aircraft operational until 1962.

In November 1950 a Navy pilot flying a F9F-2 was the first pilot credited with shooting down another jet fighter in combat.

Technical Data (typical to F9F-5 versions)

Crew: 1

Engine: one Pratt & Whitney turbojet

Dimensions: Width: 38 feet; length 35 feet 10 inches; height 12 feet 5 inches.

Weight: Empty 10,150 pounds; gross 18,700 pounds.

Performance: max speed 580 mph at 5,000 feet; cruising speed 481 mph; service ceiling 42,700 feet; range 1,300 miles.

Armament: four fixed forward shooting 20-millimeter cannons in the nose.

Douglas AD-5, AD-6 Skyraider
(Dive Bomber, Bomber)

The Skyraider was developed during World War II as a carrier-based dive-bomber, but was too late to see service during the war. It was such a well-built and versatile airplane that it was used extensively during the Korean conflict and Vietnam. The last production model was built in 1957, but the Navy actually thought about re-introducing it in the mid-60's for Vietnam use. The Navy retired the last of the Skyraider's in 1972. Known as the "Spad" by pilots who liked its reliability, the Skyraider flew off *Hornet* from 1953 until 1959. Production of the AD-5 version began in 1951.

Fifteen weapons-mounting points under the fuselage and wings allowed for an 8,000-pound payload, almost equal to the B17-E Flying Fortress!

Only about 1,000 of the AD-5s were built in several variations, including the AD-5N for night operations, AD-5Q for electronic countermeasures and AD-5W for anti-submarine warfare. The AD-6 was the upgraded version. Overall, 3,180 of the Skyraiders were built.

Technical Data (typical to AD-6 versions)

Crew: 1
Engine: one 2,700 hp Wright (propeller)
Dimensions: Width: 50 feet (26 feet 4 inches with wings folded); length 38 feet 10 inches; height 15 feet 8 inches.
Weight: Empty 12,100 pounds; gross 25,000 pounds.
Performance: max speed 343 mph at 20,000 feet; cruising speed 195 mph; service ceiling 25,400 feet; range 1,300 miles.
Armament: four fixed forward shooting 20-millimeter cannons in the wings. The Skyraider could carry up to 8,000 pounds of bombs externally.

Sikorski HSS-1 (UH-34) Seabat

(Single-rotor Helicopter)

Built by the Sikorsky Aircraft Division of United Aircraft Corporation, the HSS-1 was a military version of the civilian Model S-58 that was developed as an anti-submarine, utility and transport helicopter. It was somewhat limited in load-carrying capability, so they operated either as submarine hunters, using ASDIC for search, or as killers carrying homing torpedoes on the fuselage. They could work in pairs as a hunter/killer team, but usually they operated as hunters and called upon destroyers to attack a target when located.

The Navy had 350 of the HSS-1 built, and about half of them were HSS-1N versions for night operations. First delivered to the fleet in August 1955, they served until 1969. *Hornet* carried them from 1955 through 1964.

Technical Data (typical to HSS-1 — UH-34 versions)

Crew: four: two pilots, two crewmen. Utility versions could carry up to 18 passengers.

Engine: one 1,525 hp Wright

Dimensions: Rotor: 56 feet; length: 46 feet 9 inches; height: 15 feet 11 inches

Weight: Empty 7,900 pounds; gross 14,000 pounds

Performance: max speed 123 mph at sea level; cruising speed 98 mph; service ceiling 9,500 feet; range 182 miles

Armament: No armament. In ASW role, carried sono-buoys, ASDIC search equipment, passive sonar and could carry two homing torpedoes.

Piasecki HUP-2 (UH-25B) Retriever
(Tandem-rotor Helicopter)

Designer Frank Piasecki developed the tandem-rotor layout for the HUP series of small helicopters. It was planned that these would be used by the Coast Guard for plane-guard, search-and-rescue and utility duty. The Navy started using the HUP in 1951, eventually using 165 of them.

The HUP-2S version was equipped with radar for anti-submarine duty, but most of the HUP's were used as cargo and utility transports. They had a two or three-man crew.

The HUP was equipped with a Continental 525 hp engine and two rotors. The diameter of the rotors was 35 feet, and they could be folded for storage. The empty weight was 3,960 pounds, the loaded weight 5,750 pounds, and HUP-2 had a top speed of 120 mph. They served on *Hornet* from 1954 to 1958 and went out of service in 1964.

Technical Data

Crew: two: pilot, co-pilot plus up to four passengers
Engine: 525 hp Continental
Dimensions: rotor: 35 feet (wood); length 31 feet, 10 inches; height 12 feet, six inches.
Weight: 4,217 lbs.
Performance: 120 mph; service ceiling 12,467 feet; range 273 miles
Armament: none

The *Hornet* Museum's HUP was donated to the museum by former HUP pilot Steve Linsenmeyer of New Smyrna, Florida. The cross-country move was sponsored by Ettore Products Co. of Oakland, California. When restored, *Hornet's* HUP will be painted in the colors of the original HU-1, which operated off *Hornet* from 1954-1958.

PIASECKI (HUP) RETRIEVER. TWO VIEWS OF HORNET'S HUP TAKEN DURING ITS RESTORATION PROCESS AFTER IT HAD BEEN SANDED DOWN AND HAD ITS PAINT REMOVED.

ABOVE: AN FJ-2 FURY IN FLIGHT. BELOW, TWO VIEWS OF
HORNET'S FURY PRIOR TO RESTORATION.

North American FJ-3, FJ-4 Fury

(Swept-wing Jet Fighter)

The Fury is the naval version of the highly successful F-86 Sabre Jet, a swept-wing fighter with the large and unmistakable air intake in the nose.

The design planning started in 1951, and the first Fury was delivered to the fleet for testing in late 1952. All of the FJ-2s were assigned to the Marine Corps. The FJ-3 was delivered to the Navy beginning in September 1954. A total of 538 of the FJ-3 series and 374 of the FJ-5 series were built, and they served operationally on *Hornet* from 1956-1959.

The Fury was such a high performance aircraft that it had to land at a speed of 140 mph, which made it very interesting for the pilots to land on a carrier deck.

Technical Data (typical to FJ-4 versions)

Crew: pilot
Engine: one 7,700 lb st Wright turbojet
Dimensions: Width: 39 feet 1 inches; length 36 feet 4 inches; height 13 feet 11 inches
Weight: Empty 13,200 pounds; gross 23,700 pounds
Performance: max speed 680 mph at sea level; cruising speed 534 mph; service ceiling 46,800 feet; range 2,000 miles
Armament: four fixed forward shooting 20-millimeter cannons in the fuselage and four wing pylons for 3,000 pounds of bombs or up to four Sidewinder missiles

The Hornet Museum's FJ-2 Fury was one of 200 built, originally delivered to the Marine Corps although it did fly off the *Hancock, CV-19.* It is slightly smaller than the FJ-4 version, its General Electric turbojet engine producing 6,000 st. Its basic weight was 12,800 pounds, its gross was 16,122 pounds and it had a maximum speed of 676 mph and a cruising speed of 602 mph. Its range was 990 miles and it only carried the four 20-millimeter guns.

ABOVE: TWO VIEWS OF HORNET'S TRACKER. NOTE HOW WINGS FOLD OVER THE FUSELAGE. BELOW: A TRACKER IN FLIGHT (N.A.)

Grumman S-2F S-2 Tracker, E-1 Tracer and C-1 Trader

(Twin Engine Propeller ASW or AEW)

When *Hornet* was re-designated as an anti-submarine carrier, her air groups operated with propeller driven aircraft that were much more practical for the type of work they were required to do. The key to nuclear missile-armed anti-submarine warfare (ASW) was the early detection of the submarines, which means the search aircraft had to carry sophisticated electronic detection gear and required the ability to stay airborne for extended periods of time at low altitude.

There was a weapons bay in the fuselage, and two separate bays within it each carried up to 16 sono-buoys. Each airplane carried search radar, a magnetic anomaly detector and a 70-million candlepower searchlight.

The Tracker entered operational service in February 1954, and variations of the Tracker/Tracer were on active duty until 1976. They operated off *Hornet* from 1959 until 1970. The Trader version was designed to carry personnel, and the Tracer was used for airborne early warning (AEW). It carried the distinctive 20-foot by 30 foot AEW dome on top of the fuselage.

Technical Data (typical to S-2F S-2 versions)

Crew: four: two pilots, two radar operators
Engine: two 1,525 hp Wright (propeller)
Dimensions: Width: 72 feet 7 inches; length: 43 feet 6 inches; height: 16 feet 7 inches.
Weight: Empty 19,050 pounds; gross 26,900 pounds
Performance: max speed 253 mph at 5,000 feet; cruising speed 149 mph; service ceiling 22,000 feet; range 1,150 miles.
Armament: 4,180-pound weapons load. Fuselage weapons-bay held one depth charge or two torpedoes. Six pylons under the wings for depth charges, torpedoes or rockets, and up to 32 sono-buoys.

ABOVE: AN F8U IN FLIGHT. BELOW: TWO VIEWS OF HORNET'S RESTORED F8U. (AUTHOR'S COLLECTION).

Vought F-8 (F8U) Crusader
(Swept Wing Supersonic Jet Fighter)

The Vought F-8 Crusader never flew off the deck of *Hornet*. Although the aircraft was put into operational use in 1957, thirteen years before *Hornet* was decommissioned in 1970, the plane is too heavy to land on *Hornet's* flight deck. However, several of the *Essex*-class carriers with reinforced flight decks did carry F8U Squadrons, including *Hancock, Bon Homme Richard* and *Oriskany*. The Aircraft Carrier Hornet Museum has one fully restored F8U Crusader and another in process of restoration.

Called the "Last of the Gunfighters" the F-8 Crusader was the last Navy fighter aircraft that carried cannons and not antiaircraft missles.

Technical Data:

Crew: pilot
Engine: Pratt & Whitney turbojet
Dimensions: Width: 35 feet, 8 inches; length: 54 feet, 2 inches; height: 15 feet, 9 inches
Weight: Empty: 17,836 lbs; gross: 34,100 lbs.
Performance: Max speed, 1,133 mph at 35,000 feet; cruising speed, 570 mph at 38,600 feet; service ceiling, 52,350 feet; range 1,425 miles.
Armament: Four forward firing 20-millimeter cannons, four Sidewinder Anti-Aircraft Missiles or up to 5,000 lbs. of bombs or rockets.

The *Hornet* Museum's F8U completed a fourteen year career before being retired to China Lake Naval Weapons Station. In mid-1998 it was loaned to the museum as a display, and is being completely restored by volunteers, supported by individual and corporate donors.

Appendix 2

Hornet's Air Groups

Legend: HU (utility helicopter); HS (anti-submarine warfare helicopter); VA (attack); VAH (attack heavy); VAW (early warning); VB (bomber or dive bomber); VC (composite unit); VF (fighter); VFN (fighter, night); VFP (fighter, photo recon); VS (scouting and/or anti-submarine warfare); VT (torpedo)

Air Group 15:	December 1943 – June 1944
Detached at Pearl Harbor, assigned to *Essex*	
Air Group 2:	June 1944 – October 1944
VF-2	36 - F6F Hellcat Fighter
VB-2	33 - SB2C Helldiver Dive Bomber
VT-2	19 - TBF/TBM Avenger Torpedo Bomber
VFN-76	4 - FGF-3N Hellcat Night Fighter
Air Group 11:	October 1944 – January 1945
VF-11	40 – F6F Hellcat
VB-11	25 – SB2C Helldiver
VT-11	18 – TBF/TBM Avenger
	January 1945 – March 1945
VT-11	48 – F6F Hellcat
VB-11	28 – SB2C Helldiver
VT-11	18 – TBM Avenger
Air Group 17:	March 1945 – April 1945
VF-17	71 – F6F Hellcat
VB-17	15 – SB2C Helldiver
VT-17	15 – TBM Avenger

(Note: no air groups were assigned while Hornet was decommissioned and SCB-27A modernization)

Air Group 9:	July 1954 – June 1955
VF-91	F9F-6 Cougar jet fighter
VF-93	F9F-5 Panther jet fighter
VF-94	F9F-5 Panther jet fighter
VF-95	AD-6 Skyraider bomber
VC-3	F2H-3 Banshee jet fighter
VC-11	AD-5W Skyraider EW/ASW
VC-35	AD-5N Skyraider EW/ASW night
VC-61	F2H-4P Banshee reconnaissance
HU-1	HSS-1 Seabat helicopter
Air Group 7	June 1955 – January 1956
VF-71	F2H-3 Banshee

VF-72	F9F-2 Panther
VF-73	F9F-6 Cougar
VA-75	AD-5 Skyraider
VC-12	AD-5W Skyraider
VC-33	AD-5W Skyraider
VC-62	F9F-8 Cougar
HU-1	HSS-1 Seabat

(Note: no air groups were assigned while undergoing SCB-125 modernization)

Air Group 14	February 1957 – February 1958
VF-142	FJ-3 Fury fighter
VF-144	F9F-8 Cougar
VF-145	AD-6 Skyraider
VF-146	F9F-8 Cougar
VFP-61	F9F-8P Cougar photo recon
VAH-6	AJ-2 Savage prop bomber
HU-1	HUP-2 Retriever helicopter
Air Group ATG-4	February 1958 – May 1959
VF-94	FJ-3M Fury
VF-152	F2H-3 Banshee
VA-214	FJ-4B Fury
VA-216	AD-7 Skyraider
VAH-16	AJ-2 Savage
VAW35	AD-5N
VEP-61	F9F-8P Cougar
HU-1	HUP-2 Retriever
	May 1959 – July 1960
VS-38	S2-F Tracker
HS-8	HSS-1 Seabat
	July 1960 – July 1962
VS-37	S2-F Tracker
HA-2	HSS-1 Seabat
Air Group 57	July 1962 – September 1965
VS-35	S2-F Tracker
VS-37	S2-F Tracker
HS-2	HSS-1 Seabat
	September 1965 – June 1970
VS-35	S-2D Tracker
VS-37	S-2D Tracker
HS-2	SH-3A

Appendix 3

Hornet's Campaign Ribbons

(As displayed on the starboard side of the island)

1. Presidential Unit Citation. Awarded to *Hornet's* air groups for extraordinary heroism in action in World War II.

Air Group 2: March 29 – May 1, 1944 (Palau, Hollandia, Truk); June 11 – August 5, 1944 (Marianas, Bonis, Yap); September 6 – September 24, 1944 (Philippines, Palau).

Air Group 11: October 10 – November 22, 1944 (Ryukyus, Formosa, Philippines, Luzon); December 14 – December 16, 1944 (Luzon); January 3 – January 22, 1945 (Philippines, Formosa, China Sea, Ryukyus).

Air Group 17: February 16 – June 10, 1945 (Japan, Bonins, Ryukyus).

2. Navy Meritorious Unit Commendation with two bronze stars (for the second and third awards.)

3. China Service, 1945 – 1957, for service during the Quemoy and Matsu Islands actions.

4. American Campaign Medal for World War II

5. Asiatic – Pacific Campaign Medal for World War II. One Silver (five) and two Bronze stars denote seven battles, as follows:

Asiatic-Pacific Raids, Hollandia Operation, Marianas Campaign Western Carolina Islands Campaign, Western New Guinea Campaign, Leyte Campaign, Luzon Campaign

6. World War II Victory Medal

7. World War II European Occupation, for four days in Naples, Italy in 1954

8. National Defense Service Medal with Bronze Star

9. Armed Forces Expeditionary Medal with Bronze Star

10. Vietnam Service Medal with Silver and Bronze Star

11. Presidential Unit Citation, Philippine Republic

12. Gallantry Cross with Palm, Republic of Vietnam

13. Philippine Liberation, World War II, Philippine Republic

14. Vietnam Campaign, Republic of Vietnam

1		2	
3	4	5
6	7	8
9	10	11
12	13	14

Appendix 4

Text of *Hornet's*
Presidential Unit Citation

The President of the United States takes pleasure in presenting
the PRESIDENTIAL UNIT CITIATION to the U.S.S. *HORNET*
and her attached Air Groups participating in the following
operations:

March 29 to May 1, 1944, Palau, Hollandia, Truk; June 11 to
August 5, 1944, Marianas, Bonins, Yap; September 6 to 24, 1944,
Philippines, Palau: AG-2 (VF-2, VB-2, VT-2, Part of VFN-76).

October 10 to November 22, 1944, Ryukyus, Formosa,
Philippines, Luzon; December 14 to 16, 1944, Luzon; January 3 to 22,
1945, Philippines, Formosa, China Sea, Ryukyus: AG-11, (VF-11,
VB-11, VT-11).

February 16 to June 10, 1945, Japan, Bonins, Ryukyus: AG-17
(VF-17, VBF-17, VB-17, VT-17).

for service as set forth in the following

CITATION:
For extraordinary heroism in action against enemy Japanese forces
in the air, ashore and afloat in the Pacific War in the most forward Area
from March 29, 1944, to June 10, 1945. Operating continuously in the
most forward areas, the USS *HORNET* and their air groups struck
crushing blows toward annihilating Japanese fighting power; they
provided air cover for our amphibious forces; they fiercely countered
the enemy's aerial attacks and destroyed his planes; and they inflicted
terrific losses on the Japanese in Fleet and merchant marine units
sunk or damaged. Daring and dependable in combat, the *HORNET*
with her gallant officers and men rendered loyal service in achieving
the ultimate defeat of the Japanese Empire.

For the President

Secretary of the Navy

Appendix 5

Hornet's World War II Record

Sometimes raw numbers tell the story better than any narrative. *Hornet*, CV-12 has a most impressive World War II combat record during her 18 months at sea:

668 enemy aircraft shot down
742 enemy aircraft destroyed on the ground
1 enemy carrier, 1 cruiser and 10 destroyers sunk
Major assist on sinking the *Yamato*
42 cargo ships or transports sunk
Total enemy shipping sunk or damaged: 73 ships sunk, 37 ships
    probably sunk, 413 damaged, or 1,269,700 tons

Hornet's three air groups accomplished:
Over 23,000 arrested landings
18,570 combat sorties
Dropped 17,793 bombs, 116 torpedoes and fired 5,842 rockets
    and 4,878,000 rounds of machine gun ammunition
Burned over 5,645,000 gallons of aviation gasoline
Shot down 255 planes in a single month, a Navy record
Shot down 72 planes in a single day, another Navy record
Ten pilots become "ace in a day"

Hornet itself accomplished:
Under attack 59 times, never hit by a bomb, torpedo or kamikaze
Never tied up to a dock in 18 months, but dropped anchor 44 times
Steamed 150,000 miles, averaging 294 miles per day
Consumed 28,437,600 gallons of bunker oil
Distilled 41,231,500 gallons of seawater to make fresh water for the
    engines
Fired 7,275 rounds of 5-inch, 115,200 rounds of 40-millimeter and
    409,500 rounds of 20-millimeter ammunition.
The mess halls (food service) served over 4,200,000 meals
On 270 occasions, escorting destroyers were re-fueled by *Hornet*
    (at-sea replenishment) and on another 1,200 occasions
    destroyers or other ships transferred material, personnel or
    wounded between the two ships.

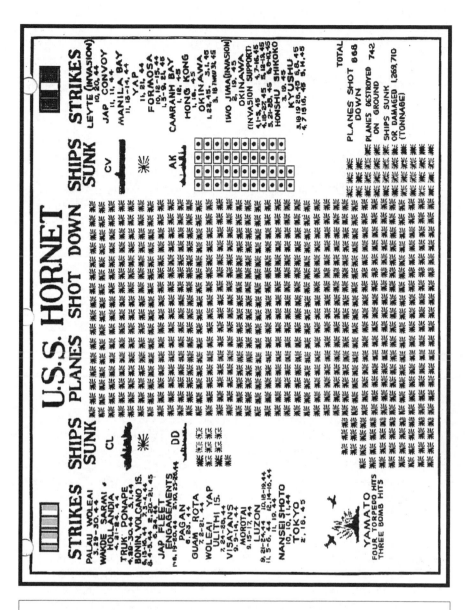

HORNET'S SCOREBOARD. THE ORIGINAL BOARD IS IN FLORIDA. THE SCOREBOARD AT THE HORNET MUSEUM IS A HAND-MADE COPY. THE BOARD DEPICTS THE 668 ENEMY AIRCRAFT SHOT DOWN BY HORNET'S PILOTS AND SHIPS CREW. ALSO LISTED IS THE AIRCRAFT CARRIER (CV), CRUISER (CL), 10 DESTROYERS (DD) AND 42 MERCHANT SHIPS (AK) HORNET'S PILOTS WERE CREDITED WITH SINKING. MILITARY SHIPS AND PLANES ARE INDICATED BY THE RISING SUN EMBLEM, CIVILIAN SHIPS BY THE SINGLE CIRCLE.

Appendix 6

Hornet's Commanding Officers

CV-12

Captain Miles M. Browning	Nov 29, 1943 – May 29, 1944
Captain William D. Sample	May 29, 1944 – Aug 9, 1944
Captain Austin K. Doyle	Aug. 9, 1944 – Aug 1, 1945
Captain C.R. Brown	Aug 1, 1945 – Feb 14, 1946
Captain Charles F. Coe	Feb 14, 1946 – Aug 14, 1946

CVA-12

Captain Francis L. Busey	Mar 20, 1951 – Apr 30, 1951
Captain Milton A. Nation	Sep 11, 1953 – Jul 19, 1954
Captain Frank A. Brandley	Jul 19, 1954 – Jul 20, 1955
Captain N.A. Campbell	Jul 20, 1955 – Aug 18, 1956
Captain William W. Hollister	Aug 18 1956 – Aug 12, 1957
Captain Thomas F. Connolly	Aug 12, 1957 – Aug 25, 1958

CVS-12

Captain Marshall W. White	Aug 25, 1958 – Nov 20, 1959
Captain Ernest E. Christensen	Nov 20, 1959 – Nov 2, 1960
Captain David C. Richardson	Nov 2, 1960 – Oct 18, 1961
Captain Hoyt D. Mann	Oct 18, 1961 – Sept 24, 1962
Captain Ellis J. Fisher	Sept 24, 1962 – Sept 25, 1963
Captain J.I. Hardy	Sept 25, 1963 – Jul 15, 1964
Captain M.A. Madden	Jul 15, 1964 – Jul 1, 1965
Captain W.M. Pardee	Jul 1, 1965 – Apr 1, 1966
Captain Van V. Eason	Apr 1, 1966 – Feb 27, 1967
Captain Gordon H. Robertson	Feb 27, 1967 – Feb 23, 1968
Captain Jackson A. Stockton	Feb 23, 1968 – May 23, 1969
Captain Carl J. Seiberlich	May 23, 1969 – Jun 26, 1970

Appendix 7

Camouflage

The Navy used ship camouflage starting in World War I and extensively in World War II. The purpose of camouflage was to confuse the enemy, particularly submarines, about which direction and speed a ship was traveling.

Several "measures" and "designs" were developed, and no two *Essex*-class carriers carried exactly the same design. A "camouflage measure" defined the color range the ship would be painted and the "camouflage design" defined the pattern the color would create. Most carriers wore more than one design during the war, and by the end of the war, the kamikaze threat required many were painted a solid color.

Hornet was the first carrier to sport the "dazzle" pattern Measure 33/3A of Pale Gray, Haze Gray and Navy Blue. The two gray colors gave *Hornet* a fairly light appearance, which was fine from the surface, however it was very visible from a higher angle. The flight deck was stained a color similar to Navy Blue, and the deck numbers were painted a dull black. *Hornet* carried these colors throughout the war, and was painted a solid gray after the war.

The drawing below is the camouflage pattern *Hornet* carried throughout the war.

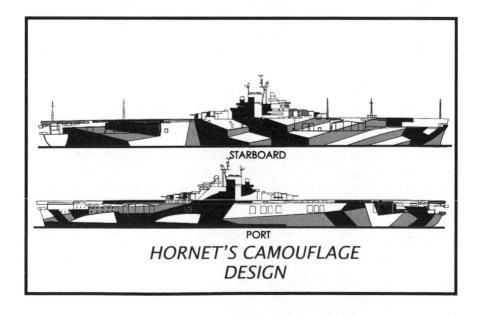

STARBOARD

PORT

HORNET'S CAMOUFLAGE DESIGN

Appendix 8

The Carriers of World War II

(Symbols: (l.) is the date the ship was launched, (d.) is the date the ship was sold for scrap.)

CV-1   *Langley,* (l.) 8/12/24, sunk off Java 2/27/42.
CV-2   *Lexington,* (l.) 10/3/25, sunk at Coral Sea, May 8, 1942
CV-3   *Saratoga,* (l.) 9/20/25, sunk as a target at the Bikini tests, 7/25/46
CV-4   *Ranger,* (l.) 2/25/33, (d.) 1/47
CV-5   *Yorktown,* (l.) 4/4/36, sunk at Midway, 4/5/42
CV-6   *Enterprise,* (l.) 10/3/36, (d.) 7/1/58
CV-7   *Wasp,* (l.) 4/4/39, sunk off Guadalcanal 9/15/42
CV-8   *Hornet,* (l.) 12/14/40, sunk at Santa Cruz, 10/27/42

Essex-Class
(Note: there were 24 *Essex*-class carriers. Missing numbers are for carriers of other classes.)

CV-9   *Essex,* (l.) 7/31/42, (d.) 6/15/75. Service: WWII, Korea, Cuban missile crisis, Apollo 7. Known as "The Oldest and the Boldest."
CV-10   *Yorktown,* (l.) 1/21/43, museum ship at Patriot's Point, South Carolina. Service: WWII and Vietnam. Known as "The Fighting Lady."
CV-11   *Intrepid,* (l.) 4/26/43, museum ship in New York City. Service: WWII, Vietnam, Aurora 7, Gemini 3. Known as "The Fighting I."
CV-12   *Hornet,* (l.) 8/29/43, museum ship at Alameda Point, California. Service: WWII, Vietnam, Apollo 11 and Apollo 12. Known as "The Grey Ghost."
CV-13   *Franklin,* (l.) 10/14/43, (d.) 10/1/64. The most heavily damaged carrier to survive an enemy attack. Known as "Big Ben."
CV-14   *Ticonderoga,* (l.) 2/7/44, (d.) 11/16/73. Service: WWII, Vietnam, Apollo 16 and Apollo 17. Known as "Big T" and "Tico."
CV-15   *Randolph,* (l.) 6/28/44, (d.) 6/15/73. Service: WWII, Liberty Bell 7, Friendship 7.
CV-16   *Lexington,* (l.) 9/26/42, museum ship in Galveston, Texas. Service: WWII, Cuban missile crisis, as a training carrier until 1991. Known as "The Blue Ghost."
CV-17   *Bunker Hill,* (l.) 12/7/42, (d.) 1/1/66. Service: WWII, severely damaged, not returned to service. Called the "Holiday Express."
CV-18   *Wasp,* (l.) 8/17/43, (d.) 7/1/72. Service: WWII, Cuban missile crisis, Gemini flights 4, 6A, 7, 9 and 12.

CV-19 *Hancock,* (l.) 1/24/44, (d.) 1/31/76. Service: WWII, Vietnam. Known as "Hannah."

CV-20 *Bennington,* (l.) 2/26/44, (d.) 12/1/94. Service: WWII, Vietnam.

CV-21 *Boxer,* (l.) 12/14/44, (d.) 12/1/69. Service: Korea and Vietnam, Cuban missile crisis. Known as "Busy B."

CV-31 *Bon Homme Richard,* (l.) 4/29/43, (d.) 2/4/92. Service: WWII, Korea and Vietenam. Known as "Bonnie Dick."

CV-32 *Leyte,* (l.) 8/23/45, (d.) 1/1/69. Service: Korea.

CV-33 *Kearsarge,* (l.) 5/5/45, (d.) 5/1/73. Service: Korea, Vietnam, Sigma 7, Faith 7. Known as "Mighty K."

CV-34 *Oriskany,* (l.) 10/13/45, (d.) 2/19/99. Service: Korea, Vietnam. Known as "Big O."

CV-36 *Antietam,* (l.) 8/20/44, (d.) 5/1/73. Service: WWII, Korea.

CV-37 *Princeton,* (l.) 7/8/45, (d.) 1/30/70. Service: Korea, Vietnam, Apollo 10.

CV-38 *Shangri-La,* (l.) 2/24/44, (d.) 8/9/88. Service: World War II, Vietnam. Known as "Tokyo Express."

CV-39 *Lake Champlain,* (l.) 11/2/44, (d.) 12/1/69. Service: Korea, Cuban missile crisis, Freedom 7, Gemini 5.

CV-40 *Tarawa,* (l.) 5/12/45, (d.) 1/1/67.

CV-45 *Valley Forge,* (l.) 11/18/45, (d.) 1/15/70. Service: Korea, Vietnam. Known as "Happy Valley."

CV-47 *Philippine Sea,* (l.) 9/5/45, (d.) 12/1/69. Service: Korea.

In addition to the large or fleet-type aircraft carriers listed above, there were over 100 other smaller carriers in service during World War II.

Bibliography

Chesneau, Roger, *Aircraft Carriers of the World, 1914 to the Present,* Wellington House, 1992

Costello, John, *The Pacific War 1941-1945,* Atlantic Communication, Inc., New York, 1982

Ewing, Steve, *USS Enterprise (CV-6),* Pictorial Histories publishing Co., 1982

Friedman, Norman, *U.S. Aircraft Carriers, An Illustrated Design History,* U.S. Naval Institute Press, 1983

Faltum, Andrew, *The Essex Aircraft Carriers,* The Nautical & Aviation Publishing Co., Baltimore, 1996

Garrison, Peter, *CV, Carrier Aviation,* Presidio Press, 1984

Glass, Kenneth and Harold Buell, *The Hornets and their Heroic Men,* American Printing and Lithographing Co., 1982

Hoyt, Edwin P. *Carrier Wars,* McGraw Hill Publishing Co., New York, 1989

Pawlowski, Gareth L., *Flat-tops and Fledglings,* Castle Books, New York, 1971

Raven, Allen, *Essex-class Carriers,* U.S. Naval Institute Press, 1988

Reynolds, Clark G., *The Fast Carriers: The Forging of an Air Navy,* Naval Institute Press, 1968

Self, Chuck, *USS Hornet, A Pictorial History*, Turner Publishing Company, 1997

Smith, Michael C., *Essex Class Carriers in Action,* Squadron/Signal Publications, 1997

Stern, Robert, *U.S. Aircraft Carriers in Action, Part 1,* Squadron/Signal Publications, Inc., 1991

Swanborough, Gordon and Peter M. Bowers: *United States Navy Aircraft Since 1911,* Putnam Books, London, 1976

GLOSSARY

ACI: Air Combat Intelligence officer

Accommodation ladder: stairway suspended over the side of the ship with a platform at the bottom, used when a ship is anchored

Aft: back end of the ship

Air Boss: nickname for the senior air officer, head of the air department

Air Group: all of the aircraft on an aircraft carrier

Air Wing: all of the aircraft on an aircraft carrier, term used after 1962

Aqueous film forming foam (AFFF) or Fog/Foam: chemical mixture, under pressure, used to extinguish a fuel fire

Armored hull: outer hall designed to minimize damage from a torpedo

Arresting gear: cables and machinery used to stop an aircraft when landing on the Flight Deck

ASW: Anti-Submarine Warfare

Battle dressing station: emergency locations where battle casualties are cared for

Berthing: sleeping quarters

Bilges: the curved portion of the ship's hull where the verticle sides meed the flat bottom

Bingo: term for a flight from the carrier to shore base

Black Shoes: non-aviator Naval officers

Blast deflector: deflects jet blast

Boat boom: a spar swung out from the side of the ship that boats are tied to.

Bogey: code for an unknown aircraft

Bolter: a missed carrier arrested landing attempt.

Bow: the front of the ship

Bridge: in the Island, where the ship is operated from

Brig: jail

Brow: walkway from a dock to the ship

Brown shoes: aviation officers

Bulkhead: a wall

Bunk: bed where officers sleep

CAG: Commander Air Group

Caliber: in a small gun, diameter or the bore in hundredths of an inch, in a large gun, the length of the barrel as expressed in number of bore diameters. A 5-inch 38 has a barrel length of 190" (the bore in inches times the caliber)

CAP: Combat Air Patrol

Capstan: a vertical revolving cylinder used for pulling lines.

Captain: person who commands the ship

CarDiv: a Carrier Division, and administrative or type of command

CARQUAL: Carrier qualifications, training to take-off and land on a carrier

Catapult: similar to a giant slingshot, used to launch aircraft off the Flight Deck.

Centerline: imaginary line down the length of the ship, compartments are numbered from it

CIC: Combat Information Center

Coaming: the raised fremework surrounding hatches to prevent water from going down them

COD: carrier on-board delivery (usually an aircraft)

Collision bulkhead: reinforced steel bulkhead behind the bow to limit collsion damage

Colors: United States flag

Combat Information Center: room where enemy contacts are tracked

Compartment: room

Conflag station: small fireproof room where firefighting can be directed

CPO: Chief Petty Officer

Crossdeck pendant: the arrestor cable stretched across the Flight Deck that is snagged by a landing plane's tailhook

CV: Navy designation for an aircraft carrier, "C" alone stands for "Cruiser" and "V" for heavier-than-air craft

CVA: Attack aircraft carrier

CVS: Anti-Submarine aircraft carrier

Cylinder and ram assembly: hydraulic ram

Davis Barrier: wire and cloth barrier stretched across the Flight Deck to trap airplanes that miss the arrestor gear

Deck: floor

Disbursing Office: bank

Displacement: the weight of the water a ship displaces

Double bottom: divided into void tanks to help with buoyancy

Draft: the depth of the ship that extends below the waterline, in feet

Essex-class: World War II built group of aircraft carriers

Escape scuttle: small round opening in a hatch used for emergency escape

Executive Officer: second-in-command of the ship

Fantail: the main deck overhanging the stern

FDC: Fire Direction Center

Fire division doors: huge rolling doors that divide the Hangar Deck into three sections to prevent the spread of fire

Fire hose station: location of fire-fighting hose

Flag Bridge: the 05 Level, used by an admiral and his staff

Flight Deck: deck from which aircraft were flown off and landed

Fo'c'sle: front of the ship where anchors are kept

Foam: used to fight fires

Frame: main structural component, attached to keel, they are 4 feet apart, and all locations within the ship are based upon the frame number

Freeboard: distance from the waterline to the Main (Hangar) Deck

Fresnel Lens: type of lens used in the Optical Landing System to enable aircraft to land on the ship

Funnel: the smokestack of a ship

Galley: where meals are prepared, i.e. the kitchen

Gallery Deck: the 02 Level, the deck directly below the Flight Deck

Gangway: place used to enter this ship

Gedunk: candy or snacks

General Quarters: condition of readiness where all hands are at their battle stations

Gyro repeater: compass card electrically connected to the gyrocompass

Gyrocompass: equipment with a heavy fly wheel, used to determine course and direction

Hangar Deck: large enclosed deck where aircraft were refueled, rearmed and repaired

Hatch: an opening through the deck (floor)

Head: Navy term for a bathroom

Hurricane bow: enclosed bow designed to keep the weather off the fo'c'sle deck

Inner hull: watertight hull inside which all vital machinery is located

Island: the structure above the Flight Deck

Jackstaff: flagpole at the bow of a ship for flying the jack

Kamikaze: aircraft flown by a pilot with the intent to commit suicide by crashing the plane into a ship

Keel: backbone of the ship, very bottom of the hull

Knee-knocker: high barrier at the bottom of doors in bulkheads, designed to prevent water from passing between compartments.

Knot: measure of speed. One knot equals 1.15 miles per hour

Ladder: stair

Level: deck above the Main Deck

List: to lean to one side

Longitudinal frame: run parallel to the keel, attached to the frames

LORAN: LOng RAnge radio Navigation system

LSO: Landing Signal Officer

MARDET: Marine Detachment

Magazine: sealed room where explosives are stored

Mast: large vertical pole that holds the radars and radio antenna

Mess: dining room

Mooring lines: large ropes used to tie the ship to a dock

Motor launch: small motorized boat

Mule: motorized cart used to move aircraft around the deck

Ordnance: military term for bombs, bullets, rockets, etc.

Outer hull: consists of the armored and unarmored hull

Overhead: the ceiling above your head

Pantry: place where food is served

Passageway: hall or corridor

Pelican hook: a hinged hook held together by a ring. When the ring is knocked off, the hook opens

Percussion fuse: gun ammunition designed to explode on contact with a target

Port: facing the bow, the left side of the ship

Pri-Fly: Primary Flight Control, located on top of the Island where the Air Boss directs operations (09 Level)

Projectile: round "or bullet" fired by a gun

Proximity fuse: type of gun ammunition designed to explode when in close proximity to a target

Purchase cable: part of the arrestor gear. One end is attached to the crossdeck pendant and the other to the arresting gear engine

Quarterdeck: area where you entered the ship

Rack: bed where enlisted personnel sleep

Radar: mechanism used to detect land, ships or planes, using technology that bounces a radio beam off an object to detect its presence

Radar repeater: equipment that indicates what a radar "sees"

Rain locker: shower

Readiness condition: determines which openings should be closed

Ready Room: where pilots meet to receive their assignments

Rivet: original method of construction of *Hornet*, subsequent builds were welded

Rudder: used to steer the ship

Rundown: curved end of the aft end of the Flight Deck

SAR: Search And Rescue

Scullery: room used for washing dishes

Scuttlebutt: drinking fountain; also a rumor

Secondary conn: secondary position where the ship can be operated from if the bridge is damaged

Sheaves: pulleys around which the purchase cable is run

Sickbay: hospital

Starboard: facing the bow, the right side of the ship

Stern: the back of the ship

Sponson: a structure protruding from the side of a ship

Stateroom: officer's quarters

Stopper: short length of chain, one end attached to the deck and the other to a pelican hook, designed to hold the anchor chain

Tattoo: signal for personnel to turn in (go to bed)

Tie down: hook recessed into the deck to tie aircraft down to prevent rolling

Unrep: Underway Replenishment, refueling and resupply at sea

Vultures row: area of the island where those not on duty can watch flight operations

Void: empty sealed tanks that can be filled with water or fuel to ballast the ship

Wardroom: room where officers eat their meals

Water closet: toilet

Water curtain: series of overhead water sprinklers designed to create a curtain of water during a fire

Waterline: line on the hull showing how much water *Hornet* should draw if fully loaded

Wave-Off: signal to pilot of a landing aircraft not to land

Wheel: as in Ships Wheel. Large wheel in the pilot house, used to steer the ship

Wildcat: a sprocket wheel on the anchor windless for grabbing the anchor chain.

Comparison between the
USS *Hornet* and the RMS *Titanic*

The two ships were almost the same size, as the numbers below will show. The largest discrepancy is in the weight of the two ships. *Titanic's* displacement at 66,750 tons was 50% more than *Hornet's* at 44,200 tons. Part of the reason for this can be found in the relative height of the two ships, keel to bridge.

The bridge on *Hornet* is 105 feet above the keel, yet it is three decks above the Flight Deck in the rather small island. *Titanic's* bridge was located on the Boat Deck, which extended for one-half the length of the ship. In other words, *Titanic* had much more mass, much higher. In addition, there were several things that created weight for *Titanic,* such as a swimming pool, hundreds of individual cabins and their fixtures, and three huge engines.

As you stand on the dock and gaze up toward the bridge of the *Hornet*, you are looking at the height of the Boat Deck on *Titanic*. *Hornet's* Flight Deck is about the same height at the two Well Decks (the lowest open decks) on *Titanic*.

	Hornet	*Titanic*
Length (overall):	894 feet	882.5 feet
Width (at waterline):	101 feet	92.5 feeet
Draft:	30 feet	31 feet
Height (bridge to keel):	105 feet	104 feet
Displacement:	44,200 tons	66,750 tons

If you enjoyed this book,
Then you might be interested in
1912 Facts About Titanic

by Lee W. Merideth

The world's most famous ocean liner carried to the bottom a treasure trove of secrets, myths, and legends. Who built RMS *Titanic*? Was it really an American owned ship? Who were the hundreds of passengers who traveled on the maiden voyage, and the dozens who didn't? Why weren't there enough lifeboats (*Titanic* carried more than were required.) What if Captain Smith hadn't delayed a major course change the day *Titanic* struck the iceberg. What if *Titanic* had missed the iceberg? How were the bodies of the dead collected and where are they buried?

1912 Facts About TITANIC doesn't follow a narrative format. It is full of easy-to-read fact "groups" that allow the reader to open the book on any page and read a rousing story. Many of the lesser-known passengers and crew are introduced and their fate is immediately divulged. Loading and launching of each of the lifeboats is listed in chronologically, as is the entire story of the great, but doomed, ship.

1912 Facts About TITANIC is jammed with little-known, hard to find and often shocking information, including a complete deck-by-deck walking tour of *Titanic* and over 50 photographs.

It will please both the serious student as well as the casual reader. This is a "must have" book if you are interested in the *Titanic* story. First published in February 1999, revised in September 2004, with over 40,000 copies sold.

You can order your copy of 1912 Facts About Titanic by sending check or money order for $18.95 ppd. for the soft cover version or $24.95 ppd. for the hard cover version (tax and postage included) to Historical Indexes,
PO Box 64142, Sunnyvale, CA 94088.
Indicate how you would like the book signed.

About the Author

Lee W. Merideth is the acclaimed author-compiler of several historical magazine indexes, including *Civil War Times and Civil War Times, Illustrated 30 Year Comprehensive Index* (1989) and the mammoth two-volume *Guide to Civil War Periodicals* (1991 and 1995). These combined 110,000 entries have helped thousands of students of the Civil War better access and utilize their extensive libraries and collections of Civil War-related periodicals.

In addition to the Civil War, Lee has been deeply interested in the *Titanic* disaster for over 40 years. In the process of his research he accumulated over 4,000 index cards with facts and figures, all of which formed the foundation for his best selling *1912 Facts About Titanic,* (1999) currently in its eighth printing with over 50,000 copies sold.

Lee's latest book is *Grey Ghost: The Story of the Aircraft Carrier Hornet* (June 2001), which is a history of the United States Navy's most decorated warship and a self-guided tour of the Aircraft Carrier Hornet Museum at Alameda Point, California.

A graduate of California Polytechnic State University in San Luis Obispo, California, and a retired United States Army officer, Lee has been in the printing and publishing business for more than 25 years and currently lives in San Jose, California where he manages his own publishing company.

* * *

To receive a personally inscribed copy of *Grey Ghost: The Story of the Aircraft Carrier Hornet, 1912 Facts About Titanic* or any of his Civil War indexes, or to schedule Lee to speak to your group, email him at historyindex@earthlink.net or write to him at P.O. Box 64142, Sunnyvale, CA 94088.

For additional information, see www.rocklinpress.com.